Over a hundred years have passed since the 'Great War' engulfed thousands of small communities. Around eighty men from Wymeswold, out of a total population of under eight hundred, are known to have served with the army during the hostilities.

The tide of history has receded, leaving thirty names on memorials to the fallen. Who were these 'lost sons'? What was the story of their lives and deaths? The number of deaths as a proportion of those who served is almost three times the national average. How did the village react?

Most people assume that villages were composed of families that had lived locally for generations. This book shows that then, as now, 'old' families and 'incomers' lived and worked side by side. As well as discovering the stories of these 'lost sons', Ivor Perry brings to life the diverse community of people who lived in Wymeswold around the start of the twentieth century.

Ivor Perry's first loves were History and then English – the subject he read at Jesus College, Cambridge. Two more degrees and several careers later he has returned to those first passions. He now researches and gives lectures about the First World War and its literature. He has lived in Wymeswold for seventeen years.

Bringing Them Home

The story of the lost sons of Wymeswold

Ivor F. Perry

WHO

WOLDS
Historical
Organisation

Bringing Them Home:

The story of the lost sons of Wymeswold

Ivor F. Perry

ISBN 978-0-951734-35-3

The publication of this book has been funded by the Heritage
Lottery Fund as part of the Bringing Them Home project.

LOTTERY FUNDED

Published by
Wolds Historical Organisation

Printed in England by Booksprint

Dedication

To my father, Jack Perry, who taught me more than I
know, and to my sons Tony and Edward. I am very
proud of you. We all stand at the crossroads between
the past and the future. We owe a debt to the one, and
a responsibility to the other.

Contents

1   Wymeswold before the Great War 1914–1918   1

2   The Lost Sons of Wymeswold   5

3   Albert Edward Bacon   12

4   Colin Bramall   16

5   John Wilfred Brookes   22

6   John Edward Clarke   27

7   Thomas Clarke   31

8   John James Collington   37

9   John William Collington   45

10   William Henry Dykes   53

11   Eric Evans   58

12   James Fermer Fletcher   65

13   Horace Giles   72

14   Ernest William Hubbard   74

15   Robert Miles Jalland   83

16   John Joseph Lamb   88

17   George Harold Marriott   94

18   Jesse Mills   100

19	John Morris	107
20	Herbert Isaac Orridge	113
21	John Robert Ovendale	119
22	Frederick Henry Robinson	127
23	Alfred Savage	133
24	Walter Foster Simpson	141
25	William Bennett Sissins	148
26	Walter Charles Smith	152
27	Bramford Sparrow	159
28	David Spicer	165
29	The Spicer Brothers: George and John Edward	170
30	George Williams	178
31	William Wilson	183
32	Wymeswold's Memorial Hall	188
33	The effect on the village: wives, children and loved ones	200

Acknowledgements

First, my grateful thanks are due to my mother, Jeanette Perry, and to my partner, Helen, who have patiently endured all my obsessions, chiefly the Great War, and now this project.

I would like to thank all those who encouraged me, whether in doing this project, or just writing: in particular Simon Vick, who walked miles of battlefields with me and patiently took photos and videos.

Thank you too, to people and organisations who have helped with research and ideas: the Wolds Historical Organisation (WHO), the Western Front Association and the Long, Long Trail. I have to pay tribute to the service offered by the Commonwealth War Graves Commission, The War Graves Photography Project, The National Archives, and The Record Office for Leicestershire, Leicester and Ruttland.

My thanks go to those who have already worked in this area; Liz Blood and her team at the Leicestershire County Council War Memorials Project, Michael Doyle, who with his late father put together an amazing database of the fallen of Leicestershire and Rutland, and Adam Llewellyn. I remember with thanks the late Alex Moretti, founder member of the WHO, who started to identify and collate the war graves information on our men. I am grateful to my present colleagues in the WHO, especially Patricia Baker and Debbie Bilham.

This document could not have been put together without the information supplied by villagers and descendants of men who gave their lives: Richard and Sue Collington, Chris Kirk, Nigel and Elizabeth Sykes, Linda Ward, Sue Easton, Sue Eliot, Frances Kent, Lily Simpson, Winnie Sleath, Peggy Mills, Sandra Brown, Elsie and Peter Hubbard, Geoff Giles and Jack Hubbard of Tweed Heads, Australia. Linda Dale supplied invaluable information about the Sissins family, as did David Morris for his family. This is their story as much as that of the thirty men we commemorate here.

If there is anyone I have forgotten, please forgive me. It was not intentional.

Chapter 1

Wymeswold before the Great War 1914–1918

Before the assassination of Archduke Ferdinand, and Austria's ultimatum to the Serbs, and all the other events that precipitated Europe headlong into war in 1914, the village of Wymeswold was a thriving place.

In April 1911, the UK census reported that the village population stood at 777 (an increase of seven since the previous census in 1901), consisting of 402 females and 375 males. In less than ten years, nearly ten percent of the male population was to die – in Flanders, France, Italy, Israel and Iraq.

Kelly's *Directory* of 1912 describes Wymeswold as a 'township, well-built village and large parish' roughly equidistant from the railway stations of East Leake and Loughborough. It was a farming community, and unlike the arable landscape of today, the land was 'largely in pasture'. The *Directory* identifies nineteen farmers, and thirteen graziers (who rented fields and raised their own livestock). Unsurprisingly, with so much pasture and cattle, there were two cattle dealers, and two cheesemakers. Albert Mills was like many Wymeswold people. In 1914 Albert, of Clay House Farm in Clay Street (now Clay House Farm, number 22) was a young, aspiring farmer. He lived with his wife and his disabled father, and farmed land behind Clay Street (now Mary's Close) and in Swift's Lane (now Swift's Close) as well as other land between Brook Street and the Burton Road. He was just establishing himself as a beef cattle farmer, investing heavily in new stock. The war would change his plans dramatically.

In order to service this busy population of nearly 800, there were a large number of local businesses; food and drink were supplied by a butcher (a second butcher appeared in the 1911 census), a baker, a miller (windmill), a shopkeeper, three grocers, and four public houses. Clothing was supplied by a shoemaker and no less than three dressmakers. Healthcare and spiritual care were provided by a doctor and a resident Church of England vicar (though the Methodist and Baptist churches were both active as well). A second doctor is recorded in the 1911 census. Unlike 2014, the village also had its own Post Office. On the other hand, the village still has a Junior School; in 1912, there were two elementary schools, one for infants (44 children) and one for juniors (50 boys and 47 girls). Today's attendance roll is not so different, though the population has almost doubled – current estimates are around 1,300 people.

Rempstone Road

Wysall Lane

West End

Wide Lane

Primitive
Methodist
chapel →

Far Street

East Road

London Lane or Street

Clay Street

Charles
Yard

The Stockwell

Church Street

St Mary's church

Methodist church

Narrow Lane

Brook Street

Fox Yard

Hoton Road

River Mantle

Burton Lane

Wymeswold in 1914 – more or less!

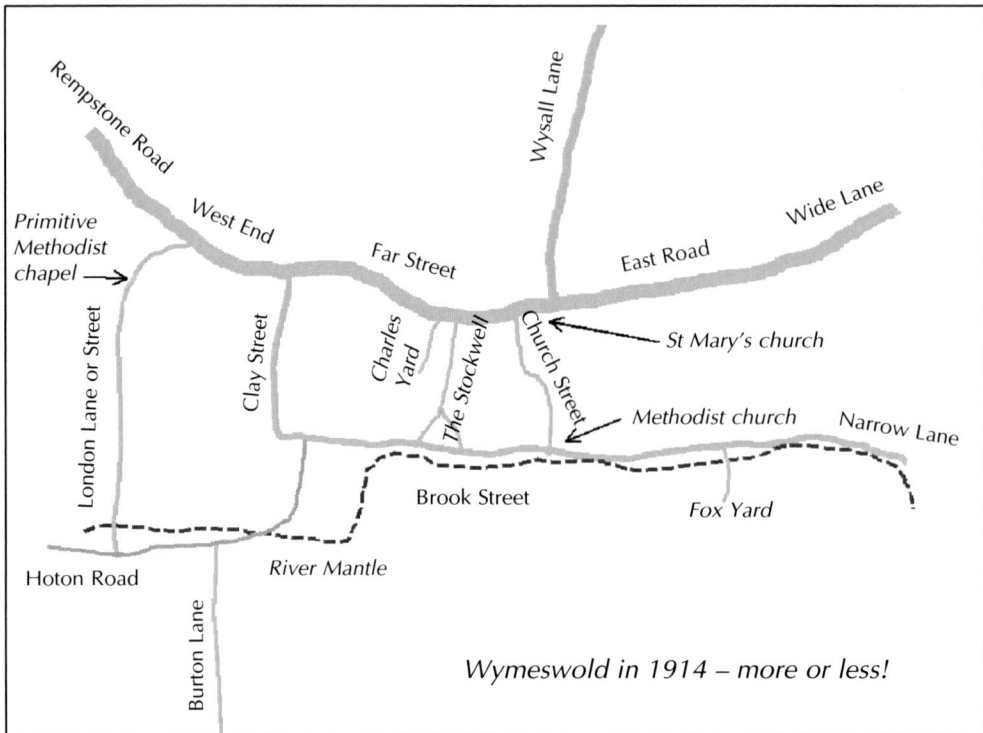

Other business people serving the community and perhaps going further afield were two carriers, a builder, a joiner, a bricklayer, two blacksmiths, a saddler, a house decorator and a cycle agent. The 1911 census has also identified a hosiery factory. Some of these trades – building work and decorating for example – still go on in the village. Others, like mending the roads, have disappeared entirely as a village occupation. In 1911 Henry Collington, aged 58, was described as a 'roadman'. He was also a grazier – multiple occupations are not a twenty-first century phenomenon! A later roadman, 'Billy' Dykes, was the father of William Henry Dykes, who was killed in 1916.

This was a self-contained community, perhaps not different from many other villages in England, but a world away from the Wymeswold of 2014, which has three pubs, a general store, and a butcher's shop. There are now very few farms, and none at all within the boundaries of the village. Most of the surrounding farmland is now arable, with some sheep, but there is very little evidence of the cattle that once populated the landscape. Perhaps the biggest difference after a hundred years is the disappearance of the local food and clothing suppliers; the contrast between shopping patterns now, and a hundred years ago, could not be more stark.

Wymeswold, or Wimeswould, as it was described in 1759, when the mediaeval field system was abolished and the land was enclosed, is in northern Leicestershire but less than a mile from the Nottinghamshire border. Unsurprisingly, some village men joined the Leicestershire regiment, while others joined the Sherwood Foresters (Notts and Derby regiment) – both were 'local' regiments so far as the community was concerned.

The village lies in a bowl-shaped valley, through which the A6006 Ashby to Melton Mowbray road passes from west to east. In the village it begins as Rempstone Road, changing its name to West End, Far Street and East Road, before exiting the village as Wide Lane. Running parallel to, and south of, the main road is Brook Street, which continues from Hoton Road until it leaves the village as Narrow Lane. Along the south side of Brook Street runs the brook itself, crossing the road just west of the Stockwell, and disappearing underground until it emerges on the north side of Hoton Road near the junction with Burton Lane. Technically, the brook is called the River Mantle, but nowadays it rarely fills its own narrow watercourse. Until the 1990s, however, it regularly flooded Brook Street in the winter, and old photographs show the street under a good foot or two of water, especially the eastern end, from the old Fox pub to the bottom of Crow Hill. In the early twentieth century the brook was used to fill the sheep wash at the junction of London Lane and Brook Street. All the streets are now surfaced with tarmac but in 1914 most, if not all, were either cobbled (like most of Clay Street) or made of compacted stone and earth, as Brook Street appears to be from old photographs. Some names have changed slightly – Swift's Lane is now Swift's Close. London Lane has also been known as London Street and Little London. Clay Street is still known to some villagers as The Clay. Since 1914, whole new streets have been created – Mantle Croft, Appleton Drive, Shepherd's Close, Orchard Way are just some of them. On the other hand, a number of the old 'yards' – little enclaves of very small cottages – have gone. The lost sons of Wymeswold would have been familiar with Dexter's Yard and Charles' Yard. Wilfred Brookes' last home was in Fox Yard.

The village had supplied soldiers in the past, and it was no stranger to wars. The Mixed School log book recorded in 1900 the names of 'old boys' who had served their country. Some had died – of disease, it is true, rather than the wholesale slaughter that was to come – but the sacrifice had been made. The headmaster, Mr Bailey, had ensured that, whether they were survivors or not, their names would be remembered:–

>John Wood (Fort Artillery)
>
>William Allen Leicestershire Regiment in Transvaal
>
>George Allen Leicestershire Regiment in Transvaal
>
>John Tyler (jnr) and John Tyler (Snr) and Alf Tyler
>
>Arthur Morris died of fever in the Mediterranean Feb 1900
>
>Ernest Brookes
>
>Samuel Knifton
>
>Albert Basford (Fort Artillery)
>
>Alexander Sheppard, died of fever in India 1898

The Sheppards would be spared another death; not so the extended Morris family. The Kniftons, too, would be touched by war through the death of Eric Evans.

Just after the turn of the century, whether inspired by the Boer War or not, at least four men of Wymeswold were regular soldiers: Amos Clarke, John Pepper, John William Collington and John James Collington. John Lamb, whose family came from the village, had joined up in 1907. George Williams, whose family lived in Wymeswold briefly, was also a pre-war 'regular'. Britain's small professional army formed the British Expeditionary Force that held up the German advance in 1914, and provided the men for the attacks at Loos and Neuve Chapelle the next year. The 'Old Army' as it is often referred to (as distinct from Kitchener's 'New Army'), would pay a high price. Of the six who were known to have been available for duty in 1914, Amos Clarke, already getting towards the maximum age for active service, was kept in England, training recruits, while four of the others were to die in the next war.

Sources

Wymeswold vicar's correspondence (DE 1728/37). The Record Office for Leicestershire, Leicester and Rutland.

Wymeswold Church of England School: log books and misc papers 1875–1983 (DE7281). The Record Office for Leicestershire, Leicester and Rutland.

Wymeswold parish registers. Online at: www.hoap.co.uk/who/localhisregister.htm [accessed June 2014].

www.firstworldwar.com [accessed 29th October 2013].

www.royalleicestershireregiment.org.uk [accessed 1 April 2014].

www.wartimememoriesproject.com/greatwar/allied/westyorkshireregiment11.php [accessed 12 February 2014].

Fromkin, D., 2004. *Europe's Last Summer: Why the world went to war in 1914.* Heinemann.

Kelly's Directory of the Counties of Derby, Nottingham, Leicester and Rutland. 1912 and 1916 editions

Reeves, J., 1962. *Georgian Poetry.* third edn. Penguin.

Smith, E., 1983. *Memories of a Country Girlhood.* First edn. Published by author.

Van Emden, R.A.H.S., 2003. *All Quiet on the Home Front.* Headline.

Chapter 2

The Lost Sons of Wymeswold

The Roll of Honour in St Mary's church contains the names of thirty men of Wymeswold who died in the Great War 1914-1918. Simply being born in Wymeswold was not a reason to be included. If it had been, then surely William Barnett, Tom Eustace Coupland and Samuel Grant would have been added to the Roll. All three, according to the Commonwealth War Graves Commission, originated from the village. The bronze plaque in the Methodist chapel adds to the confusion: it records only 28 names, omitting William Henry Dykes and Herbert Isaac Orridge. On the other hand it spells William Sissins' name correctly – the church scroll remembers William Sissons.

There is no evidence of the exact decision making process that led to the compilation of the list of names, but the fact that connects all of them is that they appear to have worked in the village at the time of enlistment, or, in the case of Ernest Hubbard, they had a large family still resident in Wymeswold. Some of them, like Alfred Savage, were Wymeswold born and bred; others, like Albert Lamb, had come here to work. Of the 'incomers', some, like John Robert Ovendale, had put down roots here; he had a wife and children in the village. Frederick Robinson, on the other hand, was new to Wymeswold, and had moved around the country for most of his adult life.

The demographics of the thirty who died show that they were very representative of those who were eligible for military service. It is commonplace to think of the Great War as a slaughter of the young, and in many ways it was. However, the ages of Wymeswold's men ranged from 18 to 36; their average age was 27. Four were under 21, and nearly two-thirds of them were under 30. Or to put it another way, over thirty percent were aged over 30. Some were married and fathers, though the majority were single. For Wymeswold, this would not be the slaughter of the young, but quite simply the slaughter of the village's menfolk.

Even in late 1914, the war must have seemed very far from Wymeswold. Some of the men would already have volunteered, or been called back to the Colours. Men like John James Collington and John William Collington, who had both been Regular Army soldiers and served their three years, and then were due to be on the Army Reserve list for nine years. As such, they were subject to recall 'if a state of War exists'. Without doubt, their families would have been worried about them, and whether the war would go on for long. Interestingly, it is a popular myth that everyone thought in August 1914 that the war would be over by Christmas. There was in fact, no united opinion in the press, parliament, or among the military about the length of the war.

It was not long before Wymeswold men were caught up in the fighting, and word quickly came back to the village. Wymeswold's earliest known casualty was John Richardson, who is listed in the school records as 'wounded at Mons'. John gave an account of his experiences to the *Loughborough Echo*. The school roll of honour (dated 1914 and 1915) contains references to other wounded, but his injury occurred in late summer 1914. He had been in the thick of the fighting around Mons and Landrecies, as the Expeditionary Force began its long retreat. The *Echo* reported:

> Richardson was fighting when he felt a sharp twinge in the
> shoulder and thought 'That's better than the head.' Then came a
> piece of shell, which cut a piece out of his wrist, and then a shot
> in the leg. 'I kept blazing away as hard as I could, and
> remembered nothing more till I woke up to find myself among
> wounded and groaning men in the hospital.'

It was however in 1915 that the war first brought tragedy into the village, with the death in January 1915 of John James Collington. His death was followed soon after by that of George Williams, in March. From the school Roll of Honour we know that there were other casualties between 1914 and 1915. In addition to John Richardson above, Fred Brooks, John Wain, Harold Morris and John Tyler are all listed as wounded, while Leonard Chadburn is a 'prisoner in Germany'. It seems that, fortunately, all five of these men survived the war. The fate of prisoners is today little talked about, but life for them was harsh. Other Ranks were expected to work, and for some conditions were appalling, especially those who were sent to the Strafe-Kommandos, or Punishment Brigades. For most prisoners, hard physical work with poor rations was occasionally punctuated by humour or acts of kindness from their 'hosts'. Those in the punishment brigades, however, were often worked for fifteen hours a day in coal or iron mines, and in consequence the death rate was significantly higher than among the prisoner population as a whole. We have to remember, of course, that as the war dragged on, and the British blockade of Germany began to bite, the German civilians themselves had less and less to eat.

The next year, 1916, saw a sharp increase in fatalities. Five Wymeswold men died that year. The relatively small number may come as a surprise to many who think of the first day of the Battle of the Somme in July 1916 as the epitome of slaughter. The fact was that the battalions in which they served were not central to the first day of the Somme, and although some of their regiments, (like the Leicesters at Bazentin Ridge in September), were to distinguish themselves in the Somme battles, the casualty rate was going to be a lottery. If your battalion were first over the top in a major battle, then your chances of death were much higher.

That said, of course, men were being killed constantly in minor battles, or in skirmishes, or while on patrol. And every day, there was the shelling. Artillery and mortar batteries on both sides would test out the enemy's defences, perfect their

6

range-finding, and experiment with different shell types by firing at least a few rounds every day. The British often referred to this as the Hun's morning or evening 'hate'. Colin Bramall's death may well have been an example. While we tend to have an image of the wholesale slaughter caused by machine guns, it appears that there were more fatalities from artillery fire than anything else. Gordon Corrigan in *Mud, Blood and Poppycock* quotes an analysis by the Royal Army Medical Corps which

showed that just over two per cent of all wounds were caused by grenades, almost thirty-nine per cent by bullets, either rifle or machine-gun, and just over *fifty-eight per cent* by shells from artillery or trench mortars. The remainder, some 0.32 per cent of the total, were due to other causes, including bayonets. (My italics)

It was in 1917 that the Wymeswold casualty rate started to rise; seven men were killed. Not a vast increase on the previous year, but a year that saw the British army heavily committed on all fronts. In France the Germans retreated strategically to the Hindenburg Line, but made the British pay dearly for the ground they gave up. The battles of Cambrai and, in Belgium, Messines Ridge and the Third Battle of Ypres (Passchendaele) claimed thousands of lives. In the Middle East, the British defeat at Kut in Iraq the previous year had been avenged, and Baghdad taken. Gaza had fallen to the British, and Allenby entered Jerusalem in December. Yet again, casualties had been high. The Mesopotamian campaign alone had resulted in 92,000 casualties between 1915 and 1917.

However, 1918 was Wymeswold's *annus horribilis* – by far its worst year. Over half Wymewold's deaths –16 out of 30 – took place in this year. In a way, this is not surprising, since in March 1918 Germany launched its last, and greatest, offensive. Germany was blockaded, almost starving at home, reduced to calling up boys and old men, and though there were only four American divisions in France, more were steadily arriving. Germany knew that unless it did something quickly, it was doomed. The only good news was the collapse of Russia in 1917 and the subsequent peace, which had released dozens of divisions from the Eastern Front. With these new armies, it planned to split the British and French forces, and to drive the British into the sea. That done, Germany could get a favourable peace treaty.

In all, Germany brought 192 divisions – nearly 3,500,000 men – into position on the Western Front. The area selected for the first strike was the British front from Arras in the north, through the Somme valleys, past St Quentin down to La Fere in the south. Here, 69 German divisions faced 33 British and Allied divisions, 10 of which were as far back as 15 miles from the front line. The offensive opened on 21st March, and within days all the British advances of 1916 and 1917 had been reversed. Haig issued his famous order: having 'our backs to the sea, and trusting in God' British forces had to hold on at all costs. These were the days of the 'cooks' battle', where every man who could hold a rifle was put into the line. It was at this time that Robert Ovendale, a musician and former Wymeswold bandsman, was to lay down his life. In fact, seven Wymeswold men died between 21st March and the end of April. Almost half of the 1918 casualties, in fact. By the end of April, the first offensive had petered out in the mud and shell holes of the Somme. But the Germans persisted,

GREAT · 1914-18 · WAR

ROLL OF HONOUR

ALBERT BACON.	JESS. MILLS.
COLIN. BRAMALL.	JOHN. MORRIS.
JOHN. W. BROOKES.	HERBERT. I. ORRIDGE.
JOHN. E. CLARKE.	ROBERT. OVENDALE.
THOMAS. CLARKE.	FREDERICK H. ROBSON.
JAMES. COLLINGTON.	ALFRED. SAVAGE.
JOHN. W. COLLINGTON.	WALTER. F. SIMPSON.
WILLIAM. H. DYKES.	WILLIAM. B. SISSONS.
ERIC. EVANS.	WALTER. C. SMITH
JAMES. F. FLETCHER.	BRAMFORD. SPARROW.
HORACE. G. GILES.	DAVID. SPICER.
ERNEST. W. HUBBARD.	GEORGE. SPICER.
ROBERT. JALLAND.	JOHN. E. SPICER.
JOHN. LAMB.	GEORGE. WILLIAMS.
GEORGE. H. MARRIOTT.	WILLIAM. WILSON.

REMEMBER WITH THANKSGIVING

The Gift of

Sgt. Major Amos. Clarke. Wymeswold.
LATE · COLDSTREAM · GUARDS ·

The Roll of Honour in St Mary's Church, Wymeswold.

The Roll of Honour in the Methodist chapel, Wymeswold.

and in May and June launched increasingly desperate attacks first against the British north of Arras, then against the French lines further south-east, drawing in British support. Another four Wymeswold men died. But by now, the writing was on the wall for Germany and Austria. The exhausted British and French armies had held, and the Americans were now pouring, not raw recruits into the training camps, but trained soldiers into the front line, mostly in the Argonne, to the east of the British.

However, Wymeswold still had a price to pay. Although the German army was on the retreat, it did not stop fighting. Every day, the German army stood and fought, even if it pulled back during the night. By the end of August, Arras was safe, and the battlefields of the Somme were back in British hands for the last time. But it was too late for Herbert Orridge and Robert Jalland, who remain there still. The last Wymeswold man to be killed was Walter Smith, who died of his wounds at the military hospital at St Sever near Rouen.

It is easy to think of the Great War as the Western Front – France and Belgium. Yet World War One was a truly global affair, with fighting in Russia, Eastern Europe, the Middle East and Africa. Australia's first major engagement of the war was the sinking of the German cruiser Emden at the Cocos and Keeling Islands in November 1914. India's contribution was enormous; over 1,500,000 troops, who fought in Western and Eastern Europe, the Dardanelles and the Middle East. Even if they did not actually fight, countries as far away as Japan and Chile had declared themselves for the Allies, and by the end of the war over 100,000 Chinese were working in France as paid labourers.

Wymeswold made its contribution outside the Western Front; John Wilfred Brookes lies in Boscon British cemetery in Italy. Presaging another conflict as yet ninety years away, John Lamb and William Sissins died in Iraq, while John Spicer was mortally wounded in present day Israel. Sadly, none of our project volunteers has been able to visit these sites; so, dear reader, if you find yourself in the area, please stop and spare a thought for a Wymeswold boy very far from home.

Sources

Census records: 1891, 1901, 1911.

Wymeswold parish registers. Online at: www.hoap.co.uk/who/localhisregister.htm [accessed June 2014].

Wymeswold Church of England School: log books and misc papers 1875–1983 (DE7281). The Record Office for Leicestershire, Leicester and Rutland.

Wymeswold vicar's correspondence (DE 1728/37). The Record Office for Leicestershire, Leicester and Rutland.

www.royalleicestershireregiment.org.uk [accessed 1 April 2014].

www.westernfrontassociation.com/great-war-on-land/73-weapons-equipment-uniforms/158-british-artillery-fire.html [accessed 4 July 2014].

Brown, M., 1999. *1918 Year of Victory*. Pan Books.

Carver, 2003. *Turkish Front 1914–18*. 2nd edn. Pan Books.

Baker, Chris / Milverton Associates, 2014. *The Long Long Trail: How men joined the British Army*. Online at: www.1914-1918.net/recruitment.htm [accessed 7 June 2014].

Corrigan, G., 2003. *Mud, Blood and Poppycock*. Cassell.

Hall, M., 2002. *In Enemy Hands: A British Territorial Soldier in Germany 1915–1919*. Tempus.

Hallifax, S., 2010. '"Over by Christmas": British popular opinion and the short war in 1914.' *First World War Studies,* 1:2, DOI: 10.1080/19475020.2010.517429, 09 October, pp. 103–121.

Hancock, E., 2001. *Bazentin Ridge*. Pen and Sword.

King, J., 2011. *Great Battles in Australian History*. Allen and Unwin.

Macdonald, L., 1997. *1915 The Death of Innocence*. Penguin .

Passingham, I., 2008. *The German Offensives of 1918*. Pen and Sword.

Pitt, B., 2003. *1918 The Last Act*. Pen and Sword.

Smith, E., 1983. *Memories of a Country Girlhood*. Published by author.

Chapter 3

Albert Edward Bacon

Albert Bacon was not a Wymeswold man; the census record shows that he was born in Loughborough, the son of Henry Bacon, a bricklayer's labourer. The family lived at 25 Factory Street in 1901, having moved there from the St Margaret's area of Leicester. In 1903 Albert's mother had died at the age of 59, and in 1911 the family was in Wheatsheaf Yard in Loughborough. By this time however Albert had left home – he was fifteen, after all – and was living and working for the Bowley (or Bouley) family as a labourer on a farm at Long Whatton. There is a known connection between Wymeswold and Long Whatton; the Mills family of Wymeswold was related by marriage to a Long Whatton family. It is almost certain that he later moved to one of the Wymeswold farms, as he was included in a list of 'residents of Wymeswold, who are serving in His Majesty's Forces'. The list, drawn up by the vicar at the time, Claud Edmunds, probably dates from 1916, but may have been added to, and subtracted from, as the war went on.

According to the Loughborough Roll of Honour, Albert joined the Leicestershire Regiment when war broke out. He would have been 19 years old. The same source says that by this time, Albert had been working on a farm at Wymeswold. Like so many soldiers, his service records have been lost – probably as a result of German bombing in the Second World War.

However, he was clearly part of the village community. He wrote a postcard from Luton (it must have been very early in his service, as the Leicesters had evidently not yet been sent abroad), to the vicar, the Rev Claud Edmunds.

> Dear Sir,
>
> I am very pleased with your kind parcels I received this morning quite safe. Please remember me to the people, I am amongst the Wymeswold boys & I am expecting a leaving the trenches for Christmas so if I get it I will give you a call. No time to write a letter at present.
>
> I am your affectionate friend. A.E.Bacon.

Albert certainly saw himself as one of the 'Wymeswold boys'. And so he is, still. The date on the postmark is illegible, but since the 6th, 7th, 8th and 9th Leicesters (the 110th Brigade) arrived in France in July 1915, it was probably sent before then.

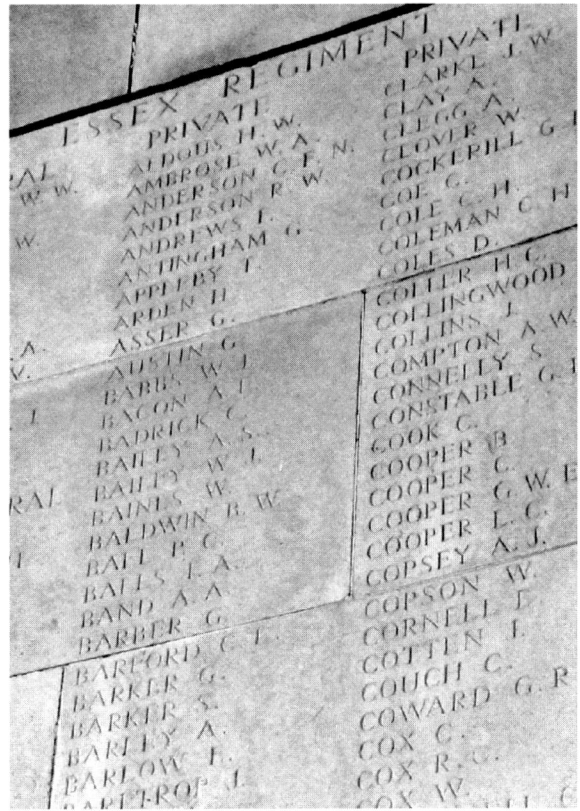

All we know for certain (from the Commonwealth War Graves Commission) is that at some point Private 16042 Bacon, Albert Edward, left the Leicestershire Regiment and became Private 43442 of the Essex Regiment. There might be all kinds of reasons for this: a simple need to reinforce the Essex Regiment; to disperse soldiers from the same home areas following the destruction of the Pals' Battalions on the Somme; or possibly Albert had been wounded, and been reassigned after convalescing. The Leicestershire Regiment website indicates that his first service number was actually 9/16042. This suggests that he was with the 9th (Service) battalion. Until the war, the regiment (like many others) had had two 'regular' battalions (1st and 2nd) and two territorial battalions (4th and 5th). The 3rd battalion was a training battalion which stayed in the UK through the war. In 1914, in response to Lord Kitchener's call for men, the regiment raised the 6th, 7th, 8th and 9th battalions for war service. They served together as the 110th Brigade, fighting with distinction at Bazentin Ridge (on the Somme) in July 1916. Such evidence as exists, therefore, suggests that Albert was one of the million-plus young men who responded to their country's call in the summer of 1914, and joined the New Army. Unfortunately, neither of his service numbers gives any idea as to when he joined the Essex regiment.

Though Albert's records have not survived, those of his brother Walter have. Taken with Albert's death they reveal a family tragedy which sadly enough must have been shared by many others across the country. Walter Peter Bacon was Albert's younger brother, born in 1896. At the age of just 19, on 12th October 1915, Walter joined up at Loughborough. His form was ratified in December and he was allocated to the Leicestershire Regiment as Private 23702. Like many British soldiers, he was not a big man – just 5 feet 2½ inches tall, with a chest measurement of only 34 inches. In fact, Australian soldiers were known to comment on the underfed appearance of their British counterparts.

Walter, now in the 10th (Service) battalion of the Leicesters, was not sent to the Western Front. Instead, in May 1916, he was sent to the 2nd Battalion and, by way of India, to the Persian Gulf and Mesopotamia (Iraq) . He was hospitalised twice; in May 1916 for pleurisy, and then in March 1917 for contusions to the face and side. He was discharged to his unit in the field on 25th March, but on 22nd April 1917, at Samara, he suffered a gunshot wound to the upper thigh, fracturing the thigh bone at the junction with his hip. He was sent to Basra, and from there to the Victoria War Hospital Bombay, via the Hospital Ship *Assage*. Surgeons had to drain a large abscess and then removed a piece of metal from his thigh. A Medical Board in July assessed him as being 'totally' unfit to work in civilian life, and 'permanently unfit' for further service. His left leg was now 1½ inches shorter. Returning to the UK, he spent months in hospital: firstly the 1/5th Northern Hospital where his wound was scraped (an X-Ray had discovered a metallic shadow and possible necrosis of the top of the thigh bone) and later at Gilroes Hospital, Leicester. He was eventually discharged in March 1918. In April, he was formally discharged from the army as an invalid. A Medical Board recommended that he should have a special boot fitted. Though several of his record sheets are stamped 'Deceased', it is likely that this was done many years later; it seems likely that Walter died in 1953, at the age of 57.

At home in George Street, Loughborough, Walter and Albert's father Henry was to receive two devastating pieces of news in 1917. Presumably the news of Walter's injury had already reached him by August, when he would have been told that Walter's elder brother, Albert, had been killed.

At the beginning of August 1917 the 2nd Essex were encamped just outside Arras, at Wilderness Camp. The battalion had been heavily involved in the battle for Arras which had raged from April until June. By trench warfare standards, it had been a great success, largely because of the capture of Vimy Ridge by the Canadians. The Germans had also been pushed back substantially from the eastern outskirts of Arras, and the city was now secure. The war had moved on – a big offensive at Ypres had just begun, and the job of the British at Arras was now to keep the enemy on their toes, and to spoil any attempts at counterattack. Orders had come from the 4th Division commander to organise a raid in strength. The battalions chosen for this were the 2nd Essex and some men from the 2nd Duke of Wellington's. The raid itself was intended to 'capture or kill as many of the enemy as possible and to obtain identification'; it had been scheduled for 8th August. After a delay in order to get artillery observers into place to guide the gunners, the raid went ahead at 7.45 p.m. on the 9th. One hundred and eighty Essex men went out into No Man's Land, covered by a 'creeping barrage'. The artillery cover was 'not very intense' and the raiders were met with heavy machine gun fire and a barrage of grenades. The war diary notes that as a result 'what remained of the raiding party had to retire'. The following day, members of the battalion were able to recover a few of the bodies of those who had been killed.

Albert was presumably killed in the raid. Maybe his was one of the bodies never recovered, since he has no known grave, and is remembered on Bay 7 of the Arras memorial to the missing. Born in mid-1895, he was just 22 when he died. At home in Loughborough, Henry Bacon, the 69 year-old widower, was told of his family's second sacrifice in a single year.

The remaining mystery around Albert Bacon is: who had his name included on the Roll of Honour? If his only involvement with the village was to have worked on a farm before the war, then he must have made his mark. Unlike George Williams, whose sister remained in the village after the rest of the family had moved, there is no discoverable family connection with Wymeswold. His elder half-brothers and his younger brother and sister do not show up on any Wymeswold records. His mother's maiden name was Bates, and there was a Bates family in the village, but there is no evidence of a family connection there either. On the other hand, two other men – Frederick Robinson and Colin Bramall – had only been in the village briefly, and they were remembered. However, both of these had 'public' roles – Colin was the local policeman and Frederick was a shop manager. Albert was a farm worker. Perhaps the family he worked for thought highly of him and wanted him remembered? Perhaps he was engaged, and a fiancée asked for his inclusion on the list? At this distance in time, we may never be sure of the exact details. It is enough perhaps, to know that he was well thought of, and that he was missed. It is a good enough epitaph for us all.

Sources

Census records: 1891, 1901, 1911.

Wymeswold parish registers. Online at: www.hoap.co.uk/who/localhisregister.htm [accessed June 2014].

Wymeswold Church of England School: log books and misc papers 1875–1983 (DE7281). The Record Office for Leicestershire, Leicester and Rutland.

Wymeswold vicar's correspondence (DE 1728/37). The Record Office for Leicestershire, Leicester and Rutland.

War Diary 2nd Battalion Essex Regiment August 1917 (WO 95/1505). The National Archives.

Medal Roll Index Cards (Series WO 373). The National Archives.

armyservicenumbers.blogspot.co.uk [accessed 18 June 2014].

www.royalleicestershireregiment.org.uk [accessed 1 April 2014].

Kelly, D., 2001. *39 Months with the 'Tigers' 1915–1918.* reprint edn. Naval and Military Press.

Richardson, M., no date. *The Tigers: 6th, 7th, 8th, 9th (Service) Battalions of the Leicestershire Regiment.*

Chapter 4

Colin Bramall

Policemen, especially when you are young, seem indestructible. They are the living proof that society has rules and order. Yet they are as vulnerable as any of us, and so was Colin Bramall. He had not been in the police service for many years, as in 1911 he was a 'pass' (probably passenger) cleaner on the railways. He was newly married to Clara, and they were living at 57 Kings Meadow Road, Nottingham.

He was not born or raised in Wymeswold; his roots were in Yorkshire, at Bradfield, near Sheffield. According to the 1891 census, his father Joseph had started out as a farm labourer in Wortley, Yorkshire, but by the census of 1901, Joseph had become a stockman in Wortley. Colin was all set to follow in his father's footsteps, as he was also working as a stockman, aged just 13. Ten years later, the family had moved to Stapleford, near Melton Mowbray, where his father had got a job as farm manager at Holly Gate Farm for the Stapleford Park estate – quite a step up in life. By 1911, the family had been in Stapleford for a few years, as Colin's youngest brother Cyril (then aged four) had been born there. Colin and his next younger brother, Reginald, had both left home, leaving Arthur (aged 19, and a cowman like his father and brother before him) as the eldest of the children still at home.

In November 1911, Colin joined the police. He was following in Reginald's footsteps – his younger brother had joined in April. The brothers must have been ideal recruits; they were tall (both 5 feet 10½ inches) and they had both already served for two years in the Territorials. Their careers followed identical paths – each of them was promoted Constable Second Class after three months, then First Class after three years. Arthur gave up farm work in July 1913 and joined them. All three brothers were in good, secure jobs with excellent prospects. Colin was evidently an enthusiastic officer – in April 1912 he was among a group of nine policemen who were awarded a gratuity (1/- for P.C.s and 1/6d for the sergeants) who had assisted at a fire. His signature in the police gratuities book shows a strong and confident writer – he was well-educated.

There is no indication of when Colin was posted to Wymeswold, but it is likely that it was somewhere between November 1912, when his first child Joseph was born, and October 1914. He was certainly living here when Florence May was born on October 5th. She was baptised in St Mary's three weeks later, on November 1st. Colin and Elizabeth were living in Brook Street, probably in the 'old police house' as it still known, at 81 Brook Street.

As Territorials, both Colin and Reginald were committed to the defence of their country in time of war. The Territorial forces, however, were originally designed to cope with internal unrest, or to defend against an invading enemy. Before 1916, when conscription was introduced, they could not be forced to fight overseas. On the other hand, they were also a source of trained men who were urgently needed. Both Reginald and Colin left the police in June 1915 and were enlisted in the Royal Artillery. Colin's service record has not survived, though his 'medal card' – the record of his medal entitlements – does. The service records for his brothers Reginald and Arthur do, however, exist, and they volunteered in May and December 1915 respectively. It is quite likely, therefore, that Colin volunteered at, or around, the same time as Reginald. From the Leicestershire Constabulary records, it is clear that though they were soldiers, their police service would continue until their return. In Colin's case, though his service was ended by his death, he was credited with 5 years and 188 days – in other words, the time between joining the Constabulary in 1911 and his death in 1917.

If Colin's war service started like his Reginald's, he was not sent abroad immediately. Indeed, most men, regardless of experience, would undergo several months' training at least. Reginald was sent to France in January 1916, and it is likely that Colin went at about the same time. He would have left Elizabeth at home with Joseph and little Florence, and pregnant with their third child. His son Colin was born in January 1916. It is likely that Elizabeth had moved to Loughborough, as Colin junior was born there, at 36 Morley Street, in January 1916.

Though all three brothers had volunteered for the Royal Artillery, they did not all serve in the same branch. Both Colin and Reginald had volunteered locally (hence the 'L' prefix on Royal Artillery service numbers). Reginald's service record confirms this – he attested in Leicester. Since both Colin and Reginald had evidently volunteered for the Royal Artillery, they were naturally assigned to the local brigade, the 176th (Leicestershire) Howitzer Brigade. After a few months in France with the 176th Reginald was transferred to the 160th (Wearside). This seems to match exactly Colin's progress. According to the Loughborough Roll of Honour, he had firstly 'joined the Howitzer Battery'. Colin junior's birth certificate shows that his father was still with the Leicestershire Howitzer Brigade in January 1916. The Loughborough Roll of Honour, and the war diary of 160th Brigade confirm that he was with them when he died.

Arthur, on the other hand, volunteered in December 1915, but was not called up until June 1917. Meanwhile, the *Melton Times* reported on 18th May 1917 that he and PC Jones, 'who have been stationed at Melton Mowbray for several years, have this week enlisted in the Royal Artillery'. Presumably they had received their call-up notices. The newspaper also reported 'We are sorry to learn that the latter's brother, Sergt. Colin Bramall, has been killed in action'. Arthur was allocated, not to the Field Artillery, but to the Royal Garrison Artillery. This group was originally responsible for coastal batteries, but because of its expertise with heavy guns, it was soon being used on both the Western Front and in the Middle East. In Arthur's case, he served in France with the 179th Siege Battery from October 1917 until the end of the war.

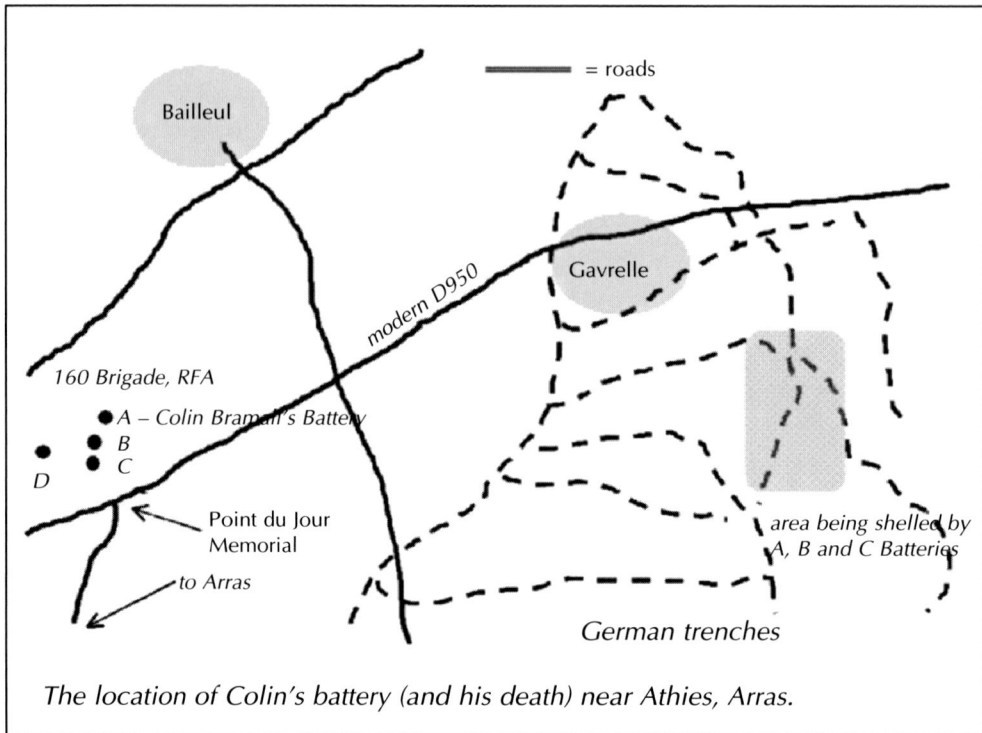

The location of Colin's battery (and his death) near Athies, Arras.

In May 1917, Colin was with the 160th Brigade, Royal Field Artillery, several miles to the east of Arras. The Brigade's war diary is terse but informative. On 1st May, they positioned their guns just north of what is now the Point Du Jour Memorial and cemetery, north of the present day suburb of Athies. Three of the four batteries of guns were drawn up beside each other. 'A' Battery, which Colin served in as a sergeant, was the most northerly, with the others strung out every fifty yards or so in a line that reached back in a south-westerly direction. Each battery would have consisted of six 18-pounder guns, capable of firing a shrapnel or high explosive shell around 6,000 yards. These were the standard British field guns, with which a well-trained crew could put 30 shells on target in a minute. The crew consisted of ten men, normally led by a sergeant (which implies that Colin was in charge of one of the guns). In addition to the business of firing the gun, and loading it, men were needed to act as replacements in case of injury, and to look after the horses. (Guns and, importantly, spare ammunition, all had to be pulled by horses).

'D' Battery was the most southerly, and therefore furthest from the German lines. Traditionally, 'D' was assigned to the single howitzer battery in the Brigade. These were heavy guns – probably 4.5-inch diameter barrels, firing a shell that weighed 35 pounds. Their range was much greater than the 18-pounders, too – 7,300 yards was standard. Each battery was targeting an area of German trenches, no more than a hundred yards wide in each case, about 4,500 yards away.

For a week or so the batteries subjected the German lines to a variety of bombardments. Sometimes they carried out 'searching' fire, probing the area behind the enemy trenches up to 400 yards in depth. Sometimes they put down 'creeping' barrages – where the shells were fired a little further every few minutes. This was standard practice when the infantry attacked, in order to give them covering fire. On the 8th they carried out a 'Chinese' attack. This consisted of a barrage, after which the guns would wait a while. The idea was that the enemy, thinking that the barrage was the beginning of a major attack, would come out of their dugouts and man their trenches. The barrage would then re-commence, hoping to catch as many enemy soldiers as possible. Colin's last action came at 3.45 a.m. on May 10th. The war diary reports 'In accordance with 9th Div: B2/401/159, of 9 May 1917, 18 pr Batteries fired 3 rds of gun fire at hostile front trenches in Battery lines'.

The war diary for May concludes with a list of casualties for the month. Among them is a reference to ' L28883 A Brammall, Sergeant, A/160, killed in action'. Since all ranks are listed, right down to Gunners, this must be a reference to L 28853 C Bramall, Wymeswold's policeman. He was the only man to die that day. The war diary makes no mention of the way he died, and ordinarily one would assume that it was just a stray German shell, or an accident. However, the local newspaper subsequently reported that he had been killed by a bomb. Though there is no mention of bombing on the day, the brigade had been attacked by an aircraft a week previously, so it is possible that it had returned. (On the other hand, the word 'bomb' in 1917 could also refer to a grenade or a trench mortar.)

Back in England, the local Press printed his death notice. On May 25th, the Melton Times announced:

> LOCAL POLICEMAN KILLED. – As briefly announced in our last issue, news has been received that Private Colin Bramall, of the Artillery, was killed on May 10th. A bomb exploded near, killing him instantaneously....he was a member of the Leicestershire Constabulary stationed first at Loughborough and then at Wymeswold, from where he enlisted in June, 1915. He leaves a widow and three children in Burder-street, Loughborough.

This confirms that Elizabeth had indeed left Wymeswold, probably because the police house was no longer available to her. Yet the memory of their stay in the village must have resonated with residents, because he was included in the Roll of Honour from the moment of its inception.

And what happened to the others in this family drama? A number of records exist to be able to piece together a story. Reginald , still with 160th Brigade, got ten days' leave ('rations allowed') two months after Colin's death. Was this a form of compassionate leave? It is impossible to say, as compassionate leave appears to have been highly discretionary at the time. However, the coincidence of dates is significant. In February 1918 he was admitted to hospital with 'Trench Fever and Deafness.' It may have been while in hospital in France that he contracted influenza, which resulted in him being shipped home in March, to be treated at the 5th Northern Hospital in Leicester. The 'flu saved him from the German Spring Offensive, and possibly saved his life. His convalescence must have been a long one,

*Colin Bramall's grave at
St Nicolas' British Cemetery,
Arras.*

since he never returned to France. He was finally demobbed in January 1919, and went home to his wife in Hinckley Road, Earl Shilton. He was back on the strength of the Leicestershire Constabulary on the 8th January 1919, and stayed with the police, rising to the rank of sergeant. In total, he served 35 years as a Police Officer until he retired in March 1946.

Arthur served with his siege battery in France, and was promoted Lance Bombardier at the beginning of October 1918. He was given leave at the end of the month, and returned to France on the 11th of November – the day of the Armistice. His guns would not fire again. Like Reginald, he was demobbed in January, and returned to his parents' home at Holygate Farm, Stapleford Park, near Melton Mowbray. He rejoined the police on 26th January 1919, and served until October 1939.

Elizabeth moved to Oxford and remarried in 1919, to Percy Oliver. Her children grew up and spent their lives in the Oxford area. The British War Cemetery at St Nicolas, a suburb of Arras, is tucked away behind houses and allotments, giving it a less austere feel than many war cemeteries. It is a beautiful and peaceful little cemetery, and it is here that Colin Bramall lies.

Sources

Birth and marriage certificates. General Register Office.

Census records: 1891, 1901, 1911.

Wymeswold parish registers. Online at: www.hoap.co.uk/who/localhisregister.htm [accessed June 2014].

Police Officers' Personnel Records (DE 3831) and Police Officers' Gratuities (DE 3831/221). The Record Office for Leicestershire, Leicester and Rutland.

Map: M/78/000042 Gavrelle 51bNW 230517. Western Front Association.

Medal Roll Index Cards (Series WO 373). The National Archives.

Service Record: 166931 Bramall, Arthur. The National Archives.

Service Record: L/29056 Bramall, Reginald. The National Archives.

War Diary 'A' Battery 160 Bde Royal Field Artillery May 1917 (WO 95/2446). The National Archives.

community.ancestry.co.uk/messages/ [accessed 2014].

www.westernfrontassociation.com/great-war-on-land/73-weapons-equipment-uniforms/158-british-artillery-fire.html [accessed 4 July 2014].

Baker, Chris / Milverton Associates, 2014. 'The Long Long Trail: Renumbering of the Territorial Force in 1917'. Online at: www.1914-1918.net/renumbering.htm [accessed 6 June 2014].

Kempf, P., no date.'Landships II'. Online at: www.landships.info/landships/artillery_articles/4_5in_Howitzer.html [accessed 4 July 2014].

Marshall, N., 2008. 'Great War Forum: Compassionate leave from France'. Online at: 1914-1918.invisionzone.com/forums/index.php?showtopic=111171 [accessed 5 July 2014].

Melton Times, 1917.

Mitchell, K., no date.'Loughborough Roll of Honour'. Online at: loughborough-rollofhonour.com/page44.htm [accessed 20 June 2014].

Chapter 5

John Wilfred Brookes

Framework knitting had been a cottage industry in Wymeswold since the eighteenth century. Machine knitting had been invented in the sixteenth century in Nottinghamshire. It had been a major improvement on hand knitting – the speed of production was almost 100 times faster. Though the industry spread, by the nineteenth century it was still focussed in Nottinghamshire, Leicestershire and Derbyshire. On the other hand, the competition from factory-made and imported goods meant that by the turn of the twentieth century it was dying out. The slow pace of the manual knitting frames in local cottages could not compare with the giant automated knitting machines in Leicester and Nottingham. The fortunes of the Brookes family mirror the changing fortunes of rural industry, and help us to see how people a hundred years ago responded to the economic challenges posed by the decline of established trades.

In 1851, there were over sixty framework knitters in Wymeswold. John Wilfred's grandfather James was one of them, working in cotton, on Far Street. We can guess at several cottages which might have been his home, as they still have the comparatively large windows needed to provide daylight to work the fabric. Business must have been fairly good, as two of his sons, John and Thomas, were working in the same trade. Another son, James, was a cotton winder and a daughter, Elizabeth, was a laceworker. Henry (John Wilfred's father) was just seven months' old. By 1871, however, Henry had joined the family business. The location is better described; still on Far Street, but between Charles Yard and North Yard. North Yard no longer exists, but Charles Yard can be seen as a driveway opposite the Three Crowns pub in Far Street.

In 1871 then, Henry, now 21, was a framework knitter in his own right, as were his elder brothers James and William, while it was the turn of his younger brothers Arthur and Frederick to be cotton winders. By 1881, Henry and his young family had moved into Charles Yard, and he was a framework knitter – in 'cotton and merino', someone has added. He was 30 and his wife Elizabeth just 25, but she worked as a sempstress, despite having three children aged between five months and six years. During the next ten years, however, the family fortunes changed. In 1891, Henry and his wife (still a seamstress) had had another two children (including John Wilfred – referred to simply as Wilfred), but significantly Henry was now an agricultural labourer. The family's address was in Far Street, but there is no reference in the census to Charles Yard or North Yard, so it is not possible to say whether they gave up their old home when they gave up the knitting frame, or whether they were able to stay.

The 1901 census shows a further two children, and perhaps a move up for Henry, who now said he was a 'labourer m. garden'. He was nevertheless a 'worker' and therefore not self-employed, though perhaps his implication that he worked in a market garden was an attempt to show that he worked on his own account as well as for an employer. If that were so, then it did not work out, as in the 1911 census Henry was a 'labourer on farm' as were the two sons still at home, James and John Wilfred. The family of four were now living in a three-roomed house in East End.

John Wilfred – known at school simply as Wilfred – merited only two mentions in the school log book. The first, when he was about eleven, was for being 'a very bad speller… Wilfred Brookes worked only one sum correctly.' On the other hand, the following year, 1912, he won a prize - *A Gospel Picture Book* – for Scripture Knowledge. For a boy probably in his final year at school, he had not distinguished himself academically. He was still in Standard iii and there were five standards of attainment that children could pass through. Perhaps he was more practically gifted, like his sister Alice. She too was considered a 'weak' speller, but in 1904, aged about eight, she and another girl were praised for their needlework – the best in the school.

Sometime between 1911 and his death, Wilfred married. The Commonwealth War Graves Commission observes that he was the 'son of Henry and Elizabeth Brookes, of Far St., Wymeswold, nr. Loughborough; husband of Mary Brookes, of Brook Street, Wymeswold, nr. Loughborough.' It is most likely that he married Mary in 1913 – the Marriage Index for Loughborough records a John W. Brookes marrying a Mary Simpson in the autumn of 1913. The Parish Baptismal records show two children were born to Mary: Frank in the January of 1914, and Florence in November 1915. It is unlikely that Wilfred was in the army at this time, as his occupation is referred to as 'labourer'. Neither does he appear on the 1914–1915 list of 'old boys' of the school, nor on the Vicar's list of early 1916. It seems likely then, that Wilfred was called up, rather than one of Lord Kitchener's early volunteers.

There was however a distant family connection to the armed services. In 1900, the school log book refers to an Ernest Brookes serving in the army – presumably during the Boer War. Ernest, born in 1877, may well have been a relative, though there is no obvious connection between the two families as far back as Wilfred's grandfather James. Additionally, Ernest's family were listed as Brooks (without the 'e') in censuses. On the other hand, the Brooks family were also framework knitters. Whether the experience of Ernest was something that encouraged Wilfred, or persuaded him not to volunteer, is something we shall never know.

What seem to be the service records of Wilfred's brother James have survived, and may give some clues as to what happened to Wilfred. James took his oath of attestation before a magistrate in December 1915, but it was not until September 1916 that he was actually taken into the army. When that happened, the 29-year old James was in for a surprise. He had expressed a preference for the 3/6th Battalion,

Wilfred's Death Plaque, kept by Mary.

Leicestershire Regiment (which, from its '3/' prefix, would have been a territorial or reserve battalion)– indicating that James had already either joined the Reserves or had friends who had). However the army, in its wisdom, sent him to the Army Service Corps. Now this actually had some logic to it; the ASC provided the transport and logistic support to the army, and James' civilian occupation was a 'roadmaker, steam (driver)'. In other words, he drove a steamroller! In an age when very few people had any acquaintance with motorised transport, James' experience must have seemed perfect for the ASC. By December he had been sent to France and attached to the 40th Auxiliary Motor Transport Company. His record shows that he served in two companies, and drove a variety of (mostly) steam engines (not rail, of course), or waggons.

It is worth noting just how significant motorisation was becoming in the few years before the war. Ted Morris drove a steam threshing machine; John Marriott, grandfather of George Marriott (killed in March 1918) was also a driver. James himself, though he lived in Woodhouse Eaves in 1916, actually worked for Bower Bros, of West Bridgford – businesses themselves were becoming more mobile, and able to extend their operations much more widely, thanks to the new forms of transport.

Like his younger brother, James had married (in October 1915). His wife was formerly Florence Emily Sykes, of Woodhouse Eaves. The couple also had two children – twins in fact: Florence Emily and Ellen Elizabeth, both born on the 1st January 1917. James was fortunate; he was to come home to his wife and little girls in March 1919. Driving lorries could be dangerous – ammunition resupply convoys in particular were targets for German artillery – but on the whole it was much less

Above: *Wilfred's two children, Frank and Florence.*

Right: *Mary, Wilfred's widow, pictured in the late 1920s or early 1930s.*

Photographs courtesy of Mrs S. Elliott.

dangerous than being in a front line battalion. James' technical skill had stood him in good stead, even though he had wanted to join a fighting unit.

Wilfred, however, was posted to just such a unit – the 11th (Service) battalion, West Riding Regiment, part of the 23rd Division. Assuming that he joined up at the same time, or later than his brother, the Division would already have fought its way through a roll call of the 'hot spots' of the Western Front: in 1916 it was at Contalmaison, the Battles of Bazentin Ridge, Pozieres, Flers-Courcelette, Morval and the Battle of Le Transloy, including the capture of Le Sars. The next year it fought in the Battle of Messines, the Battles of the Menin Road, Polygon Wood and the First and Second Battles of Passchendaele. It was not until November 1917 that the Division moved to north-eastern Italy where it took over the front line at the Montello on the 4th of December. In 1918 it fought on the Asiago Plateau, crossed the Piave and later the Monticano rivers, finally taking part in the Battle of Vittorio Veneto.

In August 1918, Wilfred's battalion was sent up into the mountains, near Asiago. In June, the Austrians had launched a 'last throw of the dice' offensive on the Allied lines along the Piave river. They had initially pushed forward, and crossed the Piave, but were thrown back within a few weeks. The British, with the Italians, were regrouping and preparing for an offensive that they now knew the Austrians would not be able to withstand. Therefore much of August saw little action on the Asiago plateau. For most of that month, the battalion was in reserve, and had time for baths, church parades, and plenty of training. The men were deployed, in their companies, on the firing ranges, as were the Lewis gun teams. It was on one of these training days, August 20th, that the

> ... vicinity of the camp was shelled by enemy heavy artillery in the evening, causing us casualties as follows:- 5 O.R. killed, 9 O.Rs. wounded.

The next day, the 21st, was described as a 'quiet day'. It was a day that John Wilfred Brookes would never see. He had died the day before, almost certainly in that short, possibly random, but devastating artillery attack.

By October, the Division had pushed north and crushed the last Austrian resistance at Vittorio Veneto. The war in Italy was effectively over. Wilfred now rests in Boscon British cemetery near the village of Cesuna, in the beautiful mountains around Asiago.

John Wilfred Brookes had died just 70 days short of the end of hostilities in northern Italy. To us, it may seem agonisingly close to the end of the war, but to Mary and the children it would have been, quite simply, the end of their lives as they knew them, and an uncertain future based around a war widow's pension, family help, and such work as Mary might find. The story has, in fact, a pragmatic ending. John's elder brother, William, was left a widower in December 1918, shortly after Wilfred's death. William had five children, and lived next door to Mary and her two children. It seemed a very practical solution that they should marry; it was, according to the family, a marriage of convenience. Being a bricklayer and builder, William simply knocked a hole in the dividing wall between the two cottages, and created one house for all of them. Though Mary went on to have another two children, she always kept a large picture of Wilfred in the hall.

Sources

Census records: 1851, 1871, 1881, 1891, 1901, 1911.

Wymeswold Church of England School: log books and misc papers 1875–1983 (DE7281). The Record Office for Leicestershire, Leicester and Rutland.

Service Record: 222486 Brookes James Henry, The National Archives.

Commonwealth War Graves Commission. 'Find War Dead' Online at: www.cwgc.org [accessed 7 February 2014].

www.wartimememoriesproject.com/greatwar/allied/westyorkshireregiment11.php [accessed 12 February 2014].

Chapter 6

John Edward Clarke

The Clarke family relationships were a bit complicated, and need explaining. Essentially Thomas Clarke, born around 1841 in Wymeswold, married twice, and had two families. One family produced the Thomas who died in 1918, and the other produced John.

John's father, also John Edward, was the son of the elder Thomas Clarke. Thomas married Harriet Savage, of East Leake, with whom he had at least four children – Hannah, Ellen, John and William. However, St Mary's parish registers show that Harriet died in September 1878, and Thomas remarried in July 1879, to Sarah Collington, of Wymeswold. His marriage to Sarah produced six children – Ann E., Amos, Lucy, Ruth, Thomas (born 1891) and Sally.

John Edward Clarke (born 1898) was therefore the grandson of Thomas the elder, and the nephew of the Thomas who was killed, although he was only eight years younger than his uncle. His time at the village school shows little formal academic promise – his performance in 1908 was described as 'weak' (a distinction incidentally that he shared with George Orridge, the elder brother of Herbert, and with Foster Simpson). It is ironic that John and Foster may have been undistinguished at school, but were good enough to put their lives on the line for their country. John did however win some praise at school. Twice he was awarded a prize for Scripture. In 1907 he was given a copy of *Pilgrim Street*, and in 1910 *The Lamplighter*. On both occasions, the books were paid for by the Jobson Fund. His siblings on the whole had less mention in the school log books, though his sister Harriet (presumably named after his late grandmother) seems to have been away ill on a number of occasions, including one period of over three months.

The 1911 census shows that John was still at school. Nearly thirteen, he would be keen, as most boys were, to leave and start working on the land. The census also gives a brief picture of how the lives of villagers were interconnected. John's elder brother William was working at Manor Farm with George Spicer (died 1916). William was a waggoner and George a cowman. The same census reveals that his sister Harriet was still living in Wymeswold, working for the Burrows family as a domestic servant. Deborah Knifton, 46, is also there as a nurse, presumably looking after the Burrows' small children. Deborah was the foster mother of Eric Evans, who was killed in the Soissons battle in May 1918.

Eliza, John's elder sister, pictured in 1948. Photograph courtesy of Muriel Camm.

The Leicestershire Regiment website says that John enlisted at Loughborough, but it does not say when. Unless he lied about his age, he could have joined in the second quarter of 1916, after his eighteenth birthday. He would have less than a year to live. He joined the 1/5th Battalion, Leicestershire Regiment, and was allocated to 'A' Company. This battalion was one of the Territorial units. The pre-war regular regiment had had two battalions (1st and 2nd) with a notional 3rd, which became used in the war as a training formation. Battalion numbers 6 to 9 were to be the 'New Army' battalions, raised following Lord Kitchener's call for men in 1916. At first, the Territorial battalions most likely to go overseas had the designation 1/ (i.e. the first wave), followed by others that were given 2/, and so on. Each of these 'waves' would be given battalion numbers that followed on from the 'old' battalions of the regiment. Therefore the Leicester Territorial battalions were 1/4 th, 1/5 th, 2/4 th, 2/5 th, 3/4 th and 3/5 th. It is worth noting that the 1/5th and the 3/5th were both raised in Loughborough, though 1/5th – John's battalion – was raised in August 1914 and the 3/5th in early 1915. This raises the possibility that John joined up before older men, like George Spicer, who joined the 3/5th. In so doing, it also raises questions about John's age when he enlisted. To join the regular or new armies, a recruit would have to be eighteen or over. John would not have been eighteen until 1916. On the other hand, seventeen year olds could join the Territorials, since they were not originally an overseas force. Historically, they had been raised to keep order in the UK. So a

John's last resting place at Noeux-Les-Mines, Nord Pas de Calais, France.

seventeen-year-old could join the Territorials, but could not be forced to serve overseas until he was eighteen. On the other hand, he could volunteer before then. Without John's service record, it is not possible to say when he actually enlisted, but he may have been very young indeed.

In May 1917 the 1/5 th Leicesters were in an area known as Fosse 10, near Angres, a couple of miles west of Lens and about three miles north of Vimy Ridge. During that month they were in and out of the line several times – it was normal practice for battalions 'at the front' to 'rotate' in the line and then in reserve, probably every four days or so. During this time there were a number of casualties. The war diary of the battalion does not always say how many were wounded or killed on a particular day – there was just so much routine shelling going on. We know, however, that in the first week there were 41 casualties.

From the 7th to the 12th the soldiers were behind the lines in Divisional Reserve, and had chance to bathe and to clean their kit and clothes. On the 12th they moved into Brigade Reserve – still behind the front lines, and with the facility of a swimming bath! Even at a distance from the first line trenches, they were not safe – four men became casualties even before they moved into their billets. From the 15th to the 18th they were in front line trenches, and subject to more serious fire. A whole Lewis gun section became casualties, probably of a German 'Priest Grenade'. The battalion held a series of outposts in the cellars of ruined houses. The war diary comments that:

> … these houses were subject to heavy trench mortaring and had
> the posts been easy for the enemy to locate, heavy casualties
> would probably have been the result.

It does not comment on how many casualties were sustained anyway.

At some point, either in the relative calm of the reserve trenches, or in the constantly-shelled front line cellars, John Edward Clarke was mortally wounded. If he had been so badly wounded that he died in the front lines, then he would probably be buried locally. Instead, he must have been evacuated to a field hospital, probably the 7th Casualty Clearing Station, about seven miles from where he was wounded. In April 1917 it had begun to use the cemetery at Noeux-Les-Mines, and this is where John was laid to rest. He was just nineteen years old.

Sources

Census records: 1861, 1871, 1881, 1901, 1911.

Wymeswold parish registers. Online at: www.hoap.co.uk/who/localhisregister.htm [accessed June 2014].

Wymeswold Church of England School: log books and misc papers 1875–1983 (DE7281). The Record Office for Leicestershire, Leicester and Rutland.

Wymeswold vicar's correspondence (DE 1728/37). The Record Office for Leicestershire, Leicester and Rutland.

Commonwealth War Graves Commission. 'Find War Dead' Online at: www.cwgc.org [accessed 7 February 2014].

War Diary 1st/5th Bn Leicestershire Regiment May 1917 (WO 95/2690). The National Archives.

www.royalleicestershireregiment.org.uk [accessed 1 April 2014].

Baker, Chris / Milverton Associates, 2014. 'The Leicestershire Regiment'. Online at: www.1914-1918.net/leicesters.htm [accessed 19 July 2014].

Chapter 7

Thomas Clarke

Thomas Clarke was actually the uncle of John Edward Clarke, but was just eight years older. The family relationships may seem strange at first, but in an age when families were large, and early death was commonplace, we should not be surprised that Thomas' father married twice, and had two families. Thomas was from the second family and therefore half-brother to John Edward Clarke's father. His mother was Sarah Collington. She and Thomas senior married in July 1879, following the death of his first wife Harriet in 1878. Within a year her first child Ann Eveline was born, and the couple went on to have a total of eight children. The second eldest, Amos, would become key to Thomas's story.

At the time of his marriage to Sarah, Thomas senior was an agricultural labourer, and was probably still living at the home had had shared with Harriet. By 1891, the family was in East Street and had six children, ranging from Ann, then eleven, to Thomas, just one month old.

By the year of Thomas' birth, all the elder children – Annie, Amos, Lucy and Sally – had won prizes for scripture or religious knowledge at the Infant School . This does not necessarily indicate that Thomas had no love of learning, or of scripture – the Infant School log books do not record prizes every year. However, the Mixed School, to which Thomas would have moved at around the age of six, does not show any great academic progress either. In contrast to his brother Amos and his sister Ruth, who both won prizes, the entries relating to Thomas are less complimentary. For example, his first mention comes on 11th October 1901 – near the end of his school career: 'During the week Standards ii to iv have been examined... In Standard iii Richard Wilson, Sam Morris and Tom Clarke did badly.' His second and last appearance in the log book occurs on 14th March 1903, with the terse 'Thos Clarke and Dor. Macer sick.' Dorothy Macer was well-known to be a delicate child, and frequently sick. Was Tom Clarke singled out because he was also a well-known absentee, or because it was unusual? The date may be significant, as it was close to his twelfth birthday – an age at which most boys would be looking forward to working (whether legally or not) on the farms.

Meanwhile, Amos, having won a number of prizes, had left school and joined the Coldstream Guards. Yet he maintained close links with his village and its school. On no less than five occasions, the school log book records his return visits, and in particular his helpfulness in taking the children for drill. Marching, according to the log books, was an integral part of the children's physical education. The entries in the log also record Amos' rise in the regiment: Corporal in 1903, Sergeant in 1905 and, by 1914, when the school Roll of Honour was started, he had been promoted Sergeant-Major. In 1916 there was a special entry:

> Feb 17 An honour to this school

The Head Master has just been informed that Sergeant Major Clarke is the smartest Officer in the Coldstream Guards, stationed at the present time at Caterham, Surrey. He is a native of this village, and of course one of our 'old boys'.

Tom, as he was referred to at school, soon established himself as a worker and something of an entrepreneur. In 1911, then just twenty, he described himself as a coal dealer. Still living at home and single, he was the only one of Thomas' and Sarah's children not to have set up their own home. Perhaps in addition to helping out with the family budget for his parents, now aged 70 and 68, he was also helpful with childcare for his niece Lois, Amos' daughter, who was staying with them at the time of the census. His single status did not last much longer, as he married Emma Bexon in May 1911, just after the census was taken. At thirty, she was ten years older than him, and had been running the family home in Loughborough, which she shared with her brother, a salt merchant, and with her two younger sisters.

By 1915, when Thomas enlisted, they had set up their own home in Far Street. He was no longer a coal dealer, but had set up as a grazier and carter – still in business on his own account, it seems. He had evidently resisted the temptation to join up in the heady days of 1914, when over a million responded to Kitchener's call. Neither had he been a member of the Territorials, as a number of village boys had. In his attestation forms, he specifically stated that he had not been a member of any of His Majesty's forces. Yet, for whatever reason, he had decided by the winter of 1915 that the time had come to join the army.

With an elder brother like Amos, what regiment should Thomas apply for but the Coldstream Guards? We do not know whether Amos 'spoke up' for him, but it would be very strange if he did not. Thomas' records have survived. The Guards regiments did not store their records with the rest of the army, and theirs were spared the bomb damage that affected so many other records. Thomas 'attested' – presented himself for enlistment – at Caterham in December 1915. It is significant that he did not join up locally and express a preference for the Coldstreams, but went directly to their home base to sign up. Again, it is strong but circumstantial evidence that he went there with Amos. However, he was not mobilized (called up) until September 1916. For the next year he was based at Caterham – did Amos try to keep him away from the front? But he was sent to France in August 1917.

While in England, he had completed a course as a first-aider and stretcher-bearer. Is that what he did in France? If so, he was in good company – it was the same duty that Ernest Hubbard carried out. Rescuing and evacuating men under fire was not a job

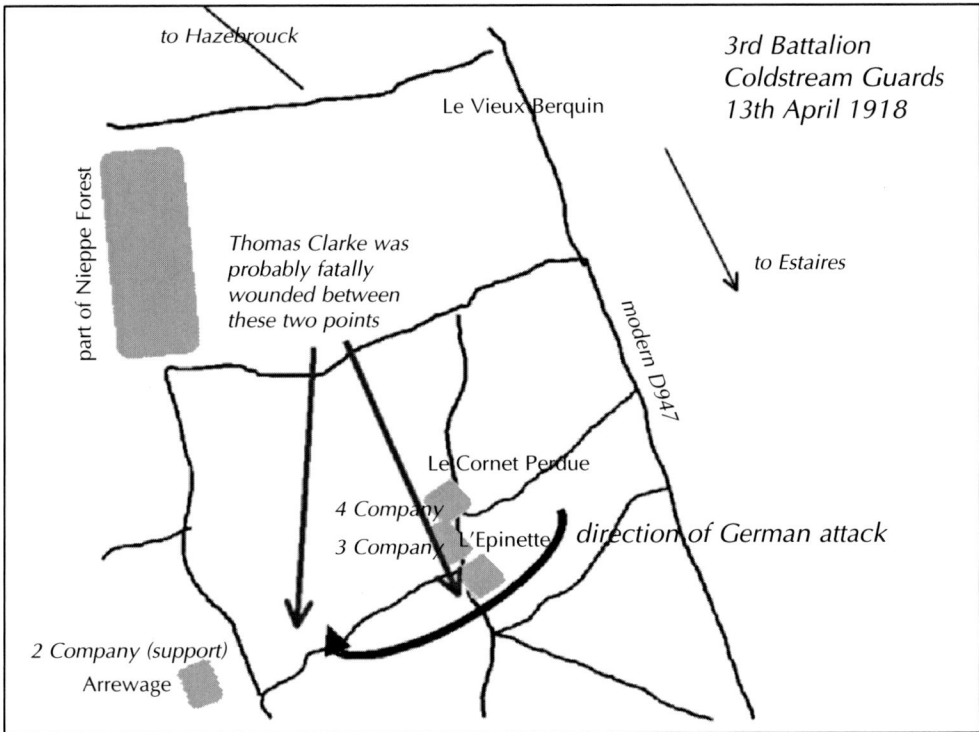

to Hazebrouck

Le Vieux Berquin

**3rd Battalion
Coldstream Guards
13th April 1918**

part of Nieppe Forest

*Thomas Clarke was
probably fatally
wounded between
these two points*

to Estaires

modern D947

Le Cornet Perdue

4 Company

3 Company   L'Epinette   *direction of German attack*

2 Company (support)
Arrewage

for the faint hearted, and stretcher-bearers were often regarded as heroes. Either way, he would have been familiar with the hardships and horrors of the Western Front. As part of the 1st Guards Brigade, Guards Division, he would have seen action in October and November at Poelcapelle and Passchendaele, as part of the 3rd battle of Ypres. He would also have been at the battle of Cambrai a few weeks later. By April 1918, the 3rd battalion Coldstream Guards was in action in the area south of Hazebrouck, in the coalfields of northern France. On the 1st April, it had come out of the trenches, and after another two days of moving positions, settled down to training and preparing for whatever might come next.

What in fact happened was a full Divisional Inspection, in ceremonial order, on the morning of the 10th, less than nine days after they had been in the mud and horror of the front line. Then, within twelve hours, they were waiting at the roadside for most of the night for buses to take them back 'up the line'. In the early hours of the 12th they reached their positions between the hamlets of L'Epinette and Le Cornet Perdu, near the town of Estaires. The locations are not named today, but they are to the west of the D947, roughly halfway between the villages of Vieux Berquin and Neuf Berquin.

The German Army had launched its last, and greatest, offensive of the war on 21st March. On the Somme, the British 5th Army had been virtually destroyed and the enemy had penetrated up to twenty miles through the British lines, across ground that had been so hard won over the last three years of war. Already five Wymeswold

33

men had died in the onslaught. In April the Germans launched the second phase of the offensive, in a series of attacks aimed at driving through the coalfields of northern France. The job of the Coldstreamers, and the rest of 4th Guards Brigade, would be to hold their ground and protect the strategic rail junction at Hazebrouck as the German Army launched a succession of hammer blows against the British lines.

On 12th April the battalion went up into the line at 2.30 a.m. It tried to get into position, but was ordered to 'side slip' to its right in order to maintain contact with the 50th Division. The Coldstreamers hardly had time to establish themselves before large numbers of the enemy started advancing at daybreak. Number One company advanced to take on the enemy, and stop him driving a wedge between the battalion and the 50th Division troops. Within an hour or so it was reduced to forty men, but hung on for most of the day. In the evening they were relieved, but the day had cost the battalion dearly: around forty dead and nearly eighty wounded, with almost ten men missing in action.

The next day was very much a repeat of the 12th. The battalion had been ordered to adjust its line of defence, but owing to problems with communication, was not completely ready when the enemy attacked at dawn. Two companies of the battalion went forward to hold up the enemy. Number One Company was now reduced to thirty-two men. Nevertheless, they again held on for most of the day, until the enemy began infiltrating around them, and they had to fight their way back to their own lines. 'Very few succeeded' is the comment in the war diary. Number Four Company was isolated with some Grenadier Guards and was completely cut off. Some remnants of the battalion, about forty men, continued a fighting retreat through farms and orchards to the hamlet of Arrewage. During the day the battalion had lost some eight officers, mostly missing: seventeen Other Ranks were known to be dead, and eighty-four wounded. Two hundred and fifty nine were missing; these were the men who had been cut off, and whose fate was unknown. Nearly half the battalion's strength was now out of combat.

It was on this day that Tom Clarke died. His service record states that he died of wounds. We will probably never know whether those wounds were sustained earlier, or whether he died in the vortex of attack and counter attack on the 13th itself.

His name is inscribed on the Memorial at Ploegsteert, some eleven miles away in Belgium. Originally the memorial to the dead of this area was to have been in Lille, but according to the Commonwealth War Graves Commission, the 'catchment area' was widened to include

> … the area from the line Caestre-Dranoutre-Warneton to the
> north, to Haverskerque-Estaires-Fournes to the south, including the
> towns of Hazebrouck, Merville, Bailleul and Armentieres, the
> Forest of Nieppe, and Ploegsteert Wood.

In all, the memorial commemorates eleven thousand men of the United Kingdom and South African Forces who have no known grave.

The Memorial to Thomas Clarke in Wymeswold Cemetery.

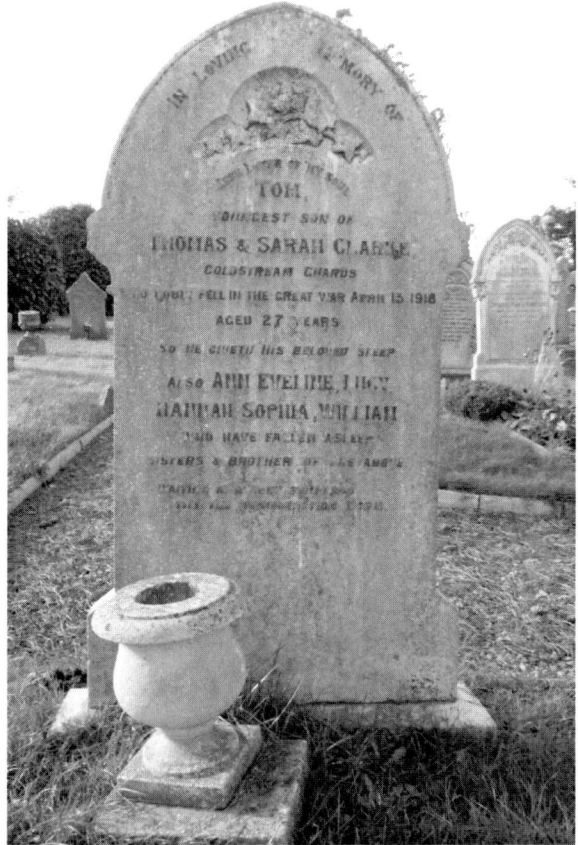

Ironically, Tom Clarke was killed just fifteen miles from Noeux les Mines Cemetery where his nephew John Edward Clarke lies, and only eight miles from Estaires cemetery, where George Williams and John James Collington are buried. Tom is also remembered at home, in the Wymeswold cemetery on Rempstone Road. His family erected a headstone in his memory, and that of his siblings who died as youngsters.

The Coldstream Guards records have an undated receipt from Emma for her late husband's war medals, but from then onward, it is impossible to trace her. It seems unlikely that she returned to Loughborough immediately, as Thomas' name does not appear on the Roll of Honour there. Of course, Emma may have gone back to her home town, and felt that inclusion on one Roll of Honour was enough. Her name is also unfortunately too common even to guess whether she remarried or not – there are a number of 'candidates' for both possibilities, over the years. With the prejudices of the time, her chances of either a career, or marriage and children, would have been stacked against her, at the age of thirty-eight. I hope she found some happiness again.

Sources

Census records: 1891, 1901, 1911.

Wymeswold parish registers. Online at: www.hoap.co.uk/who/localhisregister.htm [accessed June 2014].

Wymeswold Church of England School: log books and misc papers 1875–1983 (DE7281). The Record Office for Leicestershire, Leicester and Rutland.

Service Record: 19076 Clarke, Thomas. Coldstream Guards archive

War Diary 3Bn Coldstream Guards April 1918 (WO 95/1226). The National Archives.

Medal Roll Index Cards (Series WO 373). The National Archives.

www.wartimememoriesproject.com/greatwar/allied/coldstreamguards3-gw.php [accessed May 2014].

Baker, Chris / Milverton Associates, 2014. 'The Long Long Trail: The Coldstream Guards'. Online at: www.1914-1918.net/coldguards.htm [accessed 19 July 2014].

Passingham, I., 2008. *The German Offensives of 1918*. Pen and Sword.

Pitt, B., 2003. *1918 The Last Act*. Pen and Sword.

Chapter 8

John James Collington

John James Collington was known as James, and is still known as James by his family in Wymeswold. Other clues are on the Methodist Church memorial, where he is referred to as James, and the school log books. James was from one of the two Collington families in the village, and had been brought up on Brook Street. His father John had started as a labourer, but by 1901 was describing himself as a grazier, and by 1911 was a grazier / cattle dealer. He had made good progress in life, and he and his wife Rebecca had raised eight children, of whom James was the eldest.

James appears to have started as a good student at school, winning a prize for regular attendance at the age of six. This however was his last mention in the school log books, so it appears that, while he may not have won any more prizes, he did not attract attention for bad behaviour or absenteeism either. With a steady family background like his, it would be usual for James to follow his father and work on the farms, with the hope of becoming a grazier too.

However, in 1904 at the age of eighteen, James joined the army. The Boer War had ended two years previously, so it is unlikely that he joined up in a fit of patriotic fervour. His Attestation papers record the fact that he was already serving with the militia, so he would have been acquainted with military life and probably with former soldiers. Perhaps it was from these that he got the idea of joining up. Perhaps too, it was simply a case of a steady job with food, accommodation and prospects. After all, it had worked well for Amos Clarke, who was by this time a Corporal in the Coldstream Guards. A number of other village men had also served in the Army. The school log for 1900 records the names of eleven former pupils who had served, or were still serving.

James' enlistment had come as a result of a serious involvement with the Army. He was already a member of the Militia, and was in the 4th Battalion, Sherwood Foresters. The practice at the time was that most regiments maintained two regular battalions, with one or two militia or volunteer battalions that could be called on in times of emergency. It is also clear that James had thought about enlisting for a while, as he declared that he had received, and understood a Notice. These Notices were provided by Army recruiters, and served two purposes – to advise the potential recruit of their liabilities if they joined up, and to avoid other recruiters fighting over any potential commission or fees. The fact that James had already received such a

Notice indicates that he had already visited a recruiting agent, and had not just come in 'off the street'. He signed up for Short Service terms – three years 'with the colours' (i.e. active service), followed by nine years with the Army Reserve. This meant that he could be called up at any time if there were a national emergency. In his case, his time in the reserve would not expire until 1916. He had taken his oath of attestation on 26th February 1904, aged 18 years and 2 months. The army doctor recorded that he was 5 feet 3 inches in height, fresh-complexioned, with brown hair and brown eyes. His chest measurement was 37½ inches, and he had no physical problems apart from one defective tooth. He was accepted into the 1st Battalion, Notts and Derby regiment – the Sherwood Foresters.

The records of James' service in the peacetime army have not survived, other than a medical note that he was revaccinated against smallpox in March 1904, having been originally vaccinated in infancy. The last time that his service record mentions him before 1914 is to say that he was in B Reserve status at 25th February 1908, exactly four years after he first joined. He had therefore left the army, presumably to settle into civilian life. As a reservist, he was entitled to pay of three shillings and six pence a week – a very useful addition to his wages.

Before long he met, and in 1913 married, Julia Turkington from Quorn. The wedding at Loughborough Registry Office was celebrated in October 1913. At the time of the marriage, James was a machinist in an engineering works. Since he was still living at Brook Street, Wymeswold, it is probable (as recorded by the Loughborough Roll of Honour) that he was working at the Brush factory, as other Wymeswold men, like Charles Morris, did. As a side note, he described his father as a farmer. He may of course have still been a grazier, but this suggests that John was continuing to prosper. James, it would seem, had determined to make a success of his life too, by working with modern technology. Julia was also working in industry, as a weaver in an elastic web factory. In this she was following in her father's footsteps. The pattern of village life was changing: though Wymeswold was still dominated by an agricultural economy, with small businesses that serviced it, the pull of the town and modern industry was starting to be felt. James of course was still on the army reserve, and had to notify the authorities of his marriage (presumably so that his wife would be entitled to his property should he die on active service). Julia received the army correspondence at their new home at 17 Ratcliffe Road Loughborough, and duly sent off a copy of her marriage certificate, which was sent back on the day war broke out.

Events moved swiftly for James and Julia. A daughter, Rebecca Grace, probably named after James' mother, was born in May 1914. Then, on 4th August 1914, Britain declared war against Germany and Austria. James was mobilized at Derby on the 5th, and the life of the little Collington family would never be the same. James was posted overseas on 3rd October, and with that his period of 'home service', as far as the army was concerned, came to an end. It had lasted 10 years and 219 days. Now with the Expeditionary Force, his overseas service was to last just 118 days.

His battalion had been in India at the outbreak of war, and only returned on 2nd October. A month later, on 5th November 1914, it landed in France. By this time, the small British Expeditionary Force had been driven back from Belgium and was

John James Collington.

engaged in the 'race for the sea' – trying desperately to form a line between the sea in southern Belgium and the French forces who were themselves falling back under the massive German invasion. The Sherwood Foresters were much needed reinforcements, and were quickly thrown into battle.

By January 1915 James' battalion was in the trenches near Richebourg, not far from Arras in Artois, northern France. The year had not started kindly – they were in trenches that were at times knee deep in freezing water. Ration parties had to come over open ground, as the communication trenches were impassable. A couple of days' relief in the support lines was followed on 7th January by a return to the front line trenches. The war diary noted 'Very strong wind and rain. More rain, trenches are getting worse.' On the evening of the 9th they were relieved, and went into reserve, but were back in the front line by the 12th. There they stayed, building breastworks behind their flooded trenches in case they needed to abandon them, until the night of the 15th. By the 18th, they were on their way back up the line, and the weather had turned from rain to heavy snow. Such were the conditions that James endured in the last weeks of his life. By the 20th, a thaw had set in, and someone had responded to the appalling conditions by allowing one platoon from each company to spend the day in support trenches away from the front line.

At night, these platoons furnished working parties which continued to build up the breastworks behind the front trenches. However, the officers on the ground were unimpressed by the breastworks: '… it is difficult to see what useful purpose they will serve, they are exposed to a reverse fire, every night casualties occur in building them.' But orders, of course, are orders, so the work and the casualties continued.

Another relief on 21st was followed by a return to the front line on 24th. During this time the battalion had had a reinforcement of fifty men and an officer. The need for reinforcements on this scale tells its own story of the losses that had been suffered in the two months they had been in France. The 25th saw an increase in enemy activity, and an order from the Divisional Commanding Officer was received that 'all men are warned to be on the QUI VIVE tomorrow morning owing to it being the Kaiser's birthday'. Little is recorded for the next day, but according to the record provided by 25th Field Ambulance, it was on the 26th that James suffered a compound fracture of the skull. The casualty report for the day records with a tick that no-one was killed that day, but that twelve men were wounded. One of them was James Collington. He was evacuated to Casualty Clearing Hospital No 6 at Estaires, some four and a half miles from where he was hit. That night the battalion was relieved.

Back home in Loughborough, Julia received a letter from an army padre:

25th Fd Ambulance

8th Division

28/1/15

Dear Mrs Collington,

I am truly sorry to have to write and tell you that your husband Pte Collington No 9190 of the Sherwood Foresters died in our hospital yesterday and that I conducted his funeral today in the Cemetery here. He was shot in the head. He had died for his country, and we trust is well in God's hands. May we meet again in a happier world and may this awful war shortly come to a close.

Yours sincerely,

(Rev'd) M.W.T. Conran S S/1 CF

Church of England.

He was unconscious the whole time in our hands

James' grave at Estaires.

The Field Ambulance Brigade, and the cemetery in question, was at Estaires. In just two months it was also to become the last resting place of George Williams. The padre's account also contradicts the official record of 25th Field Ambulance that puts his death on the 28th, not the 27th. Of course, it may well be that he died in the night of 27th/28th and that the death was not formally recorded until the morning.

This was probably her first knowledge of James' death. The army's official machine swung into action fairly quickly with a formal notice sent on 12th February, that James had been killed. It is likely however, that she had already been in contact with the authorities, as they wrote to her, not at the Loughborough address, but c/o Mrs Turrington, Mountsorrel Grove, Leicester. It seems likely that in her grief she had taken her baby daughter and gone to her mother or aunt. (I am presuming that the name 'Turrington' is a mis-spelling of Julia's maiden name 'Turkington'). On the same day, the Infantry Records Office wrote to her, asking her to supply her marriage certificate, and child's birth certificate, and to complete a form, which had to be signed by 'a Police Officer not under the rank of Sergeant, who is well acquainted with you'. Goodness knows what happened to widows who were not acquainted with senior members of the local constabulary. On the 27th, the same department wrote to tell her that James was buried in Estaires Cemetery, grave No. 274. This time they got better at her mother's name and address: Mrs Turlington, Mountsorrel, Quorn.

The wheels of bureaucracy continued to grind on. In March the War Office confirmed, in its roundabout way, that she would get a widow's pension. 'The issue of Pension to soldiers' widows commences from the date following that to which Separation allowance is payable, and a further communication on the subject will be addressed to you in due course.' Clear as daylight.

The War Office also replied to her enquiry about James' Post Office account, referring her to the Controller of the Post Office Savings Bank. In July the bank wrote to her, asking her to complete a declaration (presumably that she was entitled to James' savings) and to sign it in the presence of a Justice of the Peace, or Commissioner of Oaths, or Notary Public. Some success had already come her way – a fortnight earlier, on 13th July, the War Office had sent her James' money - £3 12s 1d, together with his pay book and will. Two days later, they sent the balance of James' War Gratuity – £3. The last day of the month saw the War Office send her a confirmation of her widow's pension. She would receive fifteen shillings a week for herself and her child, starting on 16th August, when her Separation Allowance would cease. She would be able to get her money from the Post Office as she had the allowance, 'but on Wednesday instead of Monday.'

In July the Infantry records Office sent her James' effects. She received

> 1 Muffler, 1 Fork, 1 Comb
> 1 Holdall, 1 Spoon
> 1 shaving Brush
> 1 Housewife, 2 prs socks
> 1 Toothbrush, 1 Belt

Together with the request: 'A stamped addressed envelope is enclosed for favour of reply.'

Then, in August, another package arrived, containing amongst other things

> 7 Xmas cards
> 4 letters
> 1 Time Table

with the same request. These would be the last contacts she had with the man she married.

That seems to have completed her financial settlement. Now she and Rebecca were on their own, with fifteen shillings a week, and whatever help her family could give. It would not be an easy life. Within two short years she had married, had a child, looked forward to a happy life with a husband in a good job, and now the war had shattered all those dreams.

A notice was placed in the 'In Memoriam' column of the *Leicester Mercury* on 29th January 1917.

> COLLINGTON. In loving memory of Pte. J.J. Collington, 1st Batt
> Sherwood Foresters, who died of wounds 27th January 1915.
> Two years have passed away.
> Since that sad and mournful day.
> But memories, they do oft recall.
> To us, the one who gave his all.
>
> From Ethel and Guil.

I can only assume that Ethel and Guil were relatives.

In 1919, Julia was required to complete a statement of all James' living relatives for the army records. His parents and sister May continued to live in Brook Street, but his brother Alfred seems to have moved to Mountsorrel Road, Quorn – possibly staying with the Turkingtons. Julia herself is still at Mountsorrel Road, living with her mother. In this year, too, she received James' death plaque and scroll. Three years later, in 1922, she received his medals – the 1914 Star, War Medal and Victory Medal .

That is where the story of Julia and Rebecca ends, apart from fragments. There is a record of the death of a Julia Collington (the only instance of that name between 1915 and 1980) in Basford in 1946. It seems that she never remarried.

In the Collington papers at Loughborough's Carillon Museum are two documents which may be in Julia's own hand. The first details the facts of James' death as received from the War Office. The second records her choice of inscription for his gravestone.

> Look on this stone,
> Not with sorrow,
> but with pride.

It is there in France, still. Julia and Rebecca had no memorial to their suffering. This book goes some way towards that.

Sources

Census records: 1891, 1901, 1911.

Wymeswold parish registers. Online at: www.hoap.co.uk/who/localhisregister.htm [accessed June 2014].

Wymeswold Church of England School: log books and misc papers 1875–1983 (DE7281). The Record Office for Leicestershire, Leicester and Rutland.

Wymeswold vicar's correspondence (DE 1728/37). The Record Office for Leicestershire, Leicester and Rutland.

Medal Roll Index Cards (Series WO 373). The National Archives.

Service Record: 9190 Collington, John James. The National Archives.

War Diary 1Bn Sherwood Foresters January 1915 (WO 95/1721). The National Archives.

Baker, Chris / Milverton Associates, 2014. 'The Long Long Trail: Reserves and Reservists.' Online at: www.1914-1918.net/reserve.htm [accessed 19 July 2014].

Laughead, G., 2013. 'The Medical Front WW1'. Online at: www.vlib.us/medical/ [accessed June 2014].

Chapter 9

John William Collington

In 1891, there were several Collington families on Brook Street. James' family, as we have seen, was one. Another was headed by John and Sarah Collington. John, like most of the Collingtons, was born and bred in Wymeswold, but Sarah had come from the village of Cadeby. A daughter, Annie, was their eldest child, followed by John William, and then by Ethel and Sarah. By 1901, the family had moved to Wysall Lane, and two more children – Tom and Herbert – had been born. Ten years on, the family were still in Wymeswold, though only the youngest, Herbert, was still at home. Annie, however, died in that year – the only one of the six Collington children who did not reach adulthood.

John William – still referred to as Bill within the family – may be the William Collington referred to in the Infant School log for 1890, winning a prize for Religious Knowledge, and again in 1891, a prize for Scripture. He may well be the John Collington of Standard iv in the Mixed School who in December 1896 was recorded as being 'absent 20 times in the last 7 weeks.' Three items of interest come out of this little snippet: if this does refer to John William (Bill), then he would have been around twelve years old, and looking forward to leaving school. Secondly, it suggests that he attained a reasonable standard (iv) of academic attainment while at school. And thirdly, it highlights the problem of absenteeism that was the bane of the headmaster's life. Children were constantly absent, partly through poor health or cold weather, but also because they were needed, either at home or on the land, to help the family. Other absences, particularly among the boys, were due to dangerous behaviour or work injuries: Bill's youngest brother Herbert was away in July 1901 'thro' a kick by a foal'.

If Bill's school life had been uneventful, he seems to have intended a much more exciting future career. A contemporary, within a year, of both Amos Clarke and James Collington, he also joined the army. Having spent some years as a labourer, presumably on the local farms, Bill joined the army in March 1905, a couple of years after James Collington and several years after Amos Clarke. By a sheer coincidence, the service records of both Collington men have escaped the destruction of two-thirds of the First World War records by enemy bombing in the Second World War. Like James, he applied for a Short Service contract. Unlike James, he had not already been a member of the militia, so he had no military training or background. On the other hand, he had given it some thought, as he had been sent a Notice – i.e. he had been to see an Army recruiter before 'attesting' at a recruitment office. Perhaps because of Amos' example, he set his sights high – he declared that he was 'willing to be enlisted' for the Grenadier Guards. At 5 feet 106/8 inches, he would have been around the right height for that regiment. Weighing 171¾ pounds, with a chest measurement of 39 inches, he was obviously a fit young man, and, as his photos showed, very handsome, with dark brown hair and brown eyes. Instead of the Guards, however, he was sent – but it must have been with his agreement, as this was a voluntary enlistment – to the 1st Battalion, the Leicestershire Regiment. At the age of 20 years and 4 months, Bill Collington was now a soldier.

Four month's training at Leicester, during which he was transferred to the 2nd Battalion, was followed by a year at Colchester, and then the battalion was sent to India. Life there must have suited Bill, since he was still there, with the 2nd Battalion, when the census was taken in 1911. His career had had its ups and downs. He had been promoted Lance Corporal in November 1906, and received a Good Conduct badge (unpaid) in March 1907, but reverted to Private in May 1908. The reasons for this reversal no longer exist in the records, but it should be noted that his initial period of engagement ran out in March 1908. Perhaps he signed up for a further term, but had to do so at the expense of returning as a private? Or that he had elected to remain in India, even though he could have been returned to England in 1908?

Assuming that he had served a second term of Short Service, he would have been due to be sent home some time in 1911, but he was still there in 1912. He may have signed up for longer, of course, as his record indicates that he was transferred prematurely from India. That may have had something to do with his health: he had just suffered a bout of 'moderately severe' malaria. At all events, he sailed from Madras aboard the ship *Dufferin* on 21st November 1912. At that point, he must have thought his army service was over. He enrolled in the Army Reserve A list in April 1913, and was confirmed on the B list in December of that year. As a reservist, he had a small income (three shillings and six pence per week) to add to his wages.

In just nine months Bill was back in uniform. War was declared by Britain on 4th August 1914, and Bill was mobilised at Leicester on the 5th. He was re-enlisted, once again into the 1st battalion, Leicestershire Regiment. This time there would be no transfer to 2nd battalion. His unit left barracks on the 8th September 1914, and landed at St Nazaire in France on 10th. Bill was now part of the British Expeditionary Force. His wartime career is not easy to follow, as the records have been damaged, probably by the water used to put out the fires when the collection was bombed in 1940. Within months he appears to have been promoted to Lance Corporal, and full Corporal in August 1915. In December 1915 he was promoted Lance Sergeant. War, as usual, accelerated careers, and Bill was benefiting from that. After two years on the Western Front, Bill was sent back to England in August 1916, where he seems to have taken all opportunities to develop his career. During this time it is likely that he worked in training new recruits. The army had a major problem: though it had lost many experienced NCOs in the first two years of the war, it still needed experienced men like Bill to train and prepare the successive waves of volunteers and conscripts who would form the New Army.

He attended at least two courses, including in March 1917 the 36th Rifle and Lewis Gun Course at Strensall. By the beginning of 1918, however, the army in France was reaching a crisis point. The collapse of Russia in October/November 1917 had released dozens of German and Austrian divisions from the Eastern Front, and it was obvious to the Allied High Command that Germany was preparing a massive offensive somewhere in France. The aim would be to break through the British lines and drive towards the English Channel. The British would then be forced to evacuate or be surrounded. Without the British support, France would surrender. From the German point of view, all this had to happen before the Americans, now pouring men into France, could organise themselves into an effective army.

Experienced NCOs were now desperately needed, and Bill was sent back to France. He left Folkestone on 18th January 1918, joining his regiment in the field on 28th. By the beginning of March, the battalion was in reserve trenches near Favreuil, less than two miles north of Bapaume, and twelve miles south of Arras. Though it was not in the front line, the troops were not resting. They formed daily working parties. Orders had come through that the British line was to be slightly altered, and the 1st Battalion Leicesters, as part of 71st Infantry Brigade, would take up positions near Lagnicourt, with 9th Norfolks on their left, and 2nd Sherwood Foresters in reserve. The changeover happened on the 5th, and the Leicesters moved into their new positions on the front line, strengthening defences and establishing new strong points. On the 7th the war diary noted:

> Rumours of enemy attack strengthening, although no sign of same
> in forward areas. Enemy unusually quiet and his artillery inactive,
> whereas ours still more active than previously. Our patrols
> constantly active, but enemy very elusive and running no risks of
> capture.

Clearly, the Germans were working hard to give the British no clues as to their exact intentions. The British artillery kept up a heavy bombardment of the German trenches, with very little response. As we now know, the front line trenches were almost empty, as the Germans predicted that the British would attempt to deter the impending onslaught. An attack was expected at dawn on 13th, but it came to nothing, and the men were 'stood down' at 7.30 a.m..

Despite some occasional shelling, the enemy lines continued to be very quiet. The Leicesters were required to carry out a raid on a nearby strongpoint – the Magpie's Nest – in order to capture prisoners for interrogation. If successful, this would bring valuable information about the regiments opposing them, and the strength in numbers and experience of the enemy. If they were really lucky, they might gain direct information about the impending attack. The raid, by B Company, went ahead on the evening of the 16th, supported by artillery and Stokes mortars. The Magpie's Nest was deserted. No prisoners were taken. The only thing that must have been obvious was that a very big attack was coming. It must have been with some sense of relief that the Leicesters' place in the line was taken over by the 9th Norfolks on the night of the 17th / 18th.

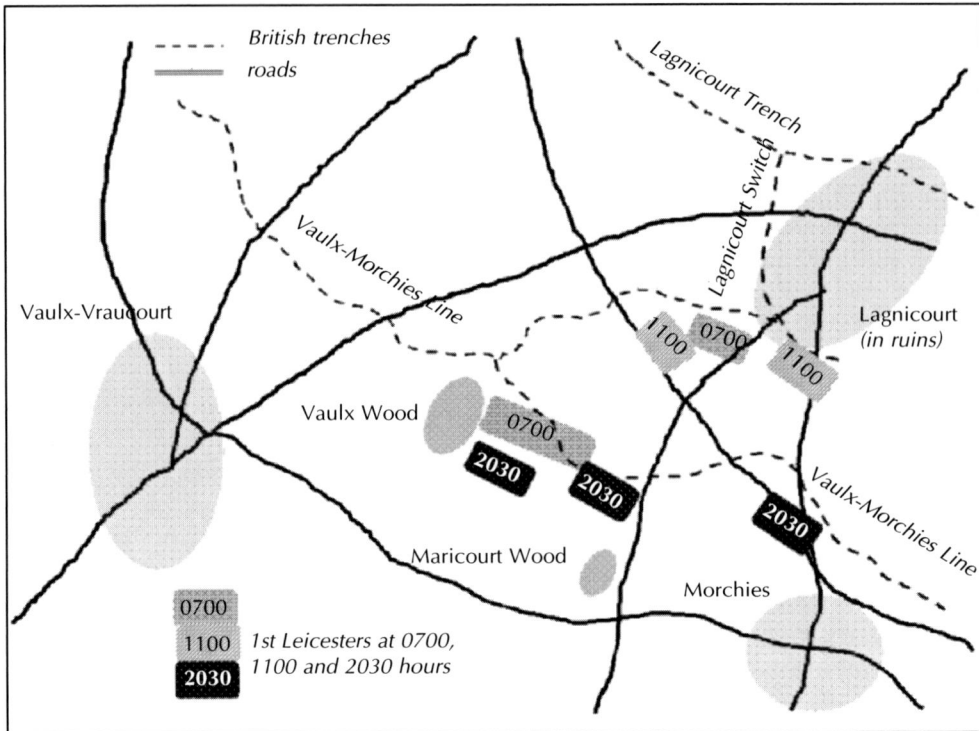

Location of Bill's death

Being back in reserve, in the area between Favreuil and Vaux, was not an opportunity for much rest. The battalion was 'stood to' at 5.05 a.m. on the 19th in order to test 'how soon battalion could be roused and be ready to march off in fighting order.' The results were not satisfactory: it took until 5.55 for the men to be ready. The war diary observes 'measures taken to expedite future moves in the event of alarm. 1½ hours Company training in morning.' Clearly, the battalion commander was unhappy. Another day of training followed, until at midnight on the 20th, an order was received to stand to at 5.30 a.m. in the morning. At 5.32 a.m., the diary records 'heavy bombardment commenced 5.30 a.m., and apparently the alarm this time was a genuine one.' I wonder whether this was grim humour, or a breathtaking understatement.

Bill would never know it for sure, but this was the first day of the 'Kaiserschlacht' – the great German Offensive of 1918, when along this part of the front line, thirty-three British Divisions faced sixty-nine German divisions. The sacrifice made by Bill and his comrades was to slow down the enemy advance until by July, the German army was exhausted, depleted and bogged down in the mud of the Somme and Artois.

On 21st March, the battalion was scarcely in a state of readiness. True, they were technically 'in reserve', but nearly 370 men and eight officers had been out all night on working parties with the result that 216 were not in their assembly areas until

48

6.30 a.m.. 'They had not returned until 5.15 a.m., and were somewhat exhausted, having marched five miles each way to work and having done a heavy night's work.' Scarcely in a fit state to take on fresh, battle-hardened assault troops. One platoon of 'A' Company was already positioned at the southern end of the village of Lagnicourt. By 11.00 a.m. 'C' and 'D' Companies, together with 9th Norfolks, were sent to the same general area. Here they tried to hold on, unsure of what was happening to both the right and the left of them. In either direction, the trenches were not continuous, so to contact other battalions they would have to go out into the open, which was almost suicidal, as machine guns and snipers were sweeping all exposed areas with constant fire.

Meanwhile, the remainder of 'A' Company, which had been placed to the left, was holding the line from the village of Vaulx-Vraucourt towards the village of Morchies, three-quarters of a mile or so further right, and south-west of the positions occupied by their comrades. By the early afternoon, 'B' Company had also moved up to this area, despite heavy machine gun fire from Vaulx wood. By late evening news had come through that the platoon of 'A' Company near Lagnicourt had been more or less wiped out and that 'C' Company was pinned down south of the village. The Vaulx-Morchies line was now held by remnants of various battalions – 9th Norfolks, 3rd Sherwood Foresters, 2nd South Lancashires, and 11th Leicesters, as well as the 1st Leicesters. The estimated strength of the battalion was put at around 370 men and fourteen officers, or around half its size. The Norfolks and the Sherwood Foresters, who had started the day in the front line, were reduced to around 120 men each. What had started as a defence of strong points and unconnected trenches had developed, by nightfall, into a grim struggle for survival.

The family tradition is that Bill was not killed in the general fog of battle. Apparently he was checking bodies on the battlefield when he was shot by a German officer. The said officer was then promptly despatched by a British soldier. Years later, on a visit to Canada, Bill's brother Herbert was able to meet and shake the hand of the man who avenged his brother's death. The story certainly implies that Bill had survived the ferocious fighting of the day, and had come out into the open in the late evening, perhaps as part of the intelligence-gathering exercise that produced the casualty figures that day. Given what we know about the exposed terrain, and the presence of snipers and concealed troops, his actions were undoubtedly courageous. As an N.C.O., he was definitely leading by example.

Without knowing which company he served with, it is not possible to identify precisely where Bill Collington died. However, using the war diary and the battle maps of the time, it is possible to narrow the area down to a triangle of ground extending a thousand yards south of Lagnicourt and then a thousand yards west towards Vaulx Wood. We know, from a certificate still in the possession of the Collington family, that the German authorities found his body and buried it near the village of Vaulx-Vraucourt. During the following German offensive, and the subsequent Allied offensive that finally drove the Germans out, his grave was lost. Bill Collington is now remembered on the Arras Memorial to the 35,000 servicemen from the UK, South Africa and New Zealand who died in the Arras sector and have no known grave.

Bill's memorial in Wymeswold cemetery.

At home, there were the usual formalities to complete. Over the next year and a half, the Army sent Bill's effects to his parents (in July 1918), and the following year they filled in the Army Form 5080 to confirm the details of all Bill's living relatives. By this time, Ethel and Sarah had married and left the area, settling in Portsmouth and Bagnall respectively. Tom had emigrated to Canada before the war, and served with the Canadian army in France. He was now back in Canada. Only Herbert, now a Sergeant and holder of the Military Medal, was still living in the area. Their form was countersigned on the 29th August 1919 by Rev Claud Edmunds, vicar of Wymeswold. For him, this must have been yet another sad occasion, one of many which had come to him again and again over the last five years. No wonder that he was thinking, possibly as he signed the document, of a fitting memorial for Bill and the other boys who would never return.

There was more contact with the Infantry records department in 1920. A disc, worn by Bill, was returned to the family. His mother wrote back a gentle but clearly emotional letter.

> I thank you kindly for sending me this Disc of my son Late J.W. Collington No. 7662 it was the Disc he worn tied on him through all his war life. I suppose it was sent from Germany.
>
> Mrs Collington

50

Bill's medals, including the 1914 Star, and Death Plaque.

His medals were sent to his parents in 1921, and Bill was further remembered on the Rolls of Honour in St Mary's and in the Methodist church. The most personal memorial however, is in Wymeswold Cemetery, on Rempstone Road. On the headstone of his sister Annie, who died in 1901, Bill's name has been added.

Also

JOHN WILLIAM COLLINGTON

1ST LEIC. REGT.

KILLED IN ACTION IN THE GREAT WAR

IN FRANCE MARCH 21, 1918

AGED 33 YEARS.

WHEN FACING THE SHADES OF DEATH

GOD'S PRESENCE WAS HIS STAY.

HE JOINED THE NOBLE ARMY OF MARTYRS

THAT PRAISE THEE O GOD.

ON THE RIVERS SILENT BRINK,

CHRIST WILL CLASP EACH BROKEN LINK.

Note:

Readers may need an explanation of the rank of Lance Serjeant. According to the Western Front Association:

… the grades of lance-sergeant and lance-corporal were not strictly ranks, but were appointments, held by selected corporals and privates, and usually carrying extra pay. The appointment was made by the man's commanding officer and could be taken away by him for disciplinary reasons, unlike full sergeants and corporals who could only be demoted by order of a court martial.

The same article explains that the spelling 'Serjeant' was the official terminology until 1946.

Sources

Census records: 1891, 1901, 1911.

Wymeswold parish registers. Online at: www.hoap.co.uk/who/localhisregister.htm [accessed June 2014].

Wymeswold Church of England School: log books and misc papers 1875–1983 (DE7281). The Record Office for Leicestershire, Leicester and Rutland.

Wymeswold vicar's correspondence (DE 1728/37). The Record Office for Leicestershire, Leicester and Rutland.

Map: M/000646 Vaulx-Vraucourt 57c NW 210318. Western Front Association.

War Diary 1Bn Leicestershire Regiment March 1918 (WO 95/1622). The National Archives.

Service Record: 7662 Collington, John William. The National Archives.

Baker, Chris / Milverton Associates, 2014. 'The Long Long Trail: How men joined the British Army'. Online at: www.1914-1918.net/recruitment.htm [accessed 7 June 2014].

Baker, Chris / Milverton Associates, 2014. 'The Long Long Trail: Renumbering of the Territorial Force in 1917'. Online at: www.1914-1918.net/renumbering.htm [accessed 6 June 2014].

Passingham, I., 2008. *The German Offensives of 1918.* Pen and Sword.

Pitt, B., 2003. *1918 The Last Act.* Barnsley: Pen and Sword.

Chapter 10

William Henry Dykes

A hundred years after the Great War, William Dykes has been perhaps the hardest of the thirty to tie to Wymeswold. There is no direct evidence that his second name was Henry, or that he was the William Henry Dykes commemorated on the Leicestershire War Memorials site. Curiously, his name does not appear on the Methodist church Roll of Honour, though it is on the rolls in the Memorial Hall and St Mary's church.

However, the Commonwealth War Graves Commission records only three W.H. Dykes as dying during the Great War. The service record of one of them survives, and shows that he was born and bred in Warrington, and seems to have had no connection with Wymeswold at all. The second is recorded as having parents William John and Elizabeth in Headcorn, Kent. Again, no connection with Wymeswold.

The third, William Henry Dykes, was in the 11th Battalion, West Yorkshire Regiment. The connection with Wymeswold is tenuous, but it is the same regiment, and the same battalion, that John Wilfred Brookes joined, admittedly after a spell with the Durham Light Infantry. His Medal Card adds little, except that he entered the theatre of war on 15th August 1915, that he became first a Lance Corporal, then Sergeant, and that he died of wounds.

The other significant detail about this William Dykes is that *Soldiers Died in the Great War* (a series of eighty volumes published in 1921 and now available via ancestry.co.uk) gives his birthplace as Smeton, Nottingham. There is no Smeton in Nottingham or Nottinghamshire, but there is a district of Nottingham called Sneinton.

Similarly, there is no obvious connection with Wymeswold in the birth and early life of a William H. Dykes. Census records reveal a number of William Dykes in the Leicestershire and Nottinghamshire area. However, there is one that stands out by reason of a Wymeswold connection. The 1911 census for Nottingham shows a William Henry Dykes living at 74 Dunscomb Road, Nottingham. He is the son of the head of the household, also William Henry Dykes, but not of his father's wife Harriet, who is evidently his stepmother. William senior and Harriet have been married just six years, while young William is seventeen. It appears that the young William's mother was Ellen Barton, who married William senior in 1892. She died in

1901, possibly in or related to childbirth – the Nottingham registers show the deaths of Ellen Dykes aged 27, and a Henry Dykes, aged 0 in the first quarter of that year.

The important detail of the 1911 census is that Harriet's widowed father is living with the Dykes family, and he was born in Wymeswold. The connection is slight, but stronger than the military connection, and shows a relationship by marriage at least with one of the Morris families of Wymeswold. The seventeen year old William is described as a motor coach builder. Tantalisingly, the census does not say which of the numerous engineering companies in the area William worked for.

Earlier censuses show that William senior had been born and raised in the Sneinton area (1891 census), while step-grandfather William Morris had been a fruiterer in Nottingham (1901 census), a widower, working from home. Much earlier, when his wife was still alive, he had been a joiner (1881 census). The son of John Morris and Elizabeth Fletcher of Wymeswold, William Morris had three brothers. Among them was Charles, the father of Jack Morris. In May 1918 Jack was also to die of wounds fifty or so miles to the north, just south of Hazebrouck.

It is at this point that the military record and the censuses come together. We now have a probable Sneinton connection and a definite Wymeswold connection for the William Henry Dykes who was born and raised in Nottingham. So did young William Dykes come to Wymeswold after 1911 to work, or perhaps more likely to live closer to a new engineering job at the Brush works or another company in Loughborough? Did he find accommodation with his great uncle Charles' family, or some of his other relatives in Wymeswold? Charles' son, also Charles, was working at the Brush when war broke out in 1914, so is it possible that William Dykes, his second cousin by marriage, also got a job there? Or did he pursue his career elsewhere, while his stepbrothers Herbert and Harold, came to live in Wymeswold? William's career seems to have become more, not less, complicated.

In March 1915, a William Henry Dykes son of a William Henry Dykes, and a Private in the 11th Battalion, West Yorkshire Regiment, married a Marion Isabel Mann in Knaresborough Yorkshire. This must be the same William Henry Dykes who wrote his will on 25th August 1915, the day before he landed in France, and left everything to '… my beloved wife, M.I. Dykes'. The will provides a link between the marriage certificate and *Soldiers Died in the Great War*, as it includes his service number, 13377. Another link between the two documents is the town of Harrogate. According to *Soldiers Died in the Great War*, this is where William enlisted, and the marriage certificate shows that Marion was resident there at the time of their marriage.

Regrettably, the marriage certificate provides no link to Wymeswold. Indeed there are three surprises. The first, easily explained, is the occupation of William's father – machinist. Four years before, William senior had been a labourer. It was now entirely possible of course that through young William, he had got a job in an engineering factory. Secondly, William gives his age as 23 when he married. Twenty-one is the age that we should expect – he was born in the quarter ending March 1894, and was married on 20th March 1915. However, his wife was already

William Dyke's Will.

INFORMAL WILL.

W.O. No.: E/319363/1   DOMICILE. *English*

Record No. 225/40986/16/17

The enclosed document dated *25/9/15.*

Name *William Henry Dykes*   and signed *W. H. Dykes,*

Regtl. No. and Rank *13344, Sergeant*   appears to have been written

Regt. *11th Bn. West Yorkshire Regt.*   or executed by the person named in the margin while

Died at *44 Casualty Clearing Station, France.*   he was "in actual military service" within the meaning of the Wills Act, 1837, and has been recognised by the

Date of Death *8. 10. 16*   War Department as constituting a valid will.

WAR OFFICE.

Date *15/2/17*   *J. P. Atkinson*

for the Assistant Financial Secretary.

27, and he may not have wanted to appear too much younger. Also, there is the slight possibility that he was still twenty, and therefore not of 'full age' to marry without formal parental consent. The third, and more puzzling entry, is that he gave his address as Terlingham Gardens, Folkestone, Kent, at his marriage. As indicated before, he is not the William H of Kent who died in WW1, since *his* father was William John. And he is the William Henry who was born at 'Smeton' (Sneinton?) in Nottingham.

The 11th (Service) Battalion, West Yorkshire Regiment had been raised in October 1914, but was not sent to France until the third week of August 1915 – which agrees exactly with William's medal card. As part of the battalion he would have been involved in the battle of Loos, and in the support of 47th Division during their defence of Vimy Ridge in late April / May of 1916. By the summer of 1916 the battalion was heavily engaged on the Somme, pushing on through the 'meat grinder' that saw the gradual capture of Contalmaison, Bazentin Ridge, Flers-Courcelette, Morval and Le Sars – all villages which today we can drive around within an hour, but which took the British and Imperial forces nearly three months to take.

At the beginning of October the battalion was in trenches in the village of Martinpuich, about six miles to the east and slightly north of the town of Albert. On

William Dykes' grave at Dernancourt, Somme. Photograph copyright The War Graves Photographic Project; reproduced with permission.

the 4th they were ordered to move up towards Le Sars, just two miles to the north-east, but very heavily defended by the Germans. They were in and around 26th Avenue – a long trench line which ran parallel to the Albert-Bapaume road, about six hundred yards to the east of it. When it came, the order to attack would mean they had to move about half a mile to the left and north, crossing the line of the road.

The battalion's war diary for the 7th is terse, but its words are chilling 'battalion attacked trenches to the left of LE SARS: objectives gained and held, losses heavy. 8 Officers and 217 OR.' In other words, the battalion, in a single attack, had lost nearly a third of its fighting strength. Le Sars would feature in the death of another Wymeswold man – Lt Robert Jalland. He was killed just a mile away, to the right of Le Sars, two years later in 1918.

William did not die on the battlefield: his medal card records that he died of wounds. He was evacuated to a Casualty Clearing Station (CCS). At the time, 45th and 56th (1st/1st South Midland) Casualty Clearing Stations were based at Dernancourt, and it was at 45 CCS that doctors tried to save his life. It was there too, that the Major in charge removed from his army paybook (known as 'AB 64') the page containing his will.

No contemporary evidence of the Dykes family in Wymeswold is currently available. However, Elsie Hubbard remembers a Billy Dykes who was the village roadman – clearing and mending the pathways and pavements. Certainly, her memory of a man who was middle aged when she was a girl in the 1930s would fit William senior. Could it be that the family moved to Wymeswold? There is one document that provides the connection. William senior's death certificate shows that he was a retired County Council roadman. He died at his home, 23 Brook Street Wymeswold, on February 23rd, 1956. His daughter in law Ida registered the death; she lived at 56 Brook Street. Evidently the Dykes family had relocated to Wymeswold, and had requested that William be remembered here, where his father and siblings lived.

Sources

Census records: 1881, 1891, 1901, 1911.

Wymeswold vicar's correspondence (DE 1728/37). The Record Office for Leicestershire, Leicester and Rutland.

Certificate of Birth, Marriage or Death. General Register Office. Online at: www.freebmd.org.uk [accessed January 2014].

Dykes W H (Will FAEJ994048), H M Government / Department of Justice.

Map: M/015197 Le Sars Sailly Saillisel 57c SW 03-09-16. Imperial War Museum / The Western Front Association.

War Diary 11Bn West Yorkshire Regiment October 1916 (WO 95/2184). The National Archives.

Medal Roll Index Cards (Series WO 373). The National Archives.

Commonwealth War Graves Commission 'Find War Dead'. Online at: www.cwgc.org [accessed 2014].

Baker, Chris / Milverton Associates, 2014. 'The Long Long Trail: How men joined the British Army'. Online at: www.1914-1918.net/recruitment.htm [accessed 7 June 2014].

Chapter 11

Eric Evans

Eric Evans is another mystery. Certainly, he was brought up in Wymeswold, and he can be traced through census and service records – his was one of the third of records that survived the bombing in the Second World War. The problem of Eric Evans is understanding who he was, and where he came from.

He first appears in Wymeswold through the 1901 census, aged five, living with Deborah Knifton and her widowed mother. Whereas Deborah's birth place, and her mother's, is Wymeswold, Eric's is shown simply as 'London'. What was his relationship to the family? 'Nurse child.' It is not a term that is used in the twenty-first century, but we have to remember that in Victorian times, children who were orphans, or whose parents were unable to care for them, were dependent either on their extended family or on whatever shelter the local workhouse could provide. The family might take the child in, and raise it with grandparents or an aunt or uncle: often, however, it would be put out to 'nurse' – in other words, someone would be paid to bring it up.

There are other records of 'nurse children' in the village. The Rev Edmunds, the vicar of Wymeswold in 1918, was writing to a brother priest in London about a nurse child who was no longer being supported by its father.

> A man named J Knowles has for the last 7 years been paying a
> woman in this parish to keep his illegitimate son at the rate of 6/-
> a week. From the last August Bank Holiday up to the last Xmas he
> has only sent 7/- every 3 weeks. Since then nothing has been
> heard of him.

The dates by the way do not fit Eric, so this was a very different case. There are relatively few children called Eric Evans who were born in London in 1896, and the most likely explanation was that he was the illegitimate child of Fanny Evans, a cook from Nottingham. The birth certificate offers no positive clue as to whether she had travelled to London to have the baby, or was working there at the time.

Deborah Knifton, then aged 36, was single in 1901. Twenty years before, she – aged 16 – and her elder sister Mary Ann – then 23 – had been domestic servants with the Burrows family in Stockwell House. The daughter of a framework knitter, Thomas

Knifton, and his seamstress wife, Harriet, Deborah would naturally have progressed, like many village girls, into service. She was obviously valued in her situation, since she was still with the same family in 1891, aged 27. Deborah's younger sister Ellen (known as Nellie) never married, though like Deborah, she had a keen interest in children, and worked for some time as a nanny. Mary Ann Knifton married into the Mills family – Peggy Mills, who has been very helpful in providing information for this book, is Deborah's great-niece.

The Kniftons seem to have lived at the western end of the village – in 1881 and 1901 Deborah's parents (later her widowed mother) lived at Little London, and London Street, the same road that is now known as London Lane. In 1891, however, Harriet was living at West End. The family are remembered by Peggy Mills, however, as living in London Lane, a few doors away from Hilder's Cottage. The Knifton sisters come across, even after a hundred years, as caring and warm people. Eric Evans was clearly loved, and included not only into the Knifton family, but also into the wider Mills family too.

Eric first distinguished himself at school by winning a prize for proficiency in Religious Knowledge, being awarded a copy of *Jesus of Nazareth* by the Jobson Trustees in 1902, aged six. The following year, as a member of the older group in the Infant School , he won again in Religious Knowledge. Moving up to the Mixed School in 1904, he was awarded a Religious Knowledge prize again, this time as part of the Lower Division of the school. In 1905 he was one of 37 children to receive prizes for regular attendance. He had been present 420 times out of a possible 428. His book (we do not know if he chose it or not) was *The Dog Crusoe*. In 1906 he was presented, courtesy of the Jobson Trustees, with a copy of *The Pilgrim's Progress* for his attainments in Religious Knowledge, and a copy of *The Wide World, England and Wales* for attending 422 times, without a single absence. In this case, the prizes were provided by the Leicestershire County Council.

The following year he again won a regular attendance prize, this time a copy of *The Young Fur Traders* – again for a maximum possible 429 attendances. Additionally he won a prize for Religious Knowledge – this time *In Prison and Out*. It is at this point that his name disappears from the school log books. This may not be surprising, because by this time, Eric would be eleven, and the following year he may well have been given dispensation to work part-time, before leaving at thirteen. The picture of Eric is of an orderly, well-behaved and attentive child, who must have been valued at school.

By 1911, he was employed as a servant on a farm – the kind of work that would be expected for a village boy in the early 1900s. However, it appears that he was determined to advance himself in life. He seems to have worked for some time as a decorator. When Susan and Keith Easton were redecorating their house at 1 London Lane, some years ago, they found a pencilled note on the wall, under the old wallpaper. It simply said that the writer had gone for lunch and would be back soon. The writer was Eric Evans. Susan and Keith covered the note up; it should still be there.

Photo of Eric sent to his pal Eustace Hubbard in August 1917. Note he is wearing the uniform of the Yorks and Lancs Regiment. Photograph courtesy of Elsie Hubbard.

Eric's career soon took him away from Wymeswold. By the time he had volunteered for the army in 1915, Eric was working on the railways. In choosing this career, he may have been following one of his foster mother's relatives. An A. Knifton is recorded at Pontefract in 1888, being transferred to the Midland Railway at Cudworth. When Eric presented himself at Barnsley in November 1915, he was based in Cudworth, and employed as a signal lamp man on the railway. His forms do not specify which company he worked for, but Cudworth was associated with both the Midland and the Great Central railways.

We will never know what persuaded Eric to volunteer, as conscription was not introduced until 1916. Like other Wymeswold men who had volunteered, he had thought about it in advance, and had received a Notice from the recruiting agent, so this was no act of impulse. However we know from the school log books that he was in the school at the same time as Jesse Mills, George Marriott, William Wilson, Fred Bailey, Herbert Collington and Bramford Sparrow, all of whom we know to have served. There may of course have been more, but it is curious to note that of this list, all but two were to die in the war. The same group contained the siblings of others who joined up, like Herbert Savage, the brother of Alred Savage. We also know that he was a pal of Eustace Hubbard, the brother of Ernest, who was killed in 1917, fighting with the Australian 14th Battalion. It is thanks to Elsie Hubbard, who kept the photo of himself sent by Eric to her father Eustace, that we have this image of Eric. By the time Eric offered himself, two village men – James Collington and George Williams – had already died.

His attestation papers show that his military career was much delayed. Having gone to an Attesting Officer in 1915, his papers were not completed and authorised until May 1917, when he was appointed Private 42299, Yorks and Lancs Regiment. He was transferred in 1918 to another regiment, to become Private 81610, Durham Light Infantry (the same regiment that Wilfred Brookes joined initially, before his transfer to the West Yorkshires).

Back in 1915, Eric had confirmed that his age was 19 years and 8 months, and that he was of the Church of England – a worshipper then, at St Mary's rather than the Methodist church. His height was average – 5 feet 5¾ inches, and his chest measured 37 inches. Importantly, he gives his next-of-kin as Deborah Knifton, of West End, Wymeswold. Presumably she was now living with her mother.

In March 1917 he had been physically examined at Pontefract. Apparently he gave his birthplace as Cudworth, but I think it most likely that was a simple clerical error or a misunderstanding on his part. It seems likely that he was still living and working in Cudworth. His record shows that he served at home from May until August 1917, when he was sent to France. He was twice wounded, on each occasion by a gunshot wound to the left leg. The wounds were sufficiently serious for him to be invalided back to Britain, and to spend thirty days in hospital each time. His seven months in France with the Yorks and Lancs had been eventful, to say the least.

Eventually, on 15th March 1918, he was passed A3 fit, i.e. an Expeditionary Force soldier, ready to be returned to active duty as soon as he was fit. The date of his transfer to the 15th Battalion, Durham Light Infantry – 31st March 1918 – is perhaps significant. It was just one week after the massive German offensive on the Somme, which had virtually destroyed a number of British divisions, and reinforcements were urgently required from other regiments. The 15th DLI were part of the 21st Division, which had endured the shock of the first, ferocious onslaught at the end of March, around St Quentin. It had then fought off the next offensives around the Lys in southern Belgium and northern France – this was part of the same holocaust that claimed the lives of Jesse Mills at La Bassee and Jack Morris near Hazebrouck. It, and other British divisions like the 50th and the 8th, were due for a rest. They would be sent to the area north of Rheims, to take up positions on the ridge known as the Chemin Des Dames. They were being 'part exchanged' with some French divisions who would provide support to the British in the north, where, it was generally agreed, the German Army would continue to make its major attacks. The British and French High Command were right in thinking that the German plan was still to break the British, and force them into the sea.

What they got terribly wrong was where the Germans would strike next. The Chemin Des Dames, a long hog's back of a ridge, protected by marshy fields and the Ailette river, was considered an unlikely place for a major enemy assault. The only dissenting voice was the new American Intelligence Corps, which was sure that the next blow would fall there, and said so, loudly. The more the Americans insisted, the more the French, in whose sector this was, resisted. Worse still, the area was under the command of a general Duchesne, a man of 'choleric disposition', who was not accustomed to taking advice from anyone, even his commanding officer. General

Petain had told him to prepare his defences in depth. Instead, Duchesne squeezed as many of his forces as possible together in the front line. It was the old 1914 strategy for an attacking force, not a defensive one. Despite British concerns, and American insistence, Duchesne both ignored the possibility of a German attack, and persisted in crowding his troops into a five mile band based on the ridge. Two days before the actual attack, three French escaped prisoners reached the British lines, and told about massive troop concentrations in front of the Chemin Des Dames. Duchesne reacted angrily; he could see 'no indication' of any planned assault. The next day, two German prisoners were brought in. Under interrogation, they provided full details of the planned offensive. The British and French armies were now alerted, but it was too late to prepare a proper defence.

In early May 1918, the 15th DLI had been re-equipping and training behind the lines, near St Omer in northern France. An indication of the severe fighting it had seen (and its losses) is the number of reinforcements it received in this one month – 182 men, or almost a quarter of a fighting battalion. On 13th May, the battalion took up positions in the line near Cauroy-les-Hermonville, about eight miles north-west of Rheims. After a week they were relieved, and moved into support positions further south near Chalons-Le-Verger. They also received another draft of reinforcements, this time thirty strong. Their rest and training period was cut short though, for on the 26th, after church services, they were warned of an impending attack, and got ready to move forward into the battle zone.

Around midnight the Germans opened up with a heavy bombardment which included drenching the camp area in poison gas. At 1.30 a.m. on the 27th, the battalion marched off towards Cauroy and the battle lines, 'through dense clouds of gas'. By the time they got to the fighting area, they found the enemy had already pushed back the 9th Kings Own Yorkshire Light Infantry (KOYLI) and they made the best of the situation, reinforcing the 14th Northumberland Fusiliers, and trying to link up with the 7th Leicesters who were holding the Centre Vauban. Throughout the day the battle swung to and fro, dominated by close quarter bombing (grenade) attacks by each side. A company of Royal Engineers was brought in around 5.30 p.m. as reinforcements, and 'a stern fight ensued which lasted until darkness set in, when the enemy were forced back on the right.'

By nightfall, the British line had been pushed back to the southern edges of Cauroy, but it had not broken. The situation, though, was desperate. The unemotional text of the war diary belies just how stretched the British were. The 9th Northumberlands was a pioneer battalion, which in 'normal' conditions would be digging and repairing trenches. Engineers would usually be busy establishing communications, directing the trench building and so on. Using them as front-line infantry is as clear a statement as possible that the British were using every man who could hold a gun.

At midnight on the 28th, the battalion was ordered to withdraw, and moved back to brigade reserve. At 7.30 a.m. their camp was subjected to heavy machine gun fire: in the night, the Germans had gained control of a ridge overlooking the camp, and there was no alternative but to retreat to positions immediately south-east of

Ouvencourt. Again the enemy attacked, and succeeded in getting around their left flank. Again the battalion moved back, this time establishing what they hoped was a firmer defensive line south of Neurieux Wood, with the 9th Northumberland on their right and the 7th Leicesters on their left.

Just after midnight, the battalion was gain ordered to evacuate its position, and marched to Muizon, where they temporarily held a line on the south bank of the river Vesle, to the west of the village. They had so far retreated five miles southwards. However, those positions were heavily shelled, and 'about 2.30 p.m. instructions were received to evacuate these positions, and under intense shell fire the battalion made its way to ROSNAY' (another two miles backwards). Somewhere, in the confusion of the last three days, in the gas attacks, the machine gunning, the shellfire, and the retreat from trench to trench, shell hole to shell hole, Eric Evans was lost.

In the three days of 27th to 29th May, the battalion lost fifteen officers and 425 other ranks. Of these, 387 were either wounded and missing, or just missing. The lucky ones were prisoners, overtaken and rounded up by the Germans. The unlucky ones were the wounded who had died alone in shell holes, or been despatched by the advancing enemy. The 15th Durham Light Infantry had lost more than half its men.

Within a month the army had asked its regimental paymaster at York to confirm who, if anyone, should receive any pay or pension on Eric's behalf. The Paymaster replied that Miss Deborah Knifton had been receiving Eric's Separation Allowance, which would continue to run at 5s 10d per week until 27th January 1919, seven months after he went missing. Along with the other missing of the battle of the Aisne, and the later dead of the third battle of the Marne, he is commemorated on the Soissons Memorial in France.

It was not until April 1919 that Army Form 2090c (Acceptance of death for Official Purposes) was released by the Army, confirming that 'Reference has been made to the Record Office, the relatives, and to Germany, on the printed missing list, but no evidence of material value has been received which would indicate that he is not dead.' Two years later, Deborah Knifton received his two medals – the War medal and the Victory medal. There is no official record, but as next of kin, she would also have received his death plaque.

Eric's short life has left no trace in Wymeswold, except for his name on the Rolls of Honour. When Deborah died in 1940 there would be no 'family' left to mourn him – even her younger sister Ellen had died the year before. Let this small history help us to remember with gratitude the life of Eric Evans, the child whose parents are unknown, but who found a loving family in Wymeswold.

Sources

Census records: 1871, 1881, 1901, 1911.

Wymeswold parish registers. Online at: www.hoap.co.uk/who/localhisregister.htm [accessed June 2014].

Wymeswold Church of England School: log books and misc papers 1875–1983 (DE7281). The Record Office for Leicestershire, Leicester and Rutland.

Wymeswold vicar's correspondence (DE 1728/37). The Record Office for Leicestershire, Leicester and Rutland.

Certificate of Birth, Marriage or Death. General Register Office. Online at: www.freebmd.org.uk [accessed January 2014].

UK Railway Employment Records 1833–1963 page 414046742. Online at: www.ancestry.co.uk [accessed June 2014].

UK Extracted Probate Records 1269–1975. Online at: www.ancestry.co.uk

Commonwealth War Graves Commission 'Find War Dead'. Online at: www.cwgc.org [accessed 2014].

War Diary 15Bn Durham Light Infantry May 1918 (WO 95/2161). The National Archives.

Service Record: 81610 Evans, Eric. The National Archives.

Baker, Chris / Milverton Associates, 2014. 'The Long Long Trail: How men joined the British Army'. Online at: www.1914-1918.net/recruitment.htm [accessed 7 June 2014].

Conseil General de L'Aisne, 2014. 'L'Offensif de Mai 1918'. Online at: www.memorial-chemindesdames.fr/ [accessed 21 July 2014].

Kelly, D., 2001. *39 Months with the 'Tigers' 1915–1918.* reprint edn. Naval and Military Press.

Pitt, B., 2003. 1918 *The Last Act.* Barnsley: Pen and Sword.

Terraine, J., 1978. *To Win a War.* Cassell Military Paperbacks.

Chapter 12

James Fermer Fletcher

James Fermer Fletcher was ten years older than Eric Evans, and a married man with a child, but death was to bring the two men together, in the same battle. Eric was killed during the German onslaught on the Chemin Des Dames, near Reims, sometime between the 27th and 29th May 1918. James was to die less than a mile away, on the 27th, the first day of the battle.

Wymeswold was home to both men, but their backgrounds were very different. Eric had been a nurse child, taken into the Knifton family and raised as Deborah's own. James on the other hand, was from established Leicestershire stock. His father was born in Burton on the Wolds, just a couple of miles away, but his mother was Wymeswold through and through. Elizabeth Basford had married William Fletcher, then living at Walton on the Wolds, in St Mary's church in February 1868.

Basfords had been recorded in Wymeswold since 1722, and Elizabeth herself was baptised there in December 1847. Her father was a sawyer – cutting wood to size and shape was a trade in itself during the nineteenth century. The first census after her marriage, in 1871, shows her living with her husband and two young daughters, Alice and Elizabeth, in Burton on the Wolds. William at that time was an agricultural labourer, but ten years later the family was living in Brook Street, Wymeswold, and William had become a sawyer. Elizabeth's father Joseph Basford appeared in the same census, living in Clay Street, where he was a 'late sawyer'. In other words, he had retired, and it seems that the business, or a share in it, had passed to William Fletcher. Interestingly, Joseph was living next door to another of the Basfords, John, who was a timber merchant. It seems that working with wood was a family tradition.

It was into this settled Wymeswold family that James was born in 1886. The middle name Fermer is a mystery, but the likelihood is that it was the surname of a family related to one of his parents. There were Fermers in Derbyshire and Nottingham at the time, so he may have been named after one of them. He does appear to have been named after his grandfather. There is a record of James' father William being baptised as an adult in 1915, and giving his father's name as James *Furmer* Fletcher.

There is no record of James distinguishing himself at Infant School , but in 1893 he received a prize for good attendance at the Mixed School . It was probably his first year there. Another boy who received an attendance prize was Ernest Hubbard, who was to die rescuing the wounded in 1917. James may have been a dutiful child, but

*James Fermer Fletcher.
Photograph courtesy of Linda
Ward.*

he did not shine academically in that first year. The headmaster, Mr Bailey, was uncompromising:

> Some other children... James Fletcher... are not fit to be presented
> even in Standard i, as either backward or 'mentally deficient'.

Two years on, in 1895, and matters had not improved greatly:

> Oct 18th. Spelling seems a hopeless subject with 4 boys in this
> standard (ii), viz. ... and J Fletcher.

James does not appear again in the log books. It seems likely that he would have been one of the lads who were anxious to get out of school and start working. By 1901, he was doing just that. Aged fifteen, he was described as an 'Ordinary Agricultural Labourer'. Presumably he was not following a trade or specialism, such as cowherding, the way Ernest Hubbard had done.

The family were still living in Brook Street, specifically in Fox Yard, along with at least five other families. Next door but one was John Edward Clarke, then aged just two, who was to die in May 1917. The family clearly took a full part in village life:

William Fletcher in his cricket whites. Photograph courtesy of Linda Ward.

James' father, William, obviously a keen cricketer, is shown here in his 'whites'. By 1911, James was still living in Brook Street, but by now he had been married to Florence Selby for four years, and had changed occupation – he was now a wood yard labourer. It seems he had joined the family tradition, though whether he was working for his father William in the sawing business, or for the Basfords in their timber business, is unclear.

When the census was taken, Florence must have been pregnant, as her first child, William Selby Fletcher was born in June 1911. A second child, Irene Elizabeth May, followed in the autumn of 1914.

James' service record did not survive the Blitz of 1940, so it is not possible to say with certainty when or where he enlisted, or whether he volunteered (like Eric Evans) or was conscripted. As a married man with children, aged 28 at the outbreak of war, did he patriotically rush to the colours, or did he take his time, like Ernest Hubbard did, and volunteer in, say, 1916?

The medal card, which often gives an indication of when men joined, makes no mention of his 'theatre of war first served in'. His military number – 203860 – helps a lot. Up to the end of 1916 men in each TF unit (infantry battalion, artillery brigade, field ambulance, etc) were numbered using a *system unique to that unit* – often by allocating the number 1 to the first man to join the unit on its formation in 1908 and continuing from there.

In 1917, all Territorial Force units were renumbered. Each corps (usually a regiment) was given a block of six-figure numbers. Once given a new number, the soldier would then retain it for the rest of his service, unless he was transferred to a new corps. The 4th Battalion, Leicestershire Regiment, (one of the territorial battalions of the regiment) was given the numbers 200001 to 240000. Therefore it is almost certain that James had joined the Territorials, ready to 'do his bit' on the Home Front, and to be sent to fight if need be.

Considering his service number, that call-up would have come after 1916. It is possible that he was transferred to the 7th Battalion and sent to France as late as April or even May 1918, to help replace the losses suffered in the first weeks of the German offensive from 21st March to the end of April. He had not been 'gung-ho' to go, but equally he had been keen to do his duty.

May 1918 started well for the 7th Battalion, Leicestershire Regiment. Having been through the ferocious fighting of March and April, they 'arrived in the area of the 6th French Army, which had undertaken to provide a rest-cure for four battered British Divisions composing the IX Corps.'

They were now under the command of General Duchesne, a hot-tempered man whose instinct was for attack, not defence, and ordered his forces accordingly. He had been given four extra British divisions in part replacement for French divisions that were being sent to support the British in the north, where the German Spring Offensive had caused havoc. Duchesne contradicted the orders of his own superior, General Petain, to organise a deep defence, and instead squeezed all his divisions, and their artillery, into an area at best five miles deep – leaving no real protection or support if the Germans made a successful attack.

At first, the countryside and the defences seemed pleasant, dry and secure. The British were told that very little activity occurred there, and that 'the established custom was to fire two shots if the enemy fired one, but otherwise to let sleeping dogs lie... ' D.V. Kelly, then a staff officer with 110th Brigade (6th, 7th, 8th and 9th Leicesters), observed that

> ... the forward area of this sector was a chalk plain intersected by
> the Aisne canal; our front line, unfortunately as it proved, ran east
> of the canal, at one point as much as fifteen hundred metres
> beyond it.... the canal with its deep two hundred metres marsh
> would have made an excellent front line, but as it ran close to the
> front line of our neighbours on the flank it would, so long as we
> remained out in front of it, enable the enemy to walk along it and
> so surround our troops, which is in fact what happened.

Kelly was soon to realise that things were about to change dramatically. On the 25th, his observers reported 'long strings of horses, apparently gun-teams, returning at dawn from the enemy forward areas.' The next day he himself 'watched the disturbing spectacle of enemy linesmen laying out new telephone wires.'

Kelly was not to know that the fledgling American Intelligence Corps had been furiously warning the French of an imminent attack, or that escaped French prisoners had reached the British lines on 25th with descriptions of troop movements – all of which was derided by Duchesne. It was only on the 26th, when two German prisoners were interrogated, that the scale and timing of the German attack became obvious to Duchesne, and by then it was too late. The 7th Battalion's war diary contains a communiqué from the 110th Brigade Major, warning all units that, according to information received from prisoners, the enemy would commence a bombardment at 1.00 a.m. the next day, the 27th, followed by a full-scale attack at 3.00 a.m. In the document, the 7th Battalion, which was due to be relieved, would stay in position, and be joined by the 8th Battalion. The 7th and 8th Battalions would 'use the whole of their two companies West of the Canal for holding the main line of resistance, less those troops required as a line of outposts along the Eastern bank of the Canal... .' For the men who were holding those outposts, it was to be a death sentence. Kelly commented that 'the enemy attack probably developed between 3 and 4 a.m., but as our isolated companies east of the treacherous canal were annihilated we never knew exactly.'

The battalion's war diary confirms the bombardment: trench mortars and field guns were being used on the men east of the canal, while a high proportion of the shells landing to the west were gas or smoke, to disrupt and confuse the defenders of the main line. At 3.15 a.m. the diary notes that 'the 2 front companies... fought their positions to the end.' By 7.20 the enemy had crossed the canal. A number of strongpoints held out, but the enemy were sending bombing parties along old communication trenches to outflank them. One by one the strongpoints were overwhelmed. The nearby village of Cauroy (where Eric Evans' Durham Light Infantry were fighting) was taken.

By 4 p.m., the battalion held a frontage of seven hundred yards, on high ground about three hundred yards south-west of the village of Cormicy. Their defences now consisted of 'five small posts'. Within half-an-hour these posts, too, had been cut off and surrounded. At 11 p.m. '40 Stragglers arrived at VAUX VARENNES and these with 10 men of Battalion Headquarters were handed over to form a composite battalion from the battalion under the command of the Officer Commanding 6th Battalion Leicestershires.' In other words, the 7th Battalion had ceased to exist.

The remnants of the battalion were evacuated and other troops sent in. The fighting continued another two days. The battalion's losses of known dead seem light: two officers and fifteen Other Ranks. However, 443 men and officers were missing, dead or prisoners. The total casualty list was 503, or at least two-thirds of the battalion.

James' daughter Irene visiting his grave at Sissonne. Photograph courtesy of Linda Ward.

James Fletcher, sawyer and family man, did not survive the carnage of the first day. It is not possible to say whether he was among the doomed companies east of the canal, or died in the defence of the strongpoints, or was killed in the general retreat. We know now, however, that he met his end on the same few days and within a few hundred yards of Eric Evans, ten years his junior, but also a Wymeswold man. His body lies in the British cemetery at Sissonne, about twenty miles north-east of Rheims. His medals, like his memory, are in the safe keeping of his family.

Note: Since different corps were given the same blocks of numbers, it is possible that James could have joined the Territorials of, say 5th Lancashire Fusiliers. However, in the case of Territorial units, which were always associated with their own locality it is so unlikely as to be discounted.

Sources

Census records: 1871, 1881, 1901, 1911.

Wymeswold parish registers. Online at: www.hoap.co.uk/who/localhisregister.htm [accessed June 2014].

Wymeswold Church of England School: log books and misc papers 1875–1983 (DE7281). The Record Office for Leicestershire, Leicester and Rutland.

Wymeswold vicar's correspondence (DE 1728/37). The Record Office for Leicestershire, Leicester and Rutland.

Certificate of Birth, Marriage or Death. General Register Office. Online at: www.freebmd.org.uk [accessed January 2014].

Medal Roll Index Cards (Series WO 373). The National Archives.

War Diary of 7th Battalion Leicestershire Regiment, May 1918 (WO 95/2164). The National Archives.

Chris Baker / Milverton Associates. 2014. The Long Long Trail: Renumbering of the Territorial Force in 1917. www.1914-1918.net/renumbering.htm [accessed 6 June 2014].

Conseil General de L'Aisne. 2014. 'L'Offensif de Mai 1918'. Online at www.memorial-chemindesdames.fr [accessed 21 July 2014].

Kelly, D., 2001. *39 Months with the 'Tigers' 1915–1918.* reprint edn. Naval and Military Press.

Passingham, I., 2008. *The German Offensives of 1918.* Pen and Sword.

Pitt, B., 2003. *1918 The Last Act.* Pen and Sword.

Chapter 13

Horace Giles

Horace Giles was the youngest of Wymeswold's sons to die in the war. The Giles' were a Wymeswold family – certainly Horace's grandfather, Joseph, and his father William were both born there. In 1698 one of the churchwardens was a Richard Giles, and the family name continued to appear in the parish registers throughout the eighteenth and early nineteenth centuries.

They may have been an old but not a wealthy family as, in the 1841 census, they were described as agricultural labourers. However, by 1901, Horace's father William classed himself as a 'Market Gardener, Labourer', which may indicate that the family saw itself as moving up the economic scale. Ten years on, and William said he was now a grazier, and that his sixteen year old son Herbert was helping him on the land. The census evidence shows that the Giles' were moving into a solid working class level – below farmers (themselves divided into tenants and owners) and of course below the few professional people, or 'persons of private means'. All in all, Horace, aged eleven in 1911, must have had a relatively comfortable life with his sister and three brothers in the seven-roomed house they shared in West End, Wymeswold.

Horace George Giles was born on 30th November 1899. His mother Ann was from Burton on the Wolds, where she had been born Annie Towell. In 1901 her brother, John, was staying with them when the census was taken. Although he was a platelayer on the railway at the time, he had also moved on in life, since in 1917, when he went into the army, he described himself as a 'horseman'. A second army document is more specific; it says he was a 'farm waggoner and builder's carter'. He had been called up, and had 'attested' exactly a year before, in June 1916. At the age of 39, with a wife and four children, John Towell was perhaps sensibly sent to the Army Veterinary Corps. Until the outbreak of war, Horace's life must have seemed a very settled one; a hardworking family of parents and five surviving children, with maternal relatives in Burton and Quorn, all in similar economic circumstances.

At school, Horace had some favourable reports: in April 1906, aged six, he was given a prize for good attendance at the Infant School , and was transferred up to the Mixed School in the September. No sooner had he arrived than he was 'absent for a week through illness' – not unusual when children move schools, but he missed another week in April 1907. In 1910 he won a book prize for Scripture Knowledge –

'Crippled George'. Having reached Standard iv in 1912, he was assessed as fourth out of a class of nineteen in Arithmetic, and tenth in Spelling. However, it seems he never made it to Standard v – the top standard. The record shows that he left school in the autumn of 1912 – shortly before his thirteenth birthday. Other leavers were William Sissins' little brother Leslie, and Herbert Orridge. The coming war would tear all three families apart. But for now, the world for young Horace must have seemed full of promise.

There is no evidence of Horace's working life before the army. Most likely he either went to work for a local farmer, like most of his contemporaries, or joined his father in the family business. Certainly, William was doing well. He must have paid for the insert in Kelly's *Directory* of 1916, which refers to him as a grazier of London Road. The family had moved from West End – no more than a few hundred yards, but presumably to a better house, or to be closer to the fields that they rented.

Following the Military Service Act of 1916, all males between the ages of 18 and 40 were deemed to have enlisted by March 1916. This was the first time that Britain had both introduced conscription, and universally applied it. Unless a man could show that he was exempt, he would be obliged to attest following his eighteenth birthday. For Horace, that time came in early 1918. The Act of 1916 had also removed the likelihood that men would be sent to their local units, and in any case the army was desperate to plug gaps as and when it needed to, rather than allow accidents of geography to dictate which regiments were replenished.

Horace would have enlisted and then been sent for several months' training before being sent to France, where the shortage of men was becoming desperate. By this time, the German offensive was well under way, and the British losses, in dead, wounded and captured, were threatening to compromise the army's ability to fight an attacking war. These events correlate well with the fact that his name does not appear on a list drawn up by the vicar, probably in 1917, in order to pray for parishioners at the front. The inference is that Horace, quite simply, was not in uniform at the time.

The 18th Battalion, Lancashire Fusiliers (South East Lancashire) had been raised in 1915 as a 'bantam' battalion – in other words, composed of men who were under 5 feet 3 inches, normally deemed the minimum necessary to join the army. By 1917, however, the losses of the previous two years, and the simple need to recruit, forced the battalion to give up its bantam status, and accept all heights of men. At the beginning on July 1918 it had relieved a French regiment just south of Ypres, in trenches that were 'indescribably filthy'. Over the next two weeks, it was moved from these support trenches into the line, and then back into reserve at Boeschepe, before being moved up into support trenches on 16th. When in reserve, the battalion was in billets, and spent its time in 'bathing and short parades'.

Deaths among Other Ranks were recorded in both locations, due to enemy shelling. A rather abortive raid had taken place on the night of the 14th/15th, resulting in a dozen or so casualties, almost all from the British Stokes Mortar barrage that was supposed to cover the raid. A picture of 'business as usual' on the Western Front.

Horace Giles' grave at Abeele, Belgium. Photograph courtesy of Geoffrey Giles.

Except that somewhere in all this, Horace Giles died, on July 17th. If he were killed instantly, then it would have been due to shellfire in the artillery duel that took place over his head that night. If he died of wounds, then he might have been injured in the previous shelling, or by 'friendly fire' in the raid. It is quite likely that he was wounded whilst in reserve, as twenty-five bodies buried in the French cemetery at Boeschepe between April and August 1918, were later moved to Abeele Aerodrome Military Cemetery, where his body now lies. At all events, he could not have been at the Front for more than a couple of months – possibly just a few weeks. He was eighteen years and seven months old. A fortnight later, on Friday August 2nd 1918, the Loughborough Echo carried this notice

> ROLL OF HONOUR.
>
> GILES. - Killed in action, July 16th, 1918, Pte.Horace George Giles, second son of Mr. and Mrs. Giles, of Wymeswold, in his 19th year.
>
> Greater love hath no man than this,
> That he lay down his life for his friends.
>
> From Mother, Father, Sister, Brothers, Nephews and Nieces

Sources

Census records: 1841, 1901, 1911.

Wymeswold Church of England School: log books and misc papers 1875–1983 (DE7281). The Record Office for Leicestershire, Leicester and Rutland.

Wymeswold vicar's correspondence (DE 1728/37). The Record Office for Leicestershire, Leicester and Rutland.

Commonwealth War Graves Commission. 'Find War Dead' Online at: www.cwgc.org [accessed 7 February 2014].

War Diary 18Bn Lancashire Fusiliers July 1918 (WO 95/2484). The National Archives.

Service Record: 29094 Towell, John Hallam. The National Archives.

Allinson, S., 2009. *The Bantams.* Pen and Sword.

Baker, Chris / Milverton Associates, 2014. 'The Long Long Trail: The Lancashire Fusiliers'. Online at: www.1914-1918.net/lancsfus.htm [accessed 20 July 2014].

Corrigan, G., 2003. *Mud, Blood and Poppycock.* Cassell.

Kelly's Directory of the Counties of Derby, Nottingham, Leicester and Rutland. 1916 edition.

Passingham, I., 2008. *The German Offensives of 1918.* Pen and Sword.

Pitt, B., 2003. 1918. *The Last Act.* Pen and Sword.

Chapter 14

Ernest William Hubbard

The Hubbards were an old Wymeswold family – parish records show Hubbards living in the village in 1814. Ernest's father Thomas had been brought up on East Street (now known as East Road). As a young man, Thomas worked as a carrier – a trade which was to stay in the family, through his son Eustace. Thomas' father, John, was a thatcher. This was the trade that Thomas later took up and provided a living for him and his growing family. And it was a large family, even by the standards of the nineteenth century. Between 1874 when John Joseph was born, and 1896, which saw the arrival of Eustace, the youngest, Thomas' wife Mary gave birth to eleven children.

As the family grew, the Hubbards moved home several times. The 1881 census found them in Charles' Yard, roughly opposite the Three Crowns in Far Street, while in 1891 they were in Clay Street, where they remained for a long time. At some point, the Savage family came to live next to them. Eustace Hubbard and Alfred Savage were about the same age, and would have played together in the street, and probably in the field where the Memorial Hall now stands. Eustace, of course, was a lot younger than Ernest, who was born in 1885, the eighth of the Hubbard children. Mary eventually settled (possibly after Thomas' death in 1910) in Church Lane, now known as Church Street. The cottage they lived in, now called Christmas Cottage, was to be the birthplace of Miss Elsie Hubbard, whose contribution to this book has been invaluable.

Ernest's school career took off well at first. The Infant School log books show that in 1891, still aged five, he was awarded prizes for scripture and for good attendance. That early promise seems to have tailed off quite soon. After moving up to the Mixed School , he appeared in their log books just once as a prizewinner, soon after joining. In May 1893, aged seven, he again won a Scripture prize. By 27th October of that year, now eight, things were not going so well for him. The headmaster noted:

> Examined 3 boys; John Morris, Geo. Bromhead, and Ernest
> Hubbard in arithmetic; the first boy was unable to take down his
> sums correctly, but worked them moderately well; the other two
> have not the least idea of division, and do not seem to know their
> tables correctly.

Ernest in the uniform of 14th Battalion AIF. Photograph courtesy of Jack and Elsie Hubbard.

He was not mentioned again as a prizewinner, and the next reference comes in February 1897 when he was aged eleven and given a Partial Exemption for a Labour Certificate. At that time, the school leaving age was thirteen, but boys who wanted to (and most of them did!) could apply for an Exemption Certificate so that they could work legally in school holidays etc. from the age of twelve. When Ernest got his Partial Exemption, he was still in Standard iii. This was the third of six possible standards that children could reach, so it seems that he was behind with his schooling.

His alienation from school is further demonstrated by the last entry about him, later in the same year: 'Sept 20: Ernest Hubbard, absent since March 26, present this morning.' Ernest's lack of commitment to school was nothing unusual. Children were constantly absent during harvest and planting time, and in those days when all kinds of wild produce were harvested (primroses, blackberries, wild apples etc.), there must have been long periods when children were tempted (or ordered by their parents) to abandon school.

Having left school as soon as possible, Ernest would have been an experienced worker by the time of the next census, in 1901. He was then, aged sixteen, a cattleman on John Wale's farm at Burton Bandalls. At a time when labour distinctions were much better understood than they are now, the title 'cattleman' showed that Ernest was considered knowledgeable and capable to look after the cows himself. In other words, he already had a foot on the ladder of a career in farming.

Between Wymeswold and Burton, roughly opposite the entrance to Wymeswold airfield (as it is still known), lived the Huntington family. Daniel Huntington, a shepherd, had four sons, and one of these, Felix, was to marry Ernest's sister Elizabeth. They emigrated to Australia in 1908, arriving in Brisbane, but later settled near Young, in New South Wales. Ernest followed them in 1911, arriving in Sydney aboard the *Wilcannia* on 4th January. His younger brother Albert followed him, but sailed to Brisbane, where he arrived in June 1912.

On the ship's passenger list, Ernest had given his occupation as 'farmer'. Some people might think this rather 'aspirational', as there is no evidence that he had either owned a farm, or run one. On the other hand, by 1911, he already had nearly thirteen years' farming experience behind him, and was obviously a skilled worker. It is not surprising therefore that he should be ambitious, and think of himself as a farmer – at least, one in the making. He settled in New South Wales, at Uppingham, Coorawatha, around twenty-one miles from his sister and brother in law. An entry in de Ruvigny's Roll of Honour, published after his death, describes him as a Shear Farmer. It would have been from here that he went to enlist at Cootamundra on 25th July 1916. Again he listed his occupation as farmer, though by now he may well have been on his way to farming in his own right.

In his enlistment papers, he gave his mother's name as next of kin – his father of course had died in 1910. It may seem strange that he did not give his sister as next of kin – she lived nearest to him after all – but in the early 1900s the convention would have been to list parents or wife as next of kin, regardless of distance. The single curiosity in his Attestation form was that he gave his age as 29. He was in fact 32. Was he concerned that the authorities might decide he was too old? Or was it just an oversight? Unlike many in those days, he was well aware of his age – he had given it correctly when he emigrated.

Though as a boy he hadn't appeared fully committed to school, his handwriting on the official Army documents is assured and fluid – he had obviously been a good learner when he was present. Ernest was obviously fit – at 5 feet 7 inches, with a chest measurement of 37½ inches to 40 inches (expanded), weighing 11 stone, and with no obvious health problems, he was an ideal recruit. Suntanned, with dark brown hair and grey eyes, he would have been quite a handsome young man, too. He was accepted into the 14th Battalion, Australian Imperial Force (AIF) and by the end of November 1916 he was aboard the SS Port Napier sailing for England, where he arrived just before the end of January 1917.

After a further three months' training at Codford, he was sent to France, and arrived with his battalion on 25th April 1917, nine months after signing up. Like every member of the AIF, he had volunteered. Australia never introduced conscription. The Australian government proposed it in a referendum in 1916, and again in 1917. Both were defeated: the Australian public was convinced that it should be a matter of conscience, and of choice. It is still a source of pride in Australia that every man who served in the First World War had chosen, and not been forced, to fight for the Empire.

Ernest's two younger brothers also served. Albert, already in Australia, had joined up six months before Ernest and fought with 33rd Battery, 97th Artillery Brigade. Eustace, the youngest of the family, was also a gunner, serving with the British Royal Artillery. Both survived, and went on to raise families. At the time of writing, Albert's son Jack lives in New South Wales, Australia, and Eustace's children Peter and Elsie both live in Wymeswold.

The 14th Battalion was serving in Belgium, and remained there until after Ernest died. Within the battalion structure, Ernest had been selected as a stretcher-bearer, and was commended by Major-General E.G. Sinclair MacLagan, C.B., D.S.O., Commanding Officer of 4th Division AIF, for his courage and untiring energy in saving wounded near Zonnebeke in September 1917. The battalion war diary is professional and unemotional about the battle of Polygon Wood, as it was later known, but the battalion's history, written up by Newton Wanliss (whose own son was killed in the battle), has far more detail, and names many of the Other Ranks who conducted themselves bravely that day. Although Wanliss mis-spelled Ernest's surname, he paid fitting tribute to the work of the stretcher-bearers:

> Owing to the heavy and continuous enemy barrages, the duties of the stretcher-bearers proved exceptionally dangerous, with consequent heavy casualties. They, however, worked unceasingly, with their usual gallantry. Thirty-two stretcher-bearers took part in the engagement, and at its conclusion only seven of them were fit for duty, and the whole of the eight stretchers, and most of the equipment, had been destroyed by enemy action. Outstanding work was done by the following stretcher-bearers, viz:- Ptes William Watson, John Thompson, Abraham Milner, Frank Lowe, James Cooper, *E.W. Hibberd*, Maurice Harrison, and Thomas Connors. *(My emphasis.)*

The battle of Polygon Wood was followed within a fortnight by the main thrust of the British autumn offensive – the battle of Passchendaele, which has become a byword, like the Somme, for slaughter. The 14th Battalion was sent up to the line on 13th October to relieve the 48th and 52nd battalions. It was supposed to be in reserve and support, but in practice the 14th held the front line, such as it was. Conditions were appalling. Wanliss records:

> The reserve line, in which the Battalion now found itself, was not a trench, but a series of shell holes partly filled with slush and water, and during the night it was as far as possible consolidated. In front was a swamp several hundred yards wide, tenanted on its other side by the enemy.

The battalion was heavily shelled with both high explosive and gas. Luckily, the ground was so boggy that many shells did not detonate. The R.A.P. (Regimental Aid Post) was located a little distance away, in the cellar of a soda-water factory at the Zonnebeke cross roads. The stretcher-bearers would have to negotiate the shell holes, the marsh, and avoid the shells and snipers in order to get the wounded to treatment.

Albert and his mother, after Ernest's death. Photograph courtesy of Jack Hubbard.

> …the stretcher-bearers had an arduous time, but carried out their
> duties with their usual courage and devotion.

The battalion's relief, the 15th Battalion, arrived on the 16th October, and by 8.30 p.m. the entire battalion had moved out of the line to dugouts in the rear. All except Ernest Hubbard. The war diary notes that there was just one fatality that day. In all probability that was Ernest. No detailed account of his death survives, but his niece Elsie was told that his brother was in the area, and hoped to meet up, only to be told that Ernest had been shot in the head the previous day. The family account would fit very well with the facts; it would not have been possible for his brother to contact the battalion in the line, so it is likely that he found the 14th the day after they had been relieved, and was given the news then.

Ernest's body was recovered, and was buried – his service record contains a note of the fact – but the grave was evidently lost. It was quite a common fate, in the mud of Passchendaele, or indeed anywhere on the Western Front, which was fought over two, sometimes three or four times. His memory is preserved along with his comrades of the 14th Battalion AIF, on the Menin Gate Memorial at Ypres.

Albert, Ernest's brother, got some leave in October 1917 – after Ernest died – and visited his mother in Wymeswold. He may have been granted compassionate leave; such things were very much up to the discretion of local commanders. A photograph of that meeting, taken at Frost's, in Baxtergate, Loughborough, still survives. It must have been very important to Mary to have a picture of her 'Australian' son, whom she might never see again.

Ernest's name on the Menin Gate.

Ernest was thirty-two when he died, and he had survived just six months on the Western Front. Now, every evening at 8.00 pm, the Last Post is sounded just yards from his name, under the great Menin Gate that commemorates the 54,000 British and Empire troops who died in the Ypres area in WW1, and who have no known grave. His remains may be somewhere in Belgium, but he is still remembered by his niece and nephews in Wymeswold and Australia.

Sources

Census records: 1891, 1901.

Wymeswold parish registers. Online at: www.hoap.co.uk/who/localhisregister.htm [accessed June 2014].

Wymeswold Church of England School: log books and misc papers 1875–1983 (DE7281). The Record Office for Leicestershire, Leicester and Rutland.

Wymeswold vicar's correspondence (DE 1728/37). The Record Office for Leicestershire, Leicester and Rutland.

Commonwealth War Graves Commission. 'Find War Dead' Online at: www.cwgc.org [accessed 7 February 2014].

War Diary, 4th Infantry Brigade, October 1917 (AWM4-23/4/25). The Australian War Memorial. Canberra.

Conscription referendums, 1916 and 1917: Fact sheet 161. National Archives of Australia,. Online at: www.naa.gov.au/collection/fact-sheets/fs161.aspx [accessed 21 July 2014].

Record Search: B2455 - HUBBARD E W 6755. National Archives of Australia. Online at: recordsearch.naa.gov.au [accessed January 2014].

Butler, C. A., 1940. *The Australian Army Medical Services in the War of 1914-1918 (Vol II)*. The Australian War Memorial.

Janman, B., 2007. 'The RAMC Chain of Evacuation'. Online at: www.ramc-ww1.com [accessed 19 June 2014].

King, J., 2011. *Great Battles in Australian History*. Allen and Unwin.

Laughead, G., 2013. 'The Medical Front WW1'. Online at: www.vlib.us/medical [accessed June 2014].

Marshall, N., 2008. 'Great War Forum: Compassionate leave from France'. Online at: 1914-1918.invisionzone.com/forums/index.php?showtopic=111171 [accessed 5 July 2014].

Wanliss, N., 1929. *The History of the Fourteenth Battalion, A.I.F.* Arrow Printery.

Chapter 15

Robert Miles Jalland

The Jalland family was not one of those, like the Collingtons and the Hubbards, that had lived in Wymeswold for generations. They came from Old Dalby, just a few miles away, where they had lived at least since the early nineteenth century. Robert's father, grandfather and great-grandfather had all been brought up there. In 1851, his great-grandfather Richard was described as a farmer – he was called Jallands, though the 's' disappeared within the next twenty years.

By 1871, Robert's grandfather, also Robert, seems to have taken over the farm and was then a farmer of 77 acres – a considerable landholding. However, Robert's father (another Robert) did not follow into the family business. He became a policeman. In 1891 he was an unmarried constable living in police accommodation in High Street, Peckham, within the parish of Camberwell, London. The Metropolitan Police may seem a long way from the farm in Old Dalby, but the family had a London connection. The 1851 census also revealed that Richard had a daughter-in-law, Harriet Taylor, whose birthplace was 'Middlesex, London' [see Note 1]. Perhaps Robert's great aunt or one of her relatives found the position for him?

In June 1893, Robert senior was married to Florence Miles, originally from Gosport. Their first child came soon after. Robert Miles Jalland was born at 14, Englehead Road, Catford, London, in June 1894, and his sister Dorothy Ida was born in Old Dalby in 1899. Did her mother intend to go to her in-laws for the confinement, or was she there on holiday? Robert went to school in London. St Dunstan's Red Coat school, in the Mile End Road, had been a charitable foundation dating back to 1714, but by 1900 it had been incorporated as a Church of England school into the local authority framework. In other words, he was educated in the state system, rather than privately.

However, the family was clearly upwardly mobile. Robert's father was by 1911 a sergeant in the Metropolitan Police, and Robert himself was working as a clerk. He describes his employers as 'engineers and manufacturing chemists', by which he probably means the chemical industry rather than the pharmaceutical industry. The exact nature of his work is not disclosed in the census, but a few years later, his service papers described him as a shipping clerk.

There is evidence to suggest that the family moved back to Leicestershire in this period. Perhaps Robert's father retired from the police, or perhaps his health was deteriorating – he died in late 1917, around the time that his son was promoted to the rank of officer. By this time, too, Robert senior's brother Fred had moved to Wymeswold. Fred had married Caroline Hubbard, of Wymeswold, in St Mary's church in 1901, and had settled in the village, building up a business as a butcher. It was not surprising therefore that Robert senior, with Florence, Robert Miles and Dorothy, should also settle in Wymeswold. When Robert Miles joined up in 1914, he did so in Loughborough, and certainly by September 1917 he was confirming that his permanent address was Wymeswold.

It may be difficult, a hundred years on, to understand why a young man, with a good career in front of him, should be so eager to join up as a private soldier. Robert attested in September 1914, just a month after war was declared. The patriotic fervour of those early months must have been something that we can simply guess at. The Queen's Diamond Jubilee and the Olympics in 2012 are probably the most patriotic events that this generation will see, but they do not come close to the emotions that were stirred in 1914. Patriotism was not the only driver in the 'stirring call for men' that saw 478,893 men joining the army between 4th August and 12 th September.

Professor Peter Simkins observes 'Apart from a bedrock of patriotism and a widespread collective sense of duty to King and Empire, two factors, in particular, helped to generate this boom in enlistment. One was the formation on 31 August of the Parliamentary Recruiting Committee (PRC), which placed at the disposal of the War Office the entire network of local party political organisations. The assistance which the PRC provided included the issue of a series of memorable recruiting posters designed by leading graphic artists of the day.

Another key factor in stimulating enlistment was the granting of permission to committees of municipal officials, industrialists and other dignitaries, especially in northern England, to organise locally-raised 'Pals' battalions, which men from the same community or workplace were encouraged to join on the understanding that they would train and, eventually, fight together.'

Robert was one of that half-a-million volunteers. He attested on 10th September 1914. It is impossible to say whether Robert's workmates were all joining up as well: the 8th Battalion, Leicestershire Regiment, was not one of the recognised 'Pals' battalions, but at that time it was comprised mostly of local men. Matthew Richardson, in his history of 'The Tigers' argues that the 6th, 7th, 8th and 9th battalions of the Leicesters were Pals battalions in all but name. Further, the recruits coming forward were no longer the hungry, the unemployed, the adventurers, who had characterised the old army before the war. They were:

> men with skilled occupations – hosiery hands, engineering
> apprentices, clerks and office boys....These recruits were
> predominantly taller, fitter, and better fed than their pre-war
> counterparts, and, more significantly, they were used to thinking
> for themselves...

The description fits Robert very well. He was educated, and fit. His medical report shows that he was 6 feet ½ inches tall and had a chest measurement of 38 inches. His eyes were brown, his complexion fair, and his hair was light brown. He had no medical problems, and was immediately accepted into 'Lord Kitchener's Reserve'.

The next six months or so would be spent in training, mostly at Aldershot and Perham Down. He must have been very bored at times, as he was in trouble on three occasions – confined to barracks and deprived of a few days' pay – for overstaying his leave or 'breaking out' of camp to go back to Loughborough for a couple of days. However, these indiscretions had no effect on his military career.

The battalion was sent to France at the end of June 1915, as part of the 110th Brigade – known as the Leicestershire Brigade, as it was made up of the 6th, 7th 8th and 9th battalions of the Leicesters. The first year in France was relatively quiet; D.V. Kelly, a liaison officer with the 110th Brigade, recalled that:

> My chief memory of that golden autumn and hard winter of 1915
> in the trenches south of Arras is one of peace – peace that is in
> comparison with what came after.

However, by June of 1916 it was evident that there would be a major attack by the British. Kelly's battalion was equipped with a machine gun company – something of a rarity at the time. Two weeks into the battle of the Somme, the brigade was involved in the bloody assault on Bazentin Ridge. It is less than a mile to walk from Mametz Wood to the far end of Bazentin village, but it took the brigade all day to win those two thousand yards of ground and another day to hold it before they were relieved. This was their first introduction to the carnage and confusion of battle.

Robert survived the Somme, and was promoted Lance Corporal (unpaid, 5th October 1916, and paid, 10th November). By the end of March 1917 he had been promoted Corporal (Acting), and it may be at this time that he became a machine gunner – the two entries on his record of service seem to be in the same hand. In April and May 1917 his brigade was part of the 21st Division that attacked along the Scarpe river, east of Arras. His officers had seen his potential, and he had been identified as a future officer himself. In early September, the final documentation was in place. He had been recommended by his battalion commander, who would have accepted him back as an officer: the recommendation was signed off by the brigade commander, and finally by the general commanding 21st Division, who considered 'Corpl. R.M. Jalland suitable for a temporary commission in the Regular Army, and I hope that he may be posted to the 6th Bn Leicestershire Rgt'. By the end of September 1917, he was confirmed as corporal. Just as the horrors of Passchendaele were unfolding, he was posted back to England, to report for officer training. He must have had mixed feelings, knowing that his comrades were going to be put through one of the worst experiences of the war, and yet relieved that he would be getting some peace and quiet (and training) at home.

He joined 18 th Officer Cadet Battalion at Bath on 9th November 1917, having duly submitted references: his old headmaster, Mr A. Waller, would provide an

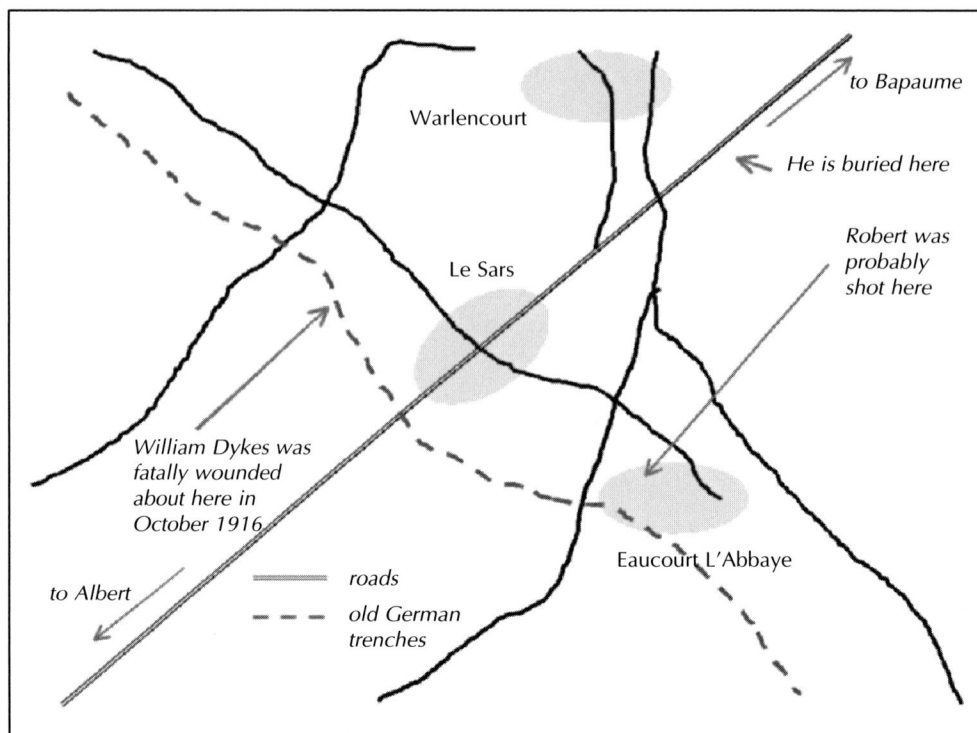

Robert Jalland was killed in this area.

educational reference, while the vicar of Wymeswold, Rev Claud Edmunds, would attest to his moral character. He did well at officer training school. His final report considered that his standard of education, military knowledge, and abilities of command and leadership were all 'very fair'. His overall summary was that he 'Has worked hard and improved greatly… [will] make a good leader'.

After four months of training, 2nd Lieutenant Robert Jalland was discharged to 6th Battalion, Leicestershire regiment, on 30th April 1918. It is unclear exactly when he returned to France, but it would have been soon after. The army by that time was desperately trying to recover from the losses suffered in the ferocious German offensive which started in March, and which was to continue, in various attacks, until June.

By July 1918 the tide was turning in favour of the Allies. The original German offensive on the Somme had petered out in the mud, shell holes and wreckage of previous battles, and the subsequent offensives to the north and east had also ground to a halt. The 6th Leicesters were back on the Somme. This time, though they were several miles west (i.e. back) from where they had fought so well at Bazentin in 1916. The valleys and woods of the Somme had to be fought over yet again. Moving from Acheux to Englebelmer, to Hamel, they alternated with other battalions in pushing the Germans back, little by little. In the wake of a massive Allied offensive launched on 8th August, the battalion reached the Ancre river on the 13th. This had

*Lieutenant Robert Jalland's
grave at Warlencourt cemetery.*

been one of the battlegrounds of July 1st 1916 – the day the Ancre ran red with blood. It was a week before they were able to cross the Ancre and fight their way up the steep hill to Thiepval ridge, where the Ulster tower now stands. They were relieved on August 22nd and returned to Englebelmer for a rest.

Events then moved swiftly, as the German army started to find itself in danger of being surrounded. Back in 1916, the area around Hamel – Auchonvillers – Thiepval – La Boiselle was the point where the Allied line turned from a north-south direction and ran eastwards. It had been seen as the 'hinge' around which the two thrusts – one coming from the west, the other from the south – would converge and cut off the Germans. It didn't work in 1916, of course, but 1918 was a much more fluid campaign, in which the Germans were no longer defending well-engineered, deep defences, but holding a series of strongpoints, based largely on old trenches and the shattered remains of those defences.

On the 24th August, Boom Ravine (south of Miraumont), which had proved so difficult in 1916, was captured, and the battalion pushed on another mile-and-a-half north eastwards to Pys. In the morning of the 25th, they were ordered to move south eastwards, crossing the Albert-Bapaume road at Le Sars, to Eaucourt L'Abbaye. They were, in fact, walking along the old front line of July 1916. At 2.00 p.m., the battalion dealt with a strong counter-attack at Eaucourt, but repulsed it, and dug in to form a defensive flank, facing south.

The following day, they turned north again, and went into Divisional Reserve at Warlencourt, about half-a-mile away. The family recalls that Robert was killed by a sniper. This is entirely consistent with the facts. The war diary of the battalion lists his date of death – 26th August, but does not record the casualties on a day-by-day basis. In theory, it is possible that he was mortally wounded earlier, but a letter to his family in March 1919 confirmed that he was buried 'about 800 yards south-east of Le Sars' – in other words, in the vicinity of Eaucourt L'Abbaye. Therefore it is most likely that he was struck by the sniper's bullet in that area. It might have happened on the 25th, just before reaching Eaucourt, or during the counter-attack, leaving him fatally wounded. It might have happened on the 26th, before the battalion moved off to Warlencourt.

In October 1920, his mother received another letter, informing her that her son's remains had been moved. In accordance with an agreement with the French and Belgian governments, all cemeteries with less than forty interments had been closed, and the bodies moved to larger burial grounds. Robert was almost certainly first buried at Hexham Road cemetery (Hexham Road was the name given by the British to the road running from Warlencourt to Eaucourt). He now lies in Warlencourt cemetery, on the main road from Albert to Bapaume.

Three women grieved for Robert; his mother, his sister, and his sweetheart in London, a Miss D. Holland. Robert left no will, so his back pay was divided between his mother Florence, who lived at Key Cottage, Brook Street, and his sister Dorothy, who, during the course of her correspondence with the army, lived at 62 Frederick Street, Loughborough, but also stayed with her uncle in Wymeswold. In September 1918, when she was writing to the army, Dorothy was in the Women's Royal Air Force, and dealing with these matters while she was on leave. She was evidently an independently-minded young woman who was as keen to 'do her bit' for the country as her brother had been.

Note . It is unclear whether Harriet Taylor was the common law wife of Edwin, Richard's elder son, or not. In 1851 she had just had a child, Alfred Taylor; by 1861 she had another, Henrietta, though both children retained the surname Taylor, and there was no adult male Taylor in evidence. In that census, too, she is described as Richard's daughter.

Sources

Census records: 1851, 1861, 1871, 1891, 1911.

Wymeswold parish registers. Online at: www.hoap.co.uk/who/localhisregister.htm [accessed June 2014].

Commonwealth War Graves Commission. 'Find War Dead' Online at: www.cwgc.org [accessed 7 February 2014].

King's College London Archives (AIM25 - Red Coat School). Online at: www.aim25.ac.uk/cgi-bin/vcdf/detail?coll_id=16661andinst_id=118 [accessed 21 July 2014].

London Guildhall Library. Online at: www.history.ac.uk/gh/18iii.htm [accessed 4 June 2014].

London Metropolitan Archives. Online at: www.nationalarchives.gov.uk /a2a/records.aspx?cat=074-p93dunandcid=305#305 [accessed 3 June 2014].

Map of M/5/000432 LeSars 57dSE57cSW 240916. Western Front Association.

Service Record: 8/15159 Jalland, Robert Miles (WO_374_36937). The National Archives.

War Diary 6Bn Leicestershire Regiment July/ Aug 1918 (WO/95/2164). The National Archives.

www.royalleicestershireregiment.org.uk [accessed 1 April 2014].

Kelly, D., 2001. *39 Months with the 'Tigers' 1915–1918.* reprint edn. Naval and Military Press.

Pitt, B., 2003. *1918 The Last Act.* Pen and Sword.

Richardson, M., no date.*The Tigers: 6th, 7th, 8th, 9th (Service) Battalions of the Leicestershire Regiment.*

Simkins, P., 2014. 'British Library: World War One'. Online at: www.bl.uk/world-war-one/articles/voluntary-recruiting [accessed 4 June 2014].

Steadman, M., 2009. *Advance to Victory 1918.* Pen and Sword.

Van Emden, R.A.H.S., 2003. *All Quiet on the Home Front.* Headline.

Chapter 16

John Joseph Lamb

The Lamb family had been in Wymeswold for over a hundred years before the start of World War One. John Lamb is recorded as marrying Mary Hickling in St Mary's church on 19th February 1810; their daughter Sarah was born in April of the same year. She grew up to have at least four children, among whom were Samuel (born 1842) and Joseph (born 1846). Their grandfather John was a wheelwright, and the two boys followed in his footsteps. When he died in January 1871, the boys appear to have taken over the business. Ten years later, they seem to have gone their separate ways, though. Joseph had married, and had had a baby daughter, Mary Ann, while Samuel still lived with his mother. Though they both still lived in Wymeswold, Joseph described himself as a joiner and wheelwright, while Samuel was a 'Master wheelwright, [employing] 1 Man, 1 Boy'.

By 1901, Samuel had married as well. His wife was Sarah Mills, a member of another old Wymeswold family and a distant relation of Jesse Mills who was killed in April 1918. Confusingly, both brothers had a daughter Mary and a son Henry. Distinguishing the two Marys is not too difficult, as Joseph's daughter was ten years older than her cousin, but the two Henrys were both born around 1893. Meanwhile, with the coming of steam driven engines and iron wheels for carts and carriages, it may be that the wheelwright business was not going too well. In 1901, both brothers described themselves as joiners, though only Joseph had dropped the term 'wheelwright' altogether.

The big change in the two families was that by 1901, Joseph had moved his family to Leicester, and they were living at 81 Mornington Street, just south of Humberstone Lane. It was a street of very pleasant, quite new terrace houses – probably a lot more comfortable than many of Wymeswold's old cottages. There is no record of when they left the village, or why, but the records of Wymeswold Infants school show that Mary Ann (Joseph's daughter) became a monitor there at the age of thirteen, in June 1894. However, in September 1895, it was noted that she had left the school. This may have been for a number of reasons, but it probably shows when the family moved.

Samuel and Joseph senior's families continued to run parallel. Mary, Samuel's daughter, also became a monitor, though in the Wymeswold Mixed School. She sat for examinations, passed, and became an assistant teacher at Somerby, before returning in June 1916 as a temporary teacher. She was welcomed by the children ('their old friend, Miss Lamb', the headmaster wrote in his log). The last entry that refers to her noted that she was absent to visit a wounded soldier in hospital at Shrewsbury. Her brother? Her cousin? A sweetheart? Regrettably the log book does not say. Samuel's Henry and possibly Joseph's Harry as well, served in the war; both Henry Lamb and Harry Lamb are on a list drawn up by the Vicar of 'residents of Wymeswold who are serving in His Majesty's Forces'.

Back in Leicester, the move may have been problematical for young John. While his elder brother George became their father's apprentice, it is likely that the family would have been unable to support another teenager who was not bringing in wages. While there is no record of what he did between the age of thirteen and seventeen, it is probable that his career prospects were not good. Because, in October 1907, he joined the army.

Joining the army before the reforms of 1908 was not exactly a 'choice of last resort', but it had been traditionally a refuge for the poor, the criminals, and the adventurers. There is no suggestion that John was any of these, but the army had never been looked on with favour by the British public until recent times, when the Imperialist vision of entrepreneurs like Rhodes, and poets like Kipling, and the lead of the Queen herself as Empress of India, made it much more respectable. However, the army could offer accommodation, food, training and a pension. For a young man with limited prospects it was bound to be an attraction. Like other Wymeswold regulars – Bill Collington, James Collington, Amos Clarke, for example – he knew what he was getting into. His service record shows that he had had a Notice (so he had been in touch with a recruiter previously) and more importantly, that he was already serving with the Militia. '

Life in the peacetime army must have been fairly agreeable, at least at first. His record shows that he remained in England, mostly at Shorncliffe Barracks in Kent, and then Aldershot, until the end of 1910, when the battalion was sent to India. He arrived in Belgaum, halfway between Mumbai and Bangalore, but moved after a few months to Madras, then north to Bareilly in Uttar Pradesh, before moving on to Ranikhet even further north in Uttarakhand. He would have been in the foothills of the Himalayas, close to the Nepalese and Tibetan borders, and some of the most dramatic scenery on earth.

In India, the battalion formed part of the Garhwal Brigade of the 7th Indian Division. After the outbreak of war, the battalion was ordered back to Europe, landing in Marseilles in October 1914. It was not long before they were in action on the Western Front. In March 1915, the Gharwal Brigade attacked with the rest of the Meerut Division at Neuve Chapelle. It was the first successful British offensive of the war; successful in that it broke into and captured the enemy positions. It also demonstrated the difficulty of breaking *through* those positions into open country beyond. Neuve Chapelle is also significant because of the major contribution of the Indian Army. The memorial to the Indian troops who have no known grave is sited just beside the battlefield.

John survived Neuve Chapelle, and in November 1915 sailed from Marseilles for Mesopotamia (Iraq). Although he and the battalion were recalled to India in March 1916, they were back in Iraq by the end of October. Still with the 7th Indian Division, the battalion 'distinguished itself in the battles of Shaikh Saad, Kut-al-Amara, the various battles of Sannaiyat, and went on to capture Baghdad'. Baghdad was liberated on 11th March, when the British commander, General Maude, issued a lengthy proclamation inviting the people of the city to '… participate in the management of your own civil affairs in collaboration with the political representatives of Great Britain' and achieve union with their fellow Arabs in the region.

Following the capture of Baghdad, Maude was faced with the classic strategic problem of securing it. He had taken Baghdad mainly to secure the strategically important town of Kut: Baghdad was of little military importance, but of enormous political significance, so when it fell into British hands, he could hardly abandon it. Therefore he started pushing outwards, testing the Turkish will to fight. John Lamb's battalion, part of the 7th Indian Division, was sent up the Tigris valley towards Masoudiyeh, a railway station at a village (now probably called Mshahdh), about twenty-five miles north of the city.

The operation began on 14th March, with John's battalion taking the left side of the railway line. It was reported that their side of the railway was the one 'most strongly held' by the enemy. They began at 4.45 p.m., advancing in open order to reduce the casualty rate, because the Turks had opened up immediately with heavy shellfire and some rifle fire. When they were about six hundred yards from the enemy they dug in and sent patrols forward throughout the night to test the enemy defences and to provide early warning against any counter-attack.

In the morning they heard that the Black Watch had entered Masoudiyeh and they began advancing again. The enemy had pulled back in the night, and they were able to reach their objective by 9 a.m.. The enemy had withdrawn entirely and 'were in full flight'. The war diary noted that 'their position had been six miles in breadth and five miles in depth'. Baghdad was secured, and the battalion made its way back on the 16th. John must have been a part of this, and fallen ill on the march. A Medical Officer noted on his hospital case form:

> Admitted 18.3.17. Had been operated on up country (19 CCS)
> three days previously. Patient had all the cardinal signs of septic
> general peritonitis and was in a moribund condition on
> admittance here. Further operative measures out of the question.
> Died 3.30 pm 19.3.17.

CCS is the abbreviation for Casualty Clearing Station. In the days before antibiotics, let alone helicopter evacuation, falling victim to acute appendicitis in a remote and hot place was likely to be a death sentence. And so it proved, in spite of the best efforts of the brigade medics to operate on him.

John's fate was not unusual. In contrast to the Western Front, death from disease in the Middle East was commonplace. The Mesopotamian campaign resulted in 92,501 casualties, of whom 13,494 were taken prisoner, and 51,386 were wounded. The causes of death were almost evenly distributed between those killed in action or died of wounds – 14,818, and those who died of disease – 12,807. John's body was interred at Amara British Cemetery, near Baghdad. Sadly, it has not been possible to obtain a photograph of his grave. The area is still considered too dangerous.

Sources

Census records: 1851, 1861 1871, 1881, 1891, 1901, 1911.

Wymeswold vicar's correspondence (DE 1728/37). The Record Office for Leicestershire, Leicester and Rutland.

Wymeswold Church of England School: log books and misc papers 1875–1983 (DE7281). The Record Office for Leicestershire, Leicester and Rutland.

Wymeswold parish registers. Online at: www.hoap.co.uk/who/localhisregister.htm [accessed June 2014].

Commonwealth War Graves Commission. 'Find War Dead' Online at: www.cwgc.org [accessed 7 February 2014].

Service Record: 8243 John Joseph Lamb. The National Archives.

War Diary 2Bn Leicestershire Regiment Feb/Mar 1917 (WO/95/5140). The National Archives.

www.royalleicestershireregiment.org.uk [Accessed 1 April 2014].

'Battles: The capture of Baghdad, 1917'. Online at: firstworldwar.com/battles/baghdad.htm [Accessed 5 June 2014].

Carver, Field Marshal Lord, 2003. *Turkish Front 1914–18*. 2nd ed. Pan Books.

Chapter 17

George Harold Marriott

There had been Marriotts in Wymeswold, on and off, since 1686, when Christiana, daughter of Bryan and Sara Marriott, was baptised at St Mary's church. Other Marriotts also figure in the parish records, indicating their connection to other Wymeswold families – the Kniftons, Hicklings, and Foxes. George's mother, Sarah Ann Marriott, was also born in Wymeswold, though her father came from Old Dalby and her mother from Pickwell, near Somerby. John, her father, was an agricultural labourer, though her brother (also John) could see the way that agriculture was moving, and by 1881 described himself as an Engine Driver (almost certainly an agricultural engine, for pulling machinery or driving a thresher etc). Unfortunately, Sarah's brother was also unemployed at the time.

By 1891, Sarah was twenty-two and a servant in the house of Eli Rischen, a mineral water manufacturer, of 67 Welford Road Leicester. Ten years later, she was back in Wymeswold, but with two children, George aged seven and Sarah aged four. Sarah had been born in Old Dalby – perhaps in the home of her grandfather John. (Her father appears to have left Wymeswold sometime previously as, although his funeral was held in St Mary's in 1899, he was described as John Marriott of Dalby).

In the census of 1901 George's mother was described as a charwoman. Life was hard for a single mother in Victorian times. George had been born in Leicester, in the autumn of 1893.

George does not figure in the Infant School records at all. It is quite possible, of course, that the family lived in Old Dalby until 1899, when George's grandfather died. If, as is likely in the case of an agricultural labourer, his home was rented then, on his death, his family would have been obliged to move out in order to provide housing for another labouring family. So Sarah found a home for herself and her children on East Street with an elderly widower, William Hawkins, who lived 'on his own means' and could therefore accommodate and pay her.

Both George and his younger sister Sarah are mentioned in the Mixed School log books. George did not get off to a good start. In 1901, probably his first year in the school, the headmaster recorded:

> Oct 11th Examined Std i in the 3 R's. The following children are
> very backward. Arthur Daft, Tom Tyler, George Marriott, Alfred
> Collington, Reuben Hickling.

Given his likely economic circumstances, and the disruption of the past two years, with losing his grandfather and moving to Wymeswold, it is probably not surprising that his performance was behind the headmaster's expectations. However, he seems to have improved. In 1904 he was awarded a prize for 'proficiency in Holy Scripture at the recent Diocesan Examination'.

By 1905 he was definitely catching up:

> Nov 1st .The following were put up a standard this morning:-
> George Marriott Jesse Mills and others.

George and Jesse were classmates and possibly pals. They were to die within a month of each other, in the bloodbath of the 'Kaiserschlacht' in 1918. At school, 1906 was probably George's best year – and probably his last, as he turned thirteen in the autumn. Both he and his sister won prizes. She was given a copy of *The Pilgrim's Progress* for her knowledge of scripture, while George was awarded a copy of *Wide World: Europe,* for attending 419 times out of a possible 422. He could not have dreamt of the kind of Europe he was to see in just eight years' time.

Details of George's life from then on are sketchy. However, we know that his mother's fortunes improved. In 1903 his mother married John Hubbard, and by 1911 they had had two children and were living in Clay Street. Later they moved to Vine Tree Terrace, Hoton, which was her address when the army recorded the interment of her son. Meanwhile by 1911 Sarah had found work as a farm servant maid with the Egglestone family at Field Farm, and George was at Highthorne Farm, working for Albert Bailey as a waggoner. Mr Bailey employed another sixteen year old lad, Tom Tyler, a cowman. Tom also served, but survived.

Both George and Tom are recorded on the Honour Roll started in the school log book by Mr Bailey, the headmaster. It appears that the list was drawn up in 1914, and added to in 1915, but there is no evidence to suggest that additions were made later. Therefore George must have been among the first to go. So too were Tom and John Tyler. George's name is numbered 23 out of 38. Since the list is not alphabetical, it suggests that he was among the later recruits in that period 1914–15. Was he a member of the Territorials, or Special Reserve as it was then called? Or had he just decided to join up? His service records have not survived, so it is unlikely that we shall ever know.

His medal card, however, provides a clue. It confirms that he first entered the 'theatre of war' (France) on 28th October 1915, and that he was originally Private 4088, the Leicestershire regiment. A four-digit number suggests very strongly that he was a Territorial as recruits to Lord Kitchener's New Army were given five digit numbers, and Territorials who changed units were renumbered with six digit numbers in 1917.

roads
railway lines

to Villers-Guislain

Heudecourt

Chapel Hill

2nd Battalion Lincolns

attempted German penetration

Battalion HQ at start

George was killed in this area.

The logical unit for him to have joined would have been the 5th (Territorial) Battalion, Leicestershire regiment. There is no evidence however of a whole Leicestershire battalion moving on 28th October 1915, so we can infer that he probably joined one of the county's battalions, most of whom, except the 2nd, were in France or Flanders.

Both Leicestershire Territorial battalions (the 4th and 5th) were assigned to the 138th Brigade, and formed part of the 46th (North Midland) Division, which was a Territorial force, composed predominantly of men from Leicestershire, Lincolnshire, Staffordshire, Derbyshire and Nottinghamshire – at least, at the beginning of the war. At some point (and the medal card gives no clues) George was transferred to the 2nd Battalion, Lincolnshire Regiment, a regular army unit. He was also given a new, five digit number – 40549.

Whenever he made the change, he would have seen action in the Somme and Flanders. He would have been involved in some of the major actions of the war. By March 1918, the 2nd Lincolns were positioned in front of the small village of Heudecourt, about 21 miles east of Albert, on the Somme. Just a year before, the 2nd Lincolns had been involved in the fighting to harry the Germans as they retired to their Hindenburg Line, less than a mile to the east of their present positions. The British defences were now a series of strong points, using old German trenches, pill

George's name on the Pozieres Memorial.

boxes and shell holes. The difficulty, of course, was that old German trenches were in ruins, and the pill boxes faced the wrong way. After three years of war, with manpower now stretched, the defences were improvised rather than solidly built.

While it was generally known that a major German attack was coming, the Lincolns' war diary makes no mention of it. The logic of an attack was obvious to most in the military. Russia had collapsed the previous November, allowing the Germans and Austrians to release dozens of divisions to the Western Front. At the same time, the Americans were beginning to pour men into France: though they were still mostly in training, they would soon be battle-ready. If the Germans did *not* attack soon, they would be destroyed later.

Unsurprisingly, much of the early part of March had been occupied in digging trenches and wiring the defences. After a number of days involved in strengthening the front line, the battalion had been put into brigade reserve on the 18th. The relief did not last long. At 5.45 a.m. on the 21st, the battalion received orders to man battle stations. This proved easier said than done, as thick fog and enemy gas shells confused and slowed up troop movements. Most of the battalion was in place by 7 a.m., but stragglers continued to come in as late as 10. Their positions were stretched out north-east of Heudecourt and west of the village of Villers-Guislain, running

INFORMAL WILL.

W.O. No.: E/561924/1 DOMICILE. English

Record No. 423/707698
18/19

Name George Harold Marriott

Regtl. No. 40549 Private
and Rank

Regt. 2nd Bn Lincolnshire

Died at in France

Date of Death 21 . 3 . 18 .

WAR OFFICE.

Date 18/10/18

The enclosed document dated Nov 3rd. 19/11/16 and signed Pte. G. H. Marriott appears to have been written or executed by the person named in the margin while he was "in actual military service" within the meaning of the Wills Act, 1837, and has been recognised by the War Department as constituting a valid will.

for the Assistant Financial Secretary.

B. 16302

George left everything to his mother.

down from Chapel Hill to a sunken road about half a mile to the south west. They were on higher ground, with another sunken road in front, so there was some natural advantage in their defensive position. On the other hand, another sunken road cut right through their lines, about half way along. Repeated attacks were beaten back, but at noon the enemy succeeded in getting into this sunken road at the heart of the Lincolns' sector, and desperate fighting followed. The battalion headquarters staff joined in the battle, and a machine gun team came up.

The Germans' concealed attack route now became a killing ground. A number were killed, and the rest, about fifty, were captured. For the rest of the day, the Lincolns clung on to their positions. In the chaos of battle, George Marriott was killed. There would have been no time to bury him, even if his body could be identified. The next day, and the day after, the battalion was ordered to retreat, as the Germans continually worked around the flanks of the British. It wasn't even possible to identify the number of casualties on a daily basis.

Ten days later, the battalion, or what was left of it, was able to catch its breath, and consider its losses. Those known to be dead amounted to thirty-one, but the other numbers are more significant: 95 were wounded, nine wounded and missing. Most telling of all, 238 were missing. Some would be prisoners, but many would be dead, or left to die in shell holes. The total losses were 373, or half the total strength of the battalion. It had all but ceased to exist as a fighting unit.

George's body was never recovered, and he is now remembered on the memorial at Pozieres, about halfway from Albert to Bapaume. The Commonwealth War Graves Commission, which maintains the memorial, and the cemetery that it surrounds, describes it:

> The Memorial commemorates over 14,000 casualties of the
> United Kingdom and 300 of the South African Forces who have
> no known grave and who died on the Somme from 21 March to
> 7 August 1918.

George was one of four Wymeswold men to die on that first day, the 21st. John William, (Bill) Collington, William Wilson and John Robert Ovendale died in the same holocaust. It was Wymeswold's worst day of losses.

Sources

Census records: 1871, 1881, 1891, 1901, 1911.

Wymeswold parish registers. Online at: www.hoap.co.uk/who/localhisregister.htm [accessed June 2014].

Wymeswold Church of England School: log books and misc papers 1875–1983 (DE7281). The Record Office for Leicestershire, Leicester and Rutland.

Wymeswold vicar's correspondence (DE 1728/37). The Record Office for Leicestershire, Leicester and Rutland.

Commonwealth War Graves Commission. 'Find War Dead' Online at: www.cwgc.org [accessed 7 February 2014].

'Find a soldier's will' service. Online at probatesearch.service.gov.uk. [Accessed June 2014]

map of. MA/001470 Heudecourt Sheet 57cSE 210318. Western Front Association.

Medal Roll Index Cards (Series WO 373). The National Archives.

War Diary 2Bn Lincolnshire regiment March 1918 (WO/95/2154). The National Archives.

Baker, Chris / Milverton Associates, 2014. 'The Long Long Trail: Renumbering of the Territorial Force in 1917'. Online at: www.1914-1918.net/renumbering.htm [accessed 6 June 2014].

Mitchinson, K. W., 1998. *Epehy*. Pen and Sword.

Passingham, I., 2008. *The German Offensives of 1918*. Pen and Sword.

Pitt, B., 2003. *1918 The Last Act*. Pen and Sword.

Chapter 18

Jesse Mills

There is a record of an Edith Mills being baptised in Wymeswold in 1640. The family is by common consent one of the old village families, and has been recorded as Mills, Millns and Milns. Yet no more Mills appear in the parish registers until the late 1700s, when the name occurs frequently, and in the twenty-five years after 1813, no less than twenty-three baptisms were recorded.

Jesse Mills' father, John, had been born in Wymeswold around 1852. He was the son of Robert and Mary Milns (later referred to in all records as Mills), baptised in January 1853. Robert had started out as an agricultural labourer, but by 1881, at the age of 55, he had become a grazier, with 36 acres. John followed in his father's footsteps. By 1881, he too was a grazier, with 38 acres, but he had had to move to Hathern to find the land. It is likely that he married Mary Hitherly in early 1878. Children followed quickly; John Robert was born in 1879, followed by William in 1880 and Marie in 1881. At least one other child, Elizabeth, died in infancy. The parish register at Wymeswold records the burial of 'Elizabeth Mills, aged 1½, of Hathern. The daughter of John and Mary Mills, granddaughter of Robert Mills'.

By 1891, John had taken over Cliff Farm, on the Six Hills road from Burton on the Wolds, but in the parish of Wymeswold. It was here, in 1894, that Jesse Mills was born, and here, in April 1899, that his father John died. Mary took over the farm, and Jesse's two elder brothers continued to work on the farm, but within a few years each had married and gone their own ways – William to farm in in Tonge, near Ashby-de-la-Zouch, and John to become a wholesale and retail dairyman in Leicester. It was left to Jesse to help his mother on the farm.

At some point, probably beginning with Jesse's grandfather, the family seems to have parted company with the Church of England because Jesse was raised as a devout Methodist. His two paternal uncles, Edward and Charles, were both for many years stewards of the Wesleyan Methodist church in Wymeswold.

Jesse was a bright and hardworking child at school. In 1906, at the Infant School , he won his first prize, for Religious Knowledge. He had just turned six, and was in the first class. His award was a copy of *Jesus Loves Me*. A younger child, in the second class, who won *Jesus of Nazareth* was Eric Evans. He was to die just five weeks after Jesse. More prizes followed – in March 1904, in the Lower Division of the Mixed

School , he was a prizewinner 'for proficiency in Holy Scripture at the recent Diocesan Examination'. Other winners in his Division were Eric Evans, and George Marriott, who was to die a month before him. In March 1905, now in the Upper Division, he was awarded a copy of *The Lamplighter*. The next year, probably his last at the school, Jesse was given *Prince of the House of David* for Religious Knowledge on 6th April. Two others receiving prizes that day were Eric Evans and Bramford Sparrow, who died a year before Jesse, in January 1917.

In addition to prizes, Jesse was one of very few children to be singled out for his academic abilities. In 1904, the headmaster observed

> Dec 23rd. Standards iii and ii read well, and show intelligence in
> their problems. Jesse Mills, Standard ii, seems a very thoughtful lad.

Just before he left the school, the log entry reads

> 1906 May 25th. To-day Standard v had an examination with
> marks for each subject: Jesse Mills and John Hickling were first
> and second respectively.

Of course, he would have needed to leave school to go and help his widowed mother on the farm. But he clearly had ability, and we can only speculate what he might have achieved if he had lived. Equally, there are twenty-nine other 'What if?' questions to be asked in this book.

At the outbreak of war, Jesse was twenty, but did not join up. It is very likely that even the authorities would have advised him against joining, as he would have been needed to work on his mother's farm. He was not a member of the Territorials either (he probably didn't have the time), so the question of enlistment would not have arisen. By 1916 however, the situation of the country had changed markedly. The losses, particularly on the Somme and Ypres, had forced a change on the government, and conscription was introduced by the Military Service Act of 27th January 1916. As of Thursday 2nd March 1916, every man over the age of 19 and under 41 was deemed to have enlisted unless he could show that he was entitled to a certificate of exemption.

Jesse enlisted at Leicester on 26th August 1916, and was immediately accepted into the Leicestershire Regiment as Private 3/32214. The prefix '3' indicates the 3rd Battalion of the regiment. In the case of the Leicesters, the 3rd Battalion was a training formation. He would inevitably be sent on somewhere else. Had it been two years earlier, he might well have stayed in the Leicesters, but by 1916 men were being allocated to units as and when there were vacancies. This appeared to be for two reasons: firstly, the acute shortage of men in battalions that had recently been in action, and secondly because the army and government were no longer willing to permit 'Pals' battalions' to go into the line. In 1914, thousands of young men had joined up in large groups – from their churches, factories, scout groups, football clubs and so on. That meant that friends and brothers all served together. It also meant that when they went over the top, they were all slaughtered together. The

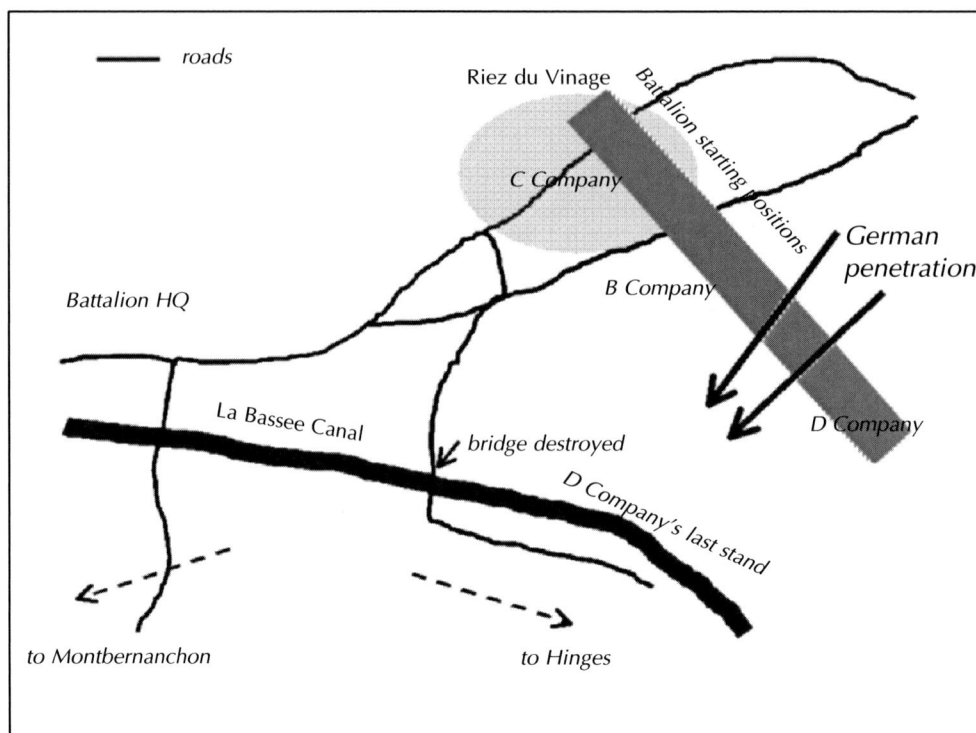

The area to the east of the Bassee Canal where Jesse's battalion was cut off.

effect on civilian morale of having whole neighbourhoods grieving at the same time was potentially destabilising to the war effort, and future recruits were dispersed through the army.

After four months training in England with the 3rd Battalion Leicestershire regiment, Jesse was posted to the Kings Own Royal Lancaster Regiment on 22nd December, and joined the 1st Battalion in Etaples on 29th. Three days later he was officially put on the strength of 'C' Company. During 1917, Jesse served with the battalion through Picardy, Pas de Calais and Flanders. The battalion's engagements are a roll call of bloody battles: Arras, the first and third battles of the Scarpe, the third Battle of Ypres, in particular Polygon Wood, Broodseinde, Poelcapelle and Passchendaele. His only respite was a few days in May when he had some dental fillings – which may have saved him from the battle of the Scarpe, which resulted in John Edward Clarke's death later in May. He would have experienced the same horrors at Polygon Wood as Ernest Hubbard who died in September 1917.

Fortunately, at the end of January 1918, he was given two weeks' leave in England. It was to be the last time he saw his family.

At the beginning of April 1918, the battalion was in the front line at Fampoux, a village just four miles east of Arras. The main German assault, on 21st March, had fallen in the Somme, just a few miles to the south, but Arras had also come under

Jesse's name (he is Private 27960) on the Loos Memorial.

attack. If it fell, it would open up an almost unbridgeable gap in the British lines. On the 2nd, a major German raiding party, about two-hundred strong, attacked their trenches

> bringing with [them] packs, barbed wire and other material as if
> sure of occupying the trench. He was ejected with loss, leaving in
> one trench 7 dead and two wounded after an hour's fighting.

The battalion took casualties though; one officer killed and fifty other ranks wounded. They were relieved (in more senses than one, probably) on the 4th and moved into brigade support near Cense La Vallee, about twenty miles to the north, just beyond the major town of Bethune.

On the 16th the battalion moved up to the front line, crossing the Bassee canal at the hamlet of Mt Bernanchon. At that point the canal bends to run south-east to the next village, Hinges. The battalion took up positions a few hundred yards to the east of the

The Communion set in the Methodist Church at Wymeswold

canal, with 'C' Company to the north, 'B' Company in the middle, and 'D' Company on the southern part of their line. 'A' Company, which had taken some casualties from shellfire when coming up to the line, was held in reserve. The situation was obvious. If the Germans wanted to take Bethune and the coalfields that surrounded it, they would have to cross the canal. The 1st Lancs had been given the job of protecting a few hundred yards of it. They could also see that they would have their backs to the canal, which would be as difficult for them to retreat over as it would be for the Germans to advance across.

In the early hours of the 17th April the Germans opened up with a barrage of heavy shells – 4.2s and 5.9s. After forty minutes it stopped, but the expected infantry attack did not materialise. Then the bombardment started up again, at 5.05 a.m., and lasted until 5.45 a.m. This time the enemy attempted to rush the Lancashire positions but were repulsed by rifle and Lewis gun fire. All went quiet during the evening and night, but the men must have been waiting for the inevitable assault to come. At 2.00 a.m. on the 18th, the enemy guns opened up again, paying special attention to the intersection between 'B' and 'D' companies. The enemy infantry eventually forced their way through a gap between the two companies; 'D' Company was gradually surrounded, and tried to fight their way back across the canal, but the nearest bridge had been destroyed. A few good swimmers made it. All the rest were lost. 'B' Company was now being attacked from the side and rear to its right, and could not make contact with 'C' Company which should have been somewhere to its left.

In fact, 'C' Company held its positions all day, but the confusion was such that 'B' Company never made contact with it. The result, as so often in the Great War, was inconclusive. The Germans now held the southern part of the battalion's ground, up to the canal. They had not crossed it. The northern part of the line, in the hamlet of Riez-du-Vinage, was still more or less in the hands of 'C' Company. Though it was still holding on it had suffered serious losses too, including a whole platoon, about a quarter of its strength. The war diary states:

> 2/Lt Wall and his platoon [had been] holding an advanced
> position were surrounded and either killed or captured.

Was Jesse in that platoon? If he was still with 'C' Company, then it is likely he was, because he was never found. Officially missing on the 18th, he was pronounced dead a year later, in March 1919.

The desperate defence of the Bassee canal had cost the 1st Royal Lancashires dearly. Their casualties, including officers, were 269, around a third of the whole battalion. Of these, 152 were missing. The lucky ones were prisoners. The others, like Jesse Mills, had been engulfed by the shelling, or drowned in the canal, or buried in makeshift graves that were never identified. He is now remembered on the Loos Memorial, which forms the side and back of Dud Corner Cemetery at Loos en Gohelle, a small village just over three miles north-west of Lens.

At home in Wymeswold, though, he is remembered in a much more personal way. In the Methodist church, there is a communion set with the simple inscription

In memory of
Jesse Mills
killed April 18th 1918.
Presented to the Trustees
of the
Wesleyan Methodist Chapel Wymesold
by the family

His memorial will be forever one of peace. The communion - the sacrifice of Christ, the Lamb of God, reconciles an imperfect and sinful world to God, and helps us to reach out, beyond the confines of nation and politics, to a shared humanity. Jesse is now part of that.

Sources

Census records: 1861, 1881, 1891, 1901, 1911

Certificate of Birth, Marriage or Death. General Register Office. Online at: www.freebmd.org.uk [accessed January 2014].

Wymeswold parish registers. Online at: www.hoap.co.uk/who/localhisregister.htm [accessed June 2014].

Wymeswold Church of England School: log books and misc papers 1875–1983 (DE7281). The Record Office for Leicestershire, Leicester and Rutland.

Wymeswold vicar's correspondence (DE 1728/37). The Record Office for Leicestershire, Leicester and Rutland.

Commonwealth War Graves Commission. 'Find War Dead' Online at: www.cwgc.org [accessed 7 February 2014].

Map: WO 297/3212 Sheet 36a SE 1918. The National Archives.

War Diary 1Bn Kings Royal Lancaster Regiment April 1918 (WO 95/1506). The National Archives.

Service Record: 27960 Mills, Jesse. The National Archives.

Baker, Chris / Milverton Associates, 2014. 'The Long Long Trail: How men joined the British Army'. Online at: Online at: www.1914-1918.net/recruitment.htm [accessed 7 June 2014].

Passingham, I., 2008. *The German Offensives of 1918*. Pen and Sword.

Chapter 19

John Morris

John – known as Jack – Morris was one of nine children, who for much of his short life lived in what is now known as Hilder's Cottage on London Lane, Wymeswold. It is named after Jack's sister, Hilda, who continued to live there for most of her life. The family was probably there as early as 1901, because the census identifies them as living in 'London Street', and the next house was in West End. This describes the location of Hilder's Cottage very well, though other houses have been built in between since then.

The house had been acquired by Charles and Caroline, Jack's parents. Caroline was a Hubbard, from another old Wymeswold family. There was another connection to families who lost sons in the Great War. It seems that Jack's father was a brother of George Morris, whose daughter Edith became the mother of Herbert Orridge. There is evidence that the families stayed quite close: in 1890 Charles and Caroline had three of their children baptised – Jesse, Everard and Walter Sam. Multiple or late baptisms were not unusual in those days - as today, there are always some things that we mean to get around to, but don't. The significance, however, is that one of George's children, Mabel, was baptised on the same day. It looks as though the whole Morris clan had decided to 'catch up' together. There was therefore a fairly strong family link between Jack's family and Herbert's family.

Jack's father, Charles, had been raised in the village, the son of John and Elizabeth Morris a grazier and his wife. In 1861, they probably lived in the cottage between the present Hall (then called The Lodge) on East Road and Church Street. The house was simply known as 'Morris' Cottage'. Even as a young man, Charles had decided that mechanisation was the future. At the age of eighteen, he is described as 'feeder to a Steam Thrashing Engine'.

He married late in life, by the standards of the time, when he was 34. Charles and Caroline's first child – also Charles – was born three years after, in 1881, and the children then arrived on a regular basis, with Jack (1882), Jesse (1886), Everard (1887), Walter Samuel (1890), Harold Hubert (1892), Frank (1895), Edward William (1897) and Hilda Alice (1898).

Mechanical farming may have been Charles' passion, but threshing machines were seasonal, and for most of the time up to 1897 he is described as a farmer, or 'small farmer'. The likelihood is that he rented some fields and farmed when he could, taking other work as it became available. Thus, when Harold was born, he was described as a labourer. However, from 1897, he seems to have established himself as a driver/engineer. At Edward's baptism he was a 'engineer on tractor' and at Hilda's he was 'an engine man'. By 1911, at the age of 69, he was an Engine Driver (Thrashing Machine). The interest in engines had been passed on: his son Everard, still at home then, was also an engine driver on threshing machines, and both Edward (Ted) and Walter (Sam) would become drivers too, working for a local corn merchant, Z. Onions and Co. The eldest boy, Charles, would work as an engineer at the Brush factory in Loughborough, but also keep up the family tradition of having a smallholding, right up to the Second World War.

Jack's school career was undistinguished. He did win a prize for geography in 1893, but in the same year the headmaster also wrote

> Oct 27 Examined 3 boys; John Morris, Geo. Bromhead, and Ernest
> Hubbard in arithmetic; the first boy was unable to take down his
> sums correctly, but worked them moderately well; the other two
> have not the least idea of division, and do not seem to know their
> tables correctly.

It was not unusual for village boys to give schooling a low priority; according to season, they could make good money potato-picking, cowslip-gathering, blackberry-picking, or gleaning after the harvest. More to the point, they also knew that they would follow their fathers on to the land when they turned thirteen.

There is no specific indication of Jack's desire to leave as soon as possible, but his brothers Jesse and Frank were certainly keen to go. Jesse had applied for a Labour (exemption) certificate at the age of eleven (children were supposed to stay in education until the age of thirteen, but could apply to leave a year early if there were a job available). In the case of Frank, the headmaster wrote in 1908:

> Sept 23 This morning there are only two children absent, viz,
> Frank Morris and Charlie Peel: both these have turned 13, and
> have asked the C.C. to release them, but their certificates have not
> arrived.

Frank had evidently taken matters into his own hands. He left two weeks later. Hilda, too, was destined for work as soon as possible: in 1991, the school entry read:

> July 21 Hilda Morris, aged 13, has left us this week to assist her
> mother.

By the age of eighteen, in 1901, Jack was a labourer/waggoner on a farm. The 1901 census does not specify which farm, but it is almost certain to have been one of the many that were in or around Wymeswold at the time. It was a trade that he stayed in: the next census sees him, at twenty-eight, still at home in Hilder's Cottage, and still working as a waggoner. It is quite probable that he continued in this occupation until he joined up.

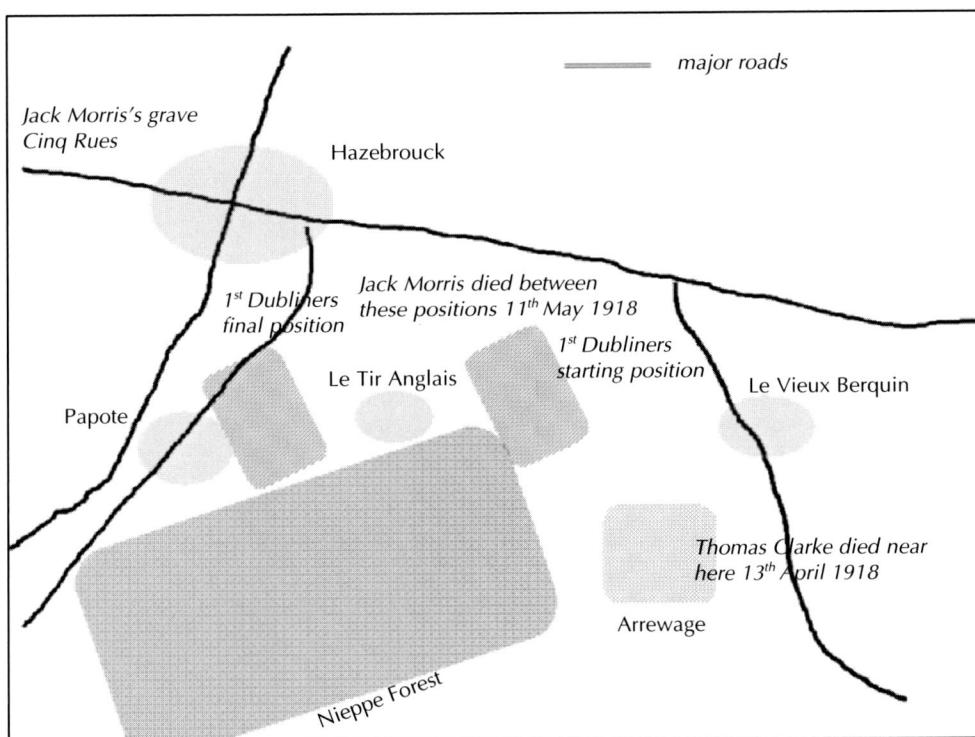

Jack was fatally wounded near Papote, or on the retreat from Vieux Berquin.

Regrettably, his service records have not survived, so it is not possible to know when, or under what circumstances he enlisted. However, his medal card provides some clues. It shows that he originally joined the Notts and Derby Regiment – the Sherwood Foresters. At the beginning of the war, it would have been expected that he would have joined either the Sherwoods or the Leicesters – the two local regiments. However, after two years of attrition, including the massive loss of life on the Somme in 1916, recruits were being sent to fill gaps as they arose. Therefore it was quite normal for a man to join up locally, and be assigned to a different regiment once he had completed his basic training. This happened, for example, to Jesse Mills, who had joined the Leicesters, but been transferred to the Royal Lancashire Rgiment.

Another clue lies in his service numbers. When he joined the Sherwoods, he was assigned a five digit number – 80105. If he had already been a member of the part-time Territorial force, he would have had a four digit number, or, after 1917, a six digit number (the original numbers were simply given a two digit prefix). Therefore, it seems that when Jack enlisted, he did so straight into the New Army. He could not have done so before 1915, or he would have been entitled to the 1914/15 Star. He might have joined in late 1915 like his brother Sam, but it is equally likely that he enlisted after conscription was introduced, in March 1916.

Not all his brothers were required to go and fight. Charles, for example, was already thirty-three on the outbreak of the war, and married with a family. More importantly,

Jack's grave at Cinque Rues cemetery, near Hazebrouck.

his work in the Brush factory kept him out of the war. Ted, too was exempt. Sam, however, volunteered for the Leicestershire Regiment in December 1915, and was transferred to the Machine Gun Corps in August 1916, before being sent to France in the September. In the family tradition, it appears that he was a transport driver rather than a gunner. Wounded in April 1918, he nevertheless returned home on his final leave a month after the war ended.

Whether Jack volunteered in late 1915, or was called up in 1916, the chances are that he fought with the 1st Battalion, Dublin Fusiliers throughout 1917 and into 1918. They fought in all three battles of the Scarpe during the Arras offensive of spring 1917, and then moved up to Flanders to fight in the battle of Langemarck. By 1918 they were back on the Somme, and were terribly mauled in the German Spring Offensive of March and April. So much so that they were amalgamated with the 2nd Battalion and, at the end of April, as part of the reorganisation of the battered British forces, they were assigned to 86th Brigade, 29th Division.

At the beginning of May, two weeks after Jesse Mills had died defending the Bassee Canal, Jack Morris' battalion was dug in just three or four miles to the north. The battle of the Lys, which had already claimed the lives of Thomas Clarke and Jesse Mills, was almost over, though Jack Morris was not to know that. The Lys was part of Operation Georgette, the second German hammer-blow against the British lines. The first, Operation Michael, had taken place on the Somme in March. The second, consisting of George I and George II (south of Ypres) and Georgette (Armentieres)

Jack Morris's memorial tree in London Lane.

was launched in April. Georgette was an attempt to capture the strategic railhead of Hazebrouck and take the French coalfields. This would have isolated the politically important town of Ypres and would have seriously weakened the British position in the north. However, by the end of April, Georgette had ground almost to a halt in the face of stubborn and well-organised resistance.

The Dubliners were acutely aware that the enemy might attack at any time – although, unsurprisingly, the German High Command had not informed them that their interest had moved elsewhere on the Western Front. The first few days of May were spent on the front line, dug in on the eastern edge of the Forest of Nieppe, close to the village of Vieux Berquin. There was little sign of the enemy, apart from sporadic shelling. On the night of 9th May though, they were relieved, and went back a few hundred yards to Le Papote, a tiny hamlet on the northern edge of the Nieppe Forest. Today, it is just an area about halfway between the little villages of Le Grand Hasard and La Motte, south of Hazebrouck. They noted 'many thousand gas shells over back areas during night and early morning'. It was an ominous observation. Again, on the 10th, the reserve area was shelled with gas. Around midnight on the 10th/11th:

> … enemy shelled reserve area especially in the vicinity of LE TIR
> ANGLAIS and PAPOTE with gas shells, estimated over 4,000.
> Direct hits obtained on numerous company billets, causing
> following casualties: 6 killed, 11 wounded and 231 gassed, some
> of whom have since died. All usual precautions were taken, but
> owing to the nature of gas shells employed (yellow cross
> 'Mustard') many men were severely blistered and burnt about the
> body.

Jack died on the 11th May, of wounds. We do not know whether they were the effects of mustard gas, or whether he had indeed been wounded considerably earlier in the fighting around Le Vieux Berquin. The cemetery at Cinq Rues was, according to the Commonwealth War Graves Commission, used by 'field ambulances and fighting units'. There is no mention of Casualty Clearing Stations (CCS) which were larger units, with more facilities. The fact that he was not taken to a CCS suggests that he died very soon after being evacuated from the front line.

He died about three miles from the place where Thomas Clarke fell, and about ten miles from the site of Jesse Mills' death. He was about eight miles north-west of Estaires, where James Collington and George Williams, victims of the fighting three years before, are buried.

Now Jack lies in the Cinque Rues British cemetery at Hazebrouck, a couple of miles north of where he fell. At home, the family planted a sycamore tree just outside Hilder's cottage. It is still there.

Sources

Census records: 1851, 1861, 1871, 1881, 1891, 1901, 1911.

Certificate of Birth, Marriage or Death. General Register Office. Online at: www.freebmd.org.uk [accessed January 2014].

Wymeswold parish registers. Online at: www.hoap.co.uk/who/localhisregister.htm [accessed June 2014].

Wymeswold Church of England School: log books and misc papers 1875–1983 (DE7281). The Record Office for Leicestershire, Leicester and Rutland.

Map: MA_004270 Lys area. Western Front Association.

War Diary 1 Bn Royal Dublin Fusiliers May 1918 (WO/95/2301). The National Archives.

Medal Roll Index Cards (Series WO 373). The National Archives.

Commonwealth War Graves Commission. 'Find War Dead' Online at: www.cwgc.org [accessed 7 February 2014].

'Ireland Casualties of WW1'. Online at: www.ancestry.co.uk [accessed 7 June 2014].

Brown, M., 1999. *1918 Year of Victory*. Pan Books.

Janman, B., 2007. 'The RAMC Chain of Evacuation'. Online at: www.ramc-ww1.com [accessed 19 June 2014].

Pitt, B., 2003. *1918 The Last Act.* Pen and Sword.

Terraine, J., 1978. *To Win a War.* Cassell Military Paperbacks.

Chapter 20

Herbert Isaac Orridge

Herbert Orridge's father William came from Wysall, not Wymeswold. In 1881, the family, then called Horridge, was headed by Isaac, and William was just four. He retained the pronunciation Horridge for at least the next ten years, because the 1891 census shows him as William H. Horridge in Basford, Nottinghham, working as farm servant. By 1901, however, he had married and dropped the 'H', and was working away from home at Cromford in Derbyshire. The mills and foundries of Cromford must have provided a lot of work at that time, because he and five other labourers were all boarding at the same house in the Mill Yard.

William married in Wymeswold, in December 1896, to Edith Eliza Morris, a cousin of Charles Morris, the father of Jack (killed May 1918). Edith came from a Wymeswold family – she was brought up, apparently, at the cottage that is now 3 East Road (next to the Hammer and Pincers), and was then at the bottom of Dexter's Yard. At the time of the 1901 census she and their two children, George aged four, and Herbert Isaac, aged one, were living on Black Path, Hoton. (Black Path still exists, as a small cul-de-sac off the A60 on the north side of Hoton.)

Herbert, always known in the family as Isaac, was born in October 1899, and baptised at St Mary's Wymeswold in August 1900. The family moved to Wymeswold and three more children were born: Florence in 1903, Edith Annie in 1905 (she died at the age of one year and two months in 1906), and Charles Edwin, who was born in 1908. At the time of Edith Annie's death, William was described as an innkeeper at the Shoulder of Mutton on Far Street. By 1911, however, William was once again a labourer, and the family was now living in Far Street. William was described as a 'general labourer – Public Works'. In the days before county councils took responsibility for the maintenance of local roads and paths, each parish provided its own 'roadman'. The family tradition is that William fulfilled this function in Wymeswold, and that Isaac, after leaving school, did so too.

Isaac's school career was not notable, and when he occasionally attracted attention, it was not for the best. True, while at the Mixed School he won a prize for Religious Knowledge in April 1910, and it was scarcely his fault that he contracted mumps in May 1909. However, the fact that his absence is recorded suggests that he had been away for a long time, which might have been due to the severity of the illness or a reluctance to go back to school. The same absence record shows that he was in

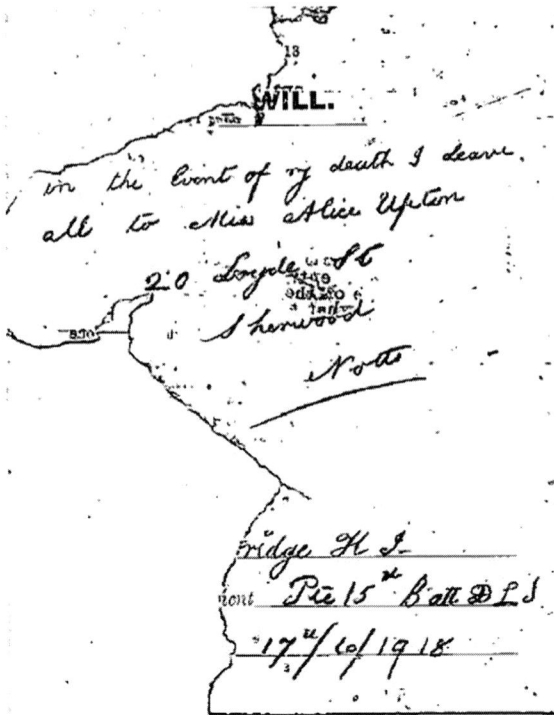

Isaac's will. Courtesy of Chris Kirk.

Standard i. In an age where children moved up through the Standards on ability and achievement, rather than age, it is significant that Isaac was eight, yet still in Standard i. Having been in the school at least a year, and maybe two, he might have been expected to be in Standard ii, or if very bright, in Standard iii. His other school records suggest that he was not engaged with education, and probably wanted to leave and start work as soon as he could. In November 1910, he had made it to Standard iii, but was placed bottom of the merit table. In August 1911, he had advanced to Standard iv, but after the annual exams, he was placed 19th out of 19 for arithmetic and 18th out of 19 for spelling.

Doubtless he was anxious to follow his brother George, who appeared in this entry for 1910:

> May 6 This week we have lost three boys:-George Orridge, aged
> 13 – gone to Farm Work.

Isaac's chance came in 1912:

> Dec 11th Below are the names of children who have left since the
> summer holidays… H Orridge'.

His name was top of the list.

The Memorial at Vis-En-Artois, near Arras.

Most of the First World War army service records were destroyed by enemy bombing in 1940. The surviving records, known as the 'burnt records' (though in fact some of them were more damaged by the water from the fire hoses than the flames from the bombing) represent only a third of the original total. Sadly, Isaac's record seems to have been among the lost documents. His medal card survives, though, and indicates that he initially joined the 5th Battalion Durham Light Infantry (service number 5/126000) before transferring to the 15th Battalion. The 5th Battalion is more usually known as the 1/5th, because it was raised as a Territorial battalion, and would have been in the first wave of support battalions in a 'normal' conflict. (There were five of these battalions prefixed '1', five with the prefix '2', indicating a second wave, and five with the prefix '3'.)

His service number – or rather the fact that it is a Territorial number – is significant. Isaac was only eighteen when he died. Therefore, he would have been too young to enlist before 1918. On the other hand, boys were entitled to volunteer for their local Territorial force when they were seventeen. Technically, as Territorials, they were not obliged to serve overseas until they were eighteen, but they could volunteer. It is possible, therefore, that Isaac volunteered for his local Territorial battalion (for example, the 3/5th Leicesters, based in Loughborough) in 1917. He might then have been transferred, before he had actually been called up, to the 1/5th DLI. This puts his enlistement somewhere between 1917 and early 1918.

Detail from the Memorial at Vis-En-Artois.

His career in the army is also something that we have to guess at. There is no indication of exactly where, when or why he joined the Durhams. The obvious inference is that he joined up at a time when men were being sent directly to battalions that were short of men. This started to happen in a major way after the battles of the Somme between July and November 1916.

Following the possibility that he had joined – if only on paper – a Leicestershire or Nottingham Territorial outfit, it would have been natural for him to have been assigned to another Territorial unit. Then, if he were still under eighteen but volunteered, to be sent to France. He could not have been with the 1/5th very long however, as it was reduced to cadre (skeleton) strength in June 1918, so Isaac's transfer to the 15th battalion probably took place no later than this.

If Isaac had stayed with the 1/5th battalion until it was reduced to a skeleton in June 1918, then he would have survived the ferocious German attack on the Somme in March, and would have fought in the same battle as Tom Clarke and Jesse Mills. If he had joined the 15th battalion earlier, he would also have survived the 'Kaiserschlacht', and gone on to defend the northern approaches to the coalfields, around Mt Keppel, north of Armentieres. Either way, he had been involved in some of the most desperate actions of the war.

Tantalisingly, the only indication of his transfer to 15th Battalion comes from his will. Like most soldiers, he was encouraged to fill in the will form in his army paybook

Isaac Orridge's Death Plaque.

(AB 64). Dated 17th June 1918, he is recorded as Private 46468 15th Battalion Durham Light infantry. At all events, it proves that he was with the 15th when he died. Yet the 15th Battalion diary refers not to fighting, but to days spent in training and preparation at that time. It was in the advanced line, but in reserve, and dug in near the village of Auchonvillers, near Albert on the Somme. This is roughly where the British army had been two years previously, immediately before the bloodbath of 1st July 1916 – the first day of the Somme. Poignantly, for a later generation, they were on Hawthorne ridge, and just a hundred yards or so from the enormous crater created by one of the mines that signalled the beginning of the carnage.

Although the battalion was in reserve, it would still have been within range of artillery fire, which was the major cause of death among British troops. We have to conclude therefore, that either a stray shell, or an accident, or possibly even illness, caused his death.

Frustratingly, the diary does not detail its casualties until the British attack of 21st August. Regrettably, at a distance of a hundred years, it is unlikely that we shall ever know the circumstances of Isaac Orridge's death.

His will suggests that he had a sweetheart – maybe he was even engaged. 'In the event of my death, I leave all to Miss Alice Upton.' There is an address in Sherwood, Nottingham. He must have been very attached to her, as it was normal for single men to leave their possessions to their parents, usually to their mother. Sadly, there is no further indication of Alice's identity. The UK census for 1911 offers at least three possible Alice Uptons in Nottingham, so it is unlikely that we shall ever be able to know what happened to her. She has no memorial to a heart broken by the war.

Curiously, Isaac is one of two men who do not appear on the Roll of Honour in the Methodist church (the other being William Henry Dykes). Yet he was on the 1922

117

list at the inception of the Memorial Hall charity, and was subsequently included on Amos Clarke's Roll of Honour in St Mary's. He is remembered on the graceful art deco memorial at Vis-en-Artois, built in 1930 to commemorate the 9,834 men who fell in the area between the Somme and Loos during the advance to victory between 8th August and the Armistice in 1918, and who have no known grave. His death plaque is currently held in trust by the Wolds Historical Organisation.

Sources

Census records: 1881, 1891, 1901, 1911.

Certificate of Birth, Marriage or Death. General Register Office. Online at: www.freebmd.org.uk [accessed January 2014].

Wymeswold parish registers. Online at: www.hoap.co.uk/who/localhisregister.htm [accessed June 2014].

Wymeswold Church of England School: log books and misc papers 1875–1983 (DE7281). The Record Office for Leicestershire, Leicester and Rutland.

Wymeswold vicar's correspondence (DE 1728/37). The Record Office for Leicestershire, Leicester and Rutland.

Commonwealth War Graves Commission. 'Find War Dead' Online at: www.cwgc.org [accessed 7 February 2014].

Map: M/5/000008 Beaumont Hamel and Serre. The Western Front Association.

War Diary 15Bn Durham Light Infantry August 1918 (WO/95/2161). The National Archives.

War Diary 1/5 Bn Durham Light Infantry Feb–Oct 1918 (WO/95/2840/1). The National Archives.

Medal Roll Index Cards (Series WO 373). The National Archives.

Brown, M., 1999. *1918 Year of Victory*. Pan Books.

Pitt, B., 2003. *1918 The Last Act*. Pen and Sword.

Steadman, M., 2009. *Advance to Victory 1918*. Pen and Sword.

Chapter 21

John Robert Ovendale

John Robert Ovendale's journey to Wymeswold was a long and eventful one, and it appears that chance and opportunity had a lot to do with it. John seems to have called himself Robert, so that is what I shall use. He was born in 1888 in Stanton, near the village of Skegby in north Nottinghamshire. His father, William, was a local man, but his mother Harriet came from the Turgoose family in Nottingham and had been born in Gedling. In the census of 1891, when Robert was just three, the family was living at 23 Bunbury Street, in the St Mary's district of Nottingham. He was the third child; his elder brother William Birkett had been born in 1884, followed by Lucy in 1888). After Robert, in 1890, came Samuel Thomas, later known as Thomas.

The houses in Bunbury Street are the bay-windowed terraced properties that are typical of late Victorian Britain. In the early 1890s, they must have been very smart – just the kind of home that Harriet, a young mother with four children under seven, would aspire to. William was in work as a miner, and their future must have seemed fairly secure. Within a year, however, all that was to change. Harriet died in early spring of the following year, 1892, probably as a result of childbirth – her daughter Lily Mary was born in the same quarter.

Exactly what happened next we do not know, except that it is evident that William was unable to cope. At some point over the next ten years, three of the children – Robert, Thomas and Lily – had been put in the Nottingham Training Institution for Pauper Children. The eldest, William Birkett, (named after his Turgoose grandfather) was living with the Turgoose family. At seventeen, he would have been old enough to contribute to the family's income, rather than be a burden. Lucy is in a 'penitentiary' in Lincoln. It is situated in Belle Vue Road, so is clearly not the workhouse, which was on Burton Road. Neither is it the prison. Since it was run by a matron, and the inmates were all young women between fifteen and twenty-two, I can only assume that it was a home for 'wayward girls'.

Robert and Thomas appear to have stayed fairly close, at least geographically. In the 1911 census, Robert is an ostler 'at a public hotel' in Loughborough. Newly married to Mary Bates (or Betts) from Burton on Trent, he was beginning to make his way in life. The couple were living at 61 Morley Street, Loughborough – right on the edge of town, near the railway station. As she and Robert filled in the census form, she may have been pregnant with their first child. Caroline Mary Elizabeth was born in the autumn of 1911. It is possible that Robert worked at one of the hotels that catered for the railway passengers. Nowadays no trace remains of the terraced houses that must have been there. Ratcliffe Road, which is opposite, gives some idea of what they would have been like – modern and roomy (the Ovendales had five rooms – more than many cottages in Wymeswold).

Meanwhile, Thomas was living and working in Wymeswold as an assistant baker, in the home of his employer, Frank Wood, who kept the baker's shop on Far Street. Their elder brother William was doing well, too: he was a coal merchant, living in Coppice Grove, Mapperley (Nottingham) with his wife and two small children. The story of their father, sadly, was a very different one. He had obviously gone downhill since his wife died nearly twenty years before. Though he described himself as a 'collier, underground' he was in fact living at the Coppice Lunatic Asylum in Nottingham.

Whether Thomas brought Robert to the Wymeswold area, or whether he found work through his contacts at the hotel, he was living in the next door village of Walton on the Wolds when his son, also John Robert, was born in 1914, on the eve of the Great War. Robert was still working with horses, though he had expanded his field, as he was now a Groom/Gardener, evidently in private service.

It is unclear whether Robert himself ever moved in to Wymeswold, though his family was certainly living here sometime after the war. However, he certainly joined in the life of the village, and was an enthusiastic member of the village band. It was an interest he took with him into the army: though his service records have not survived, the photograph here shows that he is wearing a musician's badge on his left sleeve. Without the records, it is difficult to say when he enlisted. However, his medal card gives a clue. His number – 306134 – is one of those issued to the Territorial 8th Battalion, the Notts and Derby regiment (Sherwood Foresters) in 1917. Hitherto, Territorial forces had normally issued four digit numbers. With the vast increase in the numbers of men joining the army a new numbering system was soon needed. The volunteers to Kitchener's New Army in 1916 were mostly given five digit numbers, and it was decided in 1917 to renumber the whole of the Territorial force by adding two digits to their numbers. It is quite possible that Robert was already in the Territorials (many men working on the land were), and that his number had been 6134, to which the 30 was added. It is also possible that he was called straight into the army, and given that number. Either way, it seems fairly clear that he joined in 1917 or later. It was probably while he was in uniform, therefore, that his third child Lilian was born. She arrived in the late autumn of 1917.

Like his brother William (whose records have survived) he would have been taken onto the strength of a local battalion, and then allocated to a more permanent slot. William for example was sent from the 7th Reserve Battalion of the Sherwoods to the 17th Battalion, the Yorkshire Regiment. He was then sent, perhaps because of his experience as a driver, to the Army Service Corps. Robert's last, and fatal posting, was to the 2/6th Battalion Notts and Derby Regiment (Sherwood Foresters). The 2/6th was also a Territorial battalion, but while the Territorial battalions that were prefixed

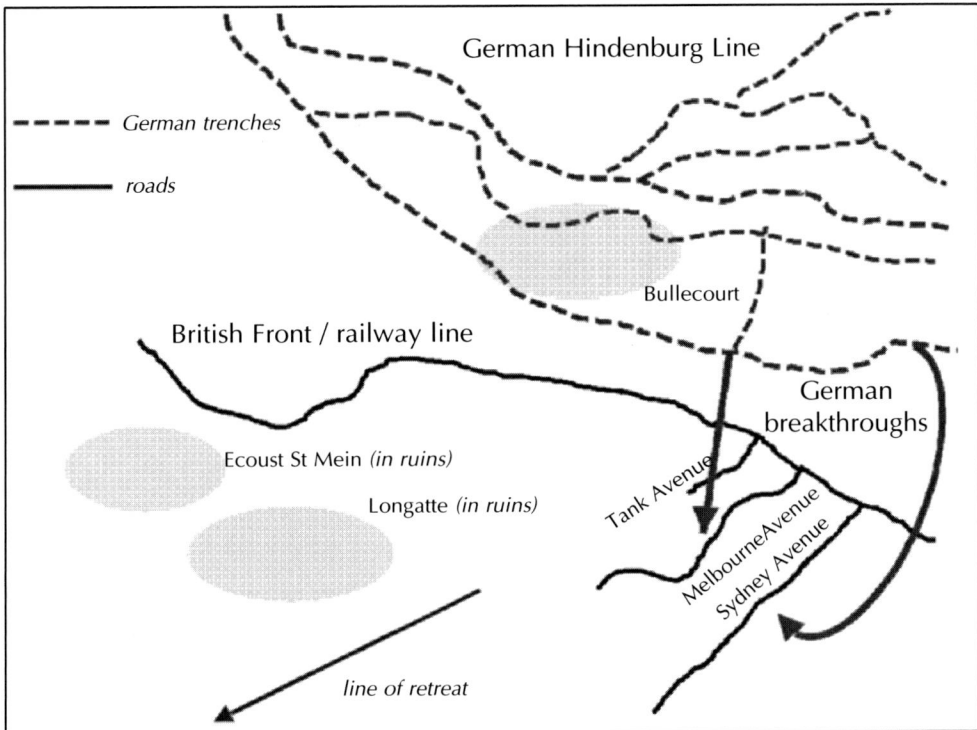

The area near Longatte where John Robert Ovendale was lost.

with a '1' would have been in the first wave of reserve units to be sent out to fight, the battalions with the '2' prefix would have been in the second wave. While the 8th battalions (the 1/8th and the 2/8th) had been on the Western Front since 1915, the 2/6th had been kept at home, seeing action only in putting down the Easter Rebellion in Ireland in 1916. It was sent out to France in February 1917, and reduced to cadre (effectively a skeleton staff) in May 1918, for reasons which will become apparent.

Robert Ovendale, the musician who loved horses and gardens, may seem an unlikely soldier, but in 1917 the country was becoming desperate for men who were fit and able to fight. Unlike Germany, where military service was part of normal life, Britain had no history of conscription until 1916, and so hundreds of thousands of men suddenly found themselves 'deemed to have enlisted'. Such was the case with his brother William, who was called up in September 1916, and initially given the number 309957 – a 7th Battalion number, close in many ways to Robert's. In the case of William, he seems to have spent all his war service in England, while Robert was sent to France.

By February 1918, the 2/6th Sherwoods were at the north edge of the Somme, a mile or so south of Arras. By stages they were ordered to Mory L'Abbaye, a couple of miles north of Bapaume, and then, at the end of the month, they marched the five miles or so to the Railway Reserve trench, just south east of Bullecourt. Their job was

Ecoust St Mein cemetery.

to construct accommodation for the reserve battalion in their sector. They had lost fifty men from their strength during the month but whether this was through transfers or enemy action, we do not know; they were surprisingly near full strength: 53 officers and 883 Other Ranks.

The British High Command knew that, with the fall of Russia, German divisions would be sent to the Western Front and an attack was imminent. What they did not know was the precise strength of the German force, or where and exactly when the blow would fall. Although Haig, the British Commander in Chief, had been complaining that he needed more men, he considered General Gough's Fifth Army on the Somme to be ready to withstand any attack. In theory, there was a man for every yard of ground. It was bound to be sufficient, wasn't it? Barrie Pitt in his book *1918, the Last Act* observed that the German Commander, Ludendorff, had assembled:

> ... sixty-nine divisions just for the attack 'along the sixty-mile
> stretch of front between Arras and La Fere. Facing this
> concentration were thirty-three British divisions, of which ten
> were as much as fifteen miles from the front line, and two were
> twenty-five.

Robert's grave at Ecoust St Mein.

What follows illustrates the success of the new German assault techniques and the weakness of the new British defence system. Having advanced in the winter of 1917, as the Germans withdrew to the Hindenburg Line, the British had left their trench systems behind, and had been preparing an 'open' system of strong points, loosely connected by trenches, some hardly dug at all. The Germans had been training with storm troops – specially picked units who would infiltrate the British lines and 'open up' the defenders for the main attack force. The battalion was now on the Railway Reserve Line, a railway embankment that runs parallel to, and south of the road from Bullecourt to Queant. It left flank was marked by Tank Avenue, and its right by Sydney Avenue (see sketch map). Today, the railway has gone, but its trace can be seen clearly as a bank and hedgerow. On the night of 20th/21st March, the battalion had been warned to expect an attack, and patrols were put out, but no evidence of preparations was found.

In 1919, the battalion's commanding officer Lt. Col. Hodgkin wrote in the war diary:

> … my patrols were very vigilant, but they failed to notice anything
> unusual in No Man's Land. (after my capture, A German told me
> that the attacking troops were lying out in front of the trenches,
> having taken up their positions earlier in the night).

At 5.00 a.m. the enemy opened up with 'a terrific bombardment' which lasted until 9.00 a.m. The effect of being in open 'strong points' or fairly shallow trenches, under a four-hour barrage, can only be guessed at. All communications were knocked out,

Robert's Death Plaque.
Photograph courtesy of Nigel
and Elizabeth Sykes.

and the men must have been to a greater or lesser extent shell shocked and disorientated. The first attack came at 9.00 a.m., but was repulsed. However, by 9.45, some of the battalion's outposts had fallen and the enemy seemed to be coming around their right flank (i.e. towards Sydney Avenue). By 10 a.m., the commanding officer was informed that the enemy was attacking in force from Tank Avenue. He last saw his left flank company 'holding on and fighting with bombs for some time', but there was no way of communicating with them. He continued:

> At 10.30 a.m. a force of the enemy moved round my flank and
> occupied SYDNEY AVENUE. the whole of the RAILWAY
> EMBANKMENT was at this time enfiladed from the south by
> trench mortars and machine guns...

 In other words, the enemy was behind him, and he was cut off. The experience of Major Clarke must have been typical of those who were captured

> As soon as the high ground north and south of us had been
> secured, [by the enemy] the Bosche in front of us advanced up to
> the Railway Embankment and lobbed bombs over. Heavy
> casualties had by this time been sustained by M.G.s [machine
> guns], Rifles and Bombs. When the L.G. [Lewis Gun] jammed I
> picked up a rifle and continued to use this till I felt a tap on the
> shoulder and on looking up, saw a Bosche with a rifle and
> bayonet standing over me.

Other survivors managed to get away or fight their way back to their own lines. By the end of the day the battalion was nine miles further back than where it had started.

It was a pattern that was unfolding all along the British line between St Quentin in the south, almost as far as Arras in the north. Not only were the British defences often

Robert with Mary and the children, Caroline and John Robert junior. Photograph created posthumously. Courtesy of Nigel and Elizabeth Sykes.

weak, the soldiers had no real training in using them, nor had the officers much idea of preparing strong second lines, to hold and trap the attackers. By contrast, the Germans were well trained for what they were doing, and had overwhelming force of numbers on their side. Somewhere in this confusion, the gentle musician was killed. His body was recovered, and now rests in the Honourable Artillery Company Cemetery at Ecoust St Mein, about two miles away.

The family has a poignant story of remembrance. Back in Wymeswold, Mary was anxious that the children should remember their father. She took a photograph of herself, Caroline and John Robert junior that had been taken a few years before, then had it merged with one that Robert had given her. It made a fine, though sad, family portrait. It is interesting that her younger daughter is not included. We can only speculate about the reason for this. The photo was evidently taken before Lilian was born: Mary had been left to bring up the children herself, and it would have been expensive to have a new photograph taken. Twelve years later, her duty done, she remarried – to Edward Brown. In 1933, Caroline married John Walton in St Mary's church. But war had not finished with the family. John, a Lewis gunner, was to die in the defence of Tobruk in December 1941.

Today, John Robert Ovendale is remembered with respect and gratitude by his family. I am sure it is a memorial that he would have wished for – to be held in the hearts of your loved ones.

Sources

Census records: 1881, 1891, 1901, 1991.

Certificate of Birth, Marriage or Death. General Register Office. Online at: www.freebmd.org.uk [accessed January 2014].

Wymeswold parish registers. Online at: www.hoap.co.uk/who/localhisregister.htm [accessed June 2014].

Wymeswold Church of England School: log books and misc papers 1875–1983 (DE7281). The Record Office for Leicestershire, Leicester and Rutland.

Wymeswold vicar's correspondence (DE 1728/37). The Record Office for Leicestershire, Leicester and Rutland.

Commonwealth War Graves Commission. 'Find War Dead' Online at: www.cwgc.org [accessed 7 February 2014].

Extracted Probate Records, 1269–1975. Online at www.ancestry.com

Map: M/78/000268 Sheet 57c NE Bullecourt/Ecoust/Noreuil. Imperial War Museum.

War Diary 2/6 Bn Sherwood Foresters Feb/Mar 1918 (WO/95/3025). The National Archives.

Service Record: 309957 Ovendale, William Birkitt. The National Archives.

Medal Roll Index Cards (Series WO 373). The National Archives.

Brown, M., 1999. *1918 Year of Victory*. Pan Books.

Baker, Chris / Milverton Associates, 2014. 'The Long Long Trail: Renumbering of the Territorial Force in 1917'. Online at: www.1914-1918.net/renumbering.htm [accessed 6 June 2014].

Passingham, I., 2008. *The German Offensives of 1918*. Pen and Sword.

Chapter 22

Frederick Henry Robinson

Frederick Robinson was not a Wymeswold man. His connection with the village seems tenuous; he seems more linked to Loughborough, where he is remembered on its Roll of Honour. On the other hand, John Joseph Lamb, Albert Bacon, Colin Bramall, Bramford Sparrow, James Collington, and David Spicer are also remembered on the Loughborough Roll of Honour. They may all have been associated with Loughborough, but some relative in Wymeswold obviously wanted them remembered here too. The inclusion of a name on a Roll of Honour is not just a recognition of the sacrifice of an individual: it is also a demonstration of the grief of those left behind. Their suffering has no memorial, except the name of their loved one on the Roll.

Our journey in the steps of Frederick Henry Robinson starts at Alverstoke, Hampshire – or possibly Staffordshire, because it was there that both his parents were born. Thomas Robinson (born around 1837) came from Stafford, while Emma Birtles was born (about 1849) in Rickerscote, just on its southern edge. There is no evidence that they knew each other while they were there, but both of them, by 1881, had moved to Alverstoke, near Gosport in Hampshire. They were living and working as servants in the home of a Yorkshire-born ship owner, William Garthorne. A year later they had married, quite late in life by the standards of the age – she must have been thirty-three, and he forty-five.

Frederick was born less than six months later, in June 1882 and his brother William (actually John William) followed in June 1883. By 1885, Emma was dead. The cause of death was 'Kidney disorder / Pregnancy / Eclampsia' The family seems to have broken up at this point. The boys' father Thomas continued to work as an attendant in mental institutions until his death, probably in 1906. He had remarried in 1900.

Meanwhile, in 1891, Frederick and William were boarders with James and Emma Heath, in the Castle Church parish of Stafford. Significantly, Castle Church includes the township of Rickerscote, their mother's home village. Perhaps James and Emma were relatives?

Another interesting detail from the 1891 census is that Emma was a grocer. Though Frederick was only eight, helping Emma in the shop may have had a bearing on his future choice of career.

From then on, Frederick's work seems to have taken him around the East Midlands. In 1901, he was still a boarder, but now, aged eighteen, he was a grocer's assistant, living in the home of Sarah Surridge, a grocer and shopkeeper of Rushden, Northamptonshire. At that time, Sarah was forty-three and unmarried, but there is a record of a Sarah Ann Surridge marrying in nearby Wellingborough in 1904, so it may be that ended her grocery business and Frederick's employment.

At all events, 1911 found him working in Hillstown, Bolsover. He was also married – to Beatrice Alice Ludlam, of Loughborough. Whether they met in the course of business, or whether he was working for a time in Loughborough, is not clear. They had married in 1907, in Norton Woodseats. She was living in the village, while he was resident in nearby Scarcliffe. It is unclear what had brought her to the area, though Frederick was working as a grocer's manager. Now they had a new, two-bedroomed house on Selwyn Street in Hillstown, providing accommodation in six rooms. It seemed that their life together was just taking off. Towards the end of 1911 their daughter Brenda Irene was born in the Mansfield district.

There is little information about Frederick's life after 1911, but since his career had been consistently in the grocery trade, there is every reason to believe that he continued as a grocery manager. Perhaps the frequent moves in the past had been because, as a junior manager, he had been sent as a relief manager to fill temporary gaps elsewhere. This also suggests that he may have worked for one of the larger chains, such as the Co-op or International Stores.

Frederick's death certificate records his home address as Stockwell Street, Wymeswold. Given his career to date, and the presence of a Co-operative store on Brook Street (between No.106, the old Fox pub, and No.94), it is highly likely that Frederick was its manager before joining the army.

The Great War was to throw Frederick's domestic arrangements into turmoil, and then destroy them. His service records have not survived, so it is impossible to say for certain when or where he joined the army. However, there are some clues. According to the Loughborough Roll of Honour (which may have had information from a local newspaper or the family), his first service number was TR/5/5061. This is a Territorial Reserve number, with the prefix 5. This prefix was given to Reserve battalions that had their Records offices either in Rugeley or Hornsea. Amongst other battalions, the 10th (Reserve) battalion, the Leicestershire Regiment was associated with Rugeley, and the 29th, 30th and 31st (Reserve) battalions, the Northumberland Fusiliers, were associated with Hornsea.

Frederick's medal card lists two different numbers, and attaches both to the Northumberland Fusiliers – TE/5/1822, and 36950. The first is a Territorial Reserve number, obviously related to one of the Northumberland Reserve battalions. The second is the number that he would have been given when actually called for duty, and assigned to a fighting battalion. There is the possibility, therefore, that he was called up while living at Loughborough or Wymeswold, and assigned to the Leicestershire Territorial Regiment, but then was sent as a relief manager in the north-east, and was transferred to the Northumberland Territorial Regiment. He was still there when called for duty, and was allocated to the Northumberland Fusiliers.

There are other scenarios, of course, but this is a reasonable hypothesis in default of other evidence. The next question is when he might have joined up. Frederick was already thirty-two when the war started. It is possible that he volunteered at the beginning of the war, and joined the Leicestershire Territorial Reserve. Equally, it is possible that he was called up in 1916 and allocated to the Territorial Reserve, firstly the Leicesters, and then the Northumberlands, until such time as he was needed. Britain was perhaps at its most desperate in late 1917. The battles of 1914-15 had destroyed much of the 'old' army, and the Somme in 1916, followed by the battles of Arras and Passchendaele (Third Ypres) had made huge inroads into the nearly one million volunteers of Kitchener's New Army.

Many of the 1917 conscripts, however, were not sent directly overseas. There was a major political battle going on between the Prime Minister, Lloyd George, and the Commander in Chief on the Western Front, Sir Douglas Haig. Lloyd George was acutely aware of the huge losses that Haig's offensives had caused, and with his politician's instinct was concerned that the public might lose the appetite for the war if those losses continued. Haig, on the other hand, was planning another offensive in the north of his sector, and argued for more recruits immediately.

In the 'war of memoirs' that followed after 1918, both men would justify their positions – Lloyd George by asserting (probably correctly) that another Haig offensive would have resulted in a massive loss of life, and that Haig thought he had enough men anyway to withstand a German attack in 1918. Haig equally asserted that because he had been starved of men, his ability to withstand the German offensive of 1918 was seriously weakened. Most historians find both accounts pretty self-serving. Ordinary soldiers like Frederick, however, would have been unaware of the in-fighting going on at the top.

The only helpful information about Frederick's army career comes from his will, signed on 21st June 1917. From that, we know that he was already Private 36950 in the 1st Battalion, Northumberland Fusiliers. Whether he had already served for many months, or whether he had recently arrived in France to replace the losses of 1916, he was still with the 1st Battalion in the period April-May 1918.

It is not possible to say exactly where and when he was wounded, but understanding the Army Medical Services will help. His Commonwealth War Graves record shows that he died of wounds and was buried in Loughborough. That means he must have been repatriated before he died – British soldiers who died overseas were buried near where they fell (as with Robert Jalland), or near to the Casualty Clearing Station they had been treated at (as with Bramford Sparrow) or the hospital they had been taken to (as with Walter Smith).

The Army Medical Services had a very efficient system of treatment and evacuation, which did an excellent job, considering the lack of modern technologies like antibiotics and blood plasma. Frederick would have been taken to a Regimental Aid

Frederick's grave in Loughborough Cemetery.

Post, which would be immediately behind the front line. He would have been 'patched up' as best they could, then sent either to an Advanced Dressing Station – still within the range of artillery fire – or directly to a Casualty Clearing Station, typically five or six miles behind the lines. The Casualty Clearing Stations were hospitals in their own right, but also had the administrative function of assessing the severity of cases, and the ability of soldiers to withstand travel, bearing in mind that roads were in a poor state, and that ambulances had limited suspension. Sometimes, for very frail cases, the CCS would direct that a wounded man be taken slowly to the nearest hospital barge, and then by canal to a hospital. Others would be taken by ambulance to the nearest railhead.

All these medical units were in what the army called the 'evacuation zone'. Behind that lay the 'distribution zone' – in other words, the main hospitals. Some of these were as large as major civilian hospitals. All were equipped in the same way as peacetime hospitals, and had specialist wards or were even specialist hospitals. They could treat men and discharge them back to their units, or send them back to the UK. According to essays submitted to the *British Medical Journal* during the First World War

> At all base hospitals the time for which serious cases may be retained is not limited, but the general rule is to transfer to Great Britain any cases which are deemed fit for transport and are not likely to be fit for active service again in less than three weeks.

In other words, Frederick's condition was known to be serious, but he could be moved. Yet he died of his wounds some time after reaching England.

130

The circumstances of Frederick's injuries may never be fully established. However, in April 1918, his battalion was in northern France, on the north side of Bethune. The first week of the month was spent in accommodating no less than 430 new recruits – half the battalion – and entirely reorganising to mix the experienced troops with the raw newcomers. The replacements were needed because the battalion – indeed the whole 3rd Division – had been badly mauled the previous month in the opening attack of the German Spring Offensive of 1918, which had pushed the British up to forty miles back and had threatened the major communications centre of Amiens.

Now the division was sent up to the coalfields of Bethune, with its flat landscapes and canals. They did not realise they were now in the path of the next German hammer blow – Operation 'Georgette'. The attack – known to the British as the Battle of the Lys – began on 9th April, and was to last for the rest of the month. It, and its subsidiary battles, were to take the life of Jesse Mills and to account for the death of Jack Morris, as well as Frederick Robinson. The 1st Battalion Northumberlands, still training and preparing themselves, were suddenly told to 'embus' for the front. It was 9th April. The following day they found themselves east of the town of Essars, near Bethune. Their sector was a stretch of the Lawe canal, about a mile and a half east of Essars, just the other side of the tiny hamlet of Hamel.

'X' Company relieved the 1/5th King's Own (Royal Lancaster Regiment) in shell holes just east of the canal, about two hundred yards east of Hamel. 'Y' company was in their support, in a 'switch' communication trench nearby, and 'W' and 'Z' Companies were just behind the canal. Their section of the 'front' was no more than five hundred yards. On the 13th 'Y' Company suffered severe casualties – we are not told how – and had to be reinforced with men from 'W'. On the 14th they were relieved in the front line but stayed close by, in support trenches. On the 18th:

> Enemy put down a considerable Barrage on Brigade front which
> also enveloped the Division on either flanks. Bombardment was
> very intense on the 1st Div. on our Right. A considerable amount
> of Phosgene was employed in this Barrage. No Infantry Attack
> materialized on the Bde front.

That night the battalion was relieved by the 1st Battalion, Royal Scots, and was able to move further back, into Brigade Reserve. Some four miles to the north, on the same day, Jesse Mills died in the defence of the Bassee canal.

We cannot be sure that Frederick was one of the 350 casualties suffered by the battalion that month. However, the necessary time taken to evacuate him from the front, assess him and then send him back to England suggests that he was wounded in the actions between the 9th and 18th April. Unlike many fatalities of the Western Front, Frederick had a death certificate. He died at the Temporary Military Hospital, Stoke on Trent, on 16th May 1918. The causes were '(1) Gunshot wound of leg, (2) Septicaemia, Exhaustion'. Thirty years later, penicillin would probably have saved his life. As it was, blood poisoning had set in, and his body's immune system could not cope. Were his family able to visit him before he died? Unfortunately there is no record of how long he had been at the hospital, so we cannot be sure.

Whether Frederick ever returned to Wymeswold after joining the army is a moot point: his will, signed on June 21st 1917, states that his wife's address is 'c/o Mrs N Harrison, 3 Chestnut Street, Loughborough.' It may be, therefore, that his wife returned to Loughborough as soon as he joined up. She may have chosen to stay with a relative, or it may be that the Stockwell house was owned by the Co-op, and needed for another manager. It seems that she never remarried. In 1962 a Beatrice Alice Robinson died in Long Whatton, leaving her estate to Brenda Irene Brodrick. Frederick and Beatrice's little girl had grown up to marry and have sons of her own. Hopefully, she had some good memories of her father before he set off on his last journey, to France and death.

Another intriguing postscript is an entry in the Parish Registers for October 1910, when Emily Cave Ludlam (Beatrice's sister) married Charles Baker in St Mary's church. It could be that, even though Beatrice moved away, Emily wanted him remembered here. If that is so, then we should be happy that the village honoured that request.

Sources

Census records: 1841, 1851, 1871, 1881, 1891, 1901, 1911

Certificate of Birth, Marriage or Death. General Register Office. Online at: www.freebmd.org.uk [accessed January 2014].

UK Extracted Probate Records 1269–1975. Online at: www.ancestry.co.uk

Wymeswold parish registers. Online at: www.hoap.co.uk/who/localhisregister.htm [accessed June 2014].

Wymeswold Church of England School: log books and misc papers 1875–1983 (DE7281). The Record Office for Leicestershire, Leicester and Rutland.

Wymeswold vicar's correspondence (DE 1728/37). The Record Office for Leicestershire, Leicester and Rutland.

UK Extracted Probate Records 1269–1975. Online at: www.ancestry.co.uk

Commonwealth War Graves Commission. 'Find War Dead' Online at: www.cwgc.org [accessed 7 February 2014].

Map: WO 297/3212 Sheet 36a SE 1918. The National Archives.

War Diary 1 Bn Northumberland Fusiliers April 1918 (WO/95/1430). The National Archives.

Baker, Chris / Milverton Associates, 2014. 'The Long Long Trail: Renumbering of the Territorial Force in 1917'. Online at: www.1914-1918.net/renumbering.htm [accessed 6 June 2014].

Laughead, G., 2013. 'The Medical Front WW1'. Online at: www.vlib.us/medical/ [accessed June 2014].

Pitt, B., 2003. *1918 The Last Act.* Pen and Sword.

Chapter 23

Alfred Savage

Like Jesse Mills, Alfred Savage came from a devout Methodist family. Like Jesse, his family's roots in Wymeswold went deep. The Parish Registers record a Deborah Savage marrying in St Mary's as long ago as 1690. Alfred's father and grandfather, both called William, were born in Costock, just two villages away. Though Alfred's grandfather had been a framework knitter, his father worked as an agricultural labourer. By the 1880s, the framework knitting industry was in sharp decline, and though it hung on in some places (there were still a few framework knitters in Wymeswold in 1911), it was simply a matter of time before the market was entirely dominated by factory-made knitwear.

In 1883, Alfred's father married Amelia Frearson, from another well-known village family in Wymeswold, and set up home in the village. By 1891, both aged twenty-seven, they already had four children: George E. aged six, William A. aged four, Henrietta aged two, and Mary aged just nine months. They were living on Brook Street, next door to John and Rebecca Collington and their little boy James, the same age as their own William. Two doors down on their other side were John and Elizabeth Spicer, whose little boy David was a couple of years older than George. James would be the first from Wymeswold to die, in January 1915, and David would follow in November 1916.

At the time of the 1891 census, Amelia must have been pregnant with Bertie, who was born in December of that year. Herbert followed in 1895, and Alfred on 3rd February 1897. At that point, with seven children under thirteen, Amelia died in March 1897 of 'Acute General Tuberculosis and Exhaustion'. She was buried later that month: Alfred was little more than a month old. However William did not fall apart, or abandon his children. He had support from his family – four years later, in the census of 1901, his younger sister Eliza was living with William and the children, and acting as housekeeper. William had not only stayed in work, but had progressed – he had become a gardener and gamekeeper.

Doubtless William's strong faith helped him in his efforts to keep the family together. The children seem to have done well at school. George, Henrietta and William all received prizes at the Infant School at various times. At the Mixed School , George had a shaky start: 'Nov 29 Ernest Charles, Fred Brookes and George Savage spelt worst in Std iii', wrote the headmaster in his log in 1893. On the other hand, three years later he observed:

Jan 20 Another case of Scarlet Fever has been reported to me this
morning, which will cause two boys to be absent for six or seven
weeks. One of them, George Savage, is one of the best
'Freehanders' in the school.

Hetty (Henrietta) had been recorded as reading 'very nicely' in 1895. Herbert started
his Mixed School career well, winning a prize on 25th March 1904 for 'for
proficiency in Holy Scripture'. Other winners in the Lower Division that day were
George Marriott and Jesse Mills. Bertie did not distinguish himself as much as
Herbert and Alfred, but in December 1904 there was ' an hour's 'arithc race' in
Standards iv and v. – 'Bills' being the subject'. Among the most successful was Bert
Savage, with '60 lines worked correctly' which made him fifth in the boys' section
and six overall.

For the next few years, though, it was Herbert and Alfred who dominated the prizes.
In 1905 Herbert had 428 attendances out of 428, and was given a copy of *Robinson
Crusoe* while Alfred had 423 out of 428, and won *The Ugly Duckling*. In November,
Herbert and his classmate George Marriott were both put up a standard. The next
year, Alfred scored the maximum of 422 out of 422 attendances, while Herbert was
close behind with 419. Both boys were awarded atlases. Among the other winners
were Eric Evans and John Spicer. Siblings of other 'old boys' who were to die
included Beatrice Sparrow and Eustace Hubbard. It was a small, close knit
community.

Alfred won again in March 1907 with 423 attendances out of 429, and got a copy of
The Dog Crusoe. Eric Evans had missed no schooling at all. Herbert's name does not
appear on the list, but he would have been twelve or thirteen and almost certainly
had left the school. This was also the last time that Alfred won any prizes. He would
have just turned ten, so there were another two or three years to go. Why were there
no more prizes? Perhaps Alfred's enthusiasm for attending had diminished, or
perhaps he was just less lucky with his health. It is true, though, that there was less
money for attendance prizes (the County Council had informed the school in 1906
that there would be just four pence per head available in future), so the number of
winners was slightly less.

The intriguing aspect of the Savages' prize history is that, apart from the one prize in
1904, none of them won awards for Scripture. With their strong Methodist
background – and we know that Alfred, at least, was a regular attendee at Sunday
School) –they might have won more. On the other hand, there were strong
divergences between the Church of England and Methodists at the time. Children
went on the Methodist outing or the Church outing, according to their family's
disposition, and the task of religious instruction at school was firmly in the hands of
the Rev. Green, the Church of England Vicar.

Meanwhile, Alfred's father, following the loss of his wife Amelia, was rebuilding his
life. We know that he had help from his sister, and that his career had prospered. In
1907 he remarried, to Mary Lamb, a widow. Mary had been born into the Hardy
family and had been brought up in Wymeswold, and had married John Lamb in

1892. The marriage only lasted three years, however, as John died in 1895, of phthisis and diarrhoea. Since phthisis is another term for tuberculosis, she and William would have had some sad experiences in common. She had found work as a cook at The Hermitage on Far Street, which is where she was living in 1901. (The Hermitage, which faces Clay Street, is often confused with the Manor House, which is two doors further east on Far Street.) By the time of her marriage to William she was living in Cross Hill, while he was in Clay Street. They were neighbours.

The Savage children were all growing up fast. By 1901 only Mary Alice, Bertie, Herbert and Alfred were still at home, and by 1911 they had all left. They must have stayed fairly close, through the church, if nowhere else. William was made a Leader in the Methodist church in 1909, and Alfred attended Sunday School until he joined up in 1914. The entry for 30th December 1914 in the Methodist Leaders' Book notes:

> Annual teachers' tea and meeting. Alf Savage having 'joined Lord
> Kitchener's Army' his name to remain on the register as a scholar.

The entry in the Leaders' Book is significant because it shows that Alfred joined up in 1914, at the outbreak of war. Further, if he 'joined Lord Kitchener's Army' he was one of the million volunteers who responded to Kitchener's call for men. He was not already a member of the militia, though. His service number is not a four digit one, like those of the 'old' army and militia, but one of the new five-digit numbers. However, it was to one of the 'old' battalions – the 1st – that he was sent.

His medal card does not help with his 'entry into theatre', though there is a medal card which probably refers to his brother Herbert , and to an embarkation in July 1915 (almost certainly the departure of the 110th Brigade). Whether he had joined the 1st Battalion directly, or had served with one of the new 'Service' battalions (6th, 7th, 8th and 9th – the 110th Brigade) he would have seen a lot of action before his last and fateful battle in September 1916. The 1st Battalion had initially been sent to the Aisne in late 1914, to help stem the German advance, and had distinguished itself the following year in the battle for Hooge, in northern France. The 110th Brigade, sent to France in July 1915, spent the autumn and winter in the trenches south of Arras. The sector was relatively quiet at the time, but the Brigade was sent to the Somme in the summer of 1916, and faced its first and bloody test in mid-July at the battle of Bazentin Ridge.

Since it is fairly unlikely that troops from the battle-weary 110th Brigade, which had been sent back to Arras, would be diverted to units about to deliver the next onslaught on the Somme, we presume that Alfred was already with the 1st Battalion by this time. It was the same battalion as Bill Collington served in, though Bill (a former professional soldier) had been posted back to England shortly before the battle of Flers-Courcelette in which Alfred died.

The arbitrary nature of death in the Great War meant that Alfred may have been mortally wounded at any time in September. Accidents, snipers, stray shells and the regular 'evening hate' artillery bombardments took their toll of all units positioned in or near the front line. However, there was one action which involved the 1st

Leicesters that may have resulted in Alfred's death. In the early part of the month the battalion had been informed of an attack planned for their sector, just south of the little village of Ginchy, on the Somme. Ginchy itself was now just a heap of rubble. It had been taken on 9th September by the Irish Division and then held by the Welsh Guards against a ferocious counter-attack. However, the British position in Ginchy was something of a salient – a bulge sticking out into German-held territory. The Leicesters were immediately south of the village, initially in support of the Sherwood Foresters and Suffolks, who advanced on 14th September and gained around two hundred yards of ground. They did not gain their objective, but the action was seen as a success.

Later that day more orders were received by the Leicesters. The enemy, it seemed, was still holding some defences on the Ginchy-Morval road, and another attack was planned, this time to take the villages of Flers, Gueudecourt, Morval and LesBoeufs. The Leicesters, just on the southern edge of Ginchy, were to advance with the 9th Norfolks on their right and the Guards on their left and move towards Morval. They would be supported by a creeping barrage that would be a hundred yards ahead of them and move forward fifty yards every minute, once the attack started. Tanks would be used, and the infantry were warned to let them have enough room to pass through.

The idea of tanks in battle is now so commonplace that they appear an inevitable part of war, just as much as rifles and machine guns. In 1916 however, they were untried. Most of the men, and all the enemy, would never have seen a tank before. The battle of Flers, set for the next day, would be their first test. The very sight of these metal monsters, able to cross trenches and crush machine gun nests, was terrifying to defenders. The Germans were to call them barbaric and weapons of mass destruction. They would soon learn to build their own, of course.

The Leicesters and Norfolks had a combined front of 250 yards. They would each advance with one company – in other words, a total of some 400 men – in each wave. The wave was subdivided into platoons, so the leading company of each battalion would advance with one platoon (around fifty men), followed thirty yards behind by the next, and so on. Each line would advance at the walk.

There has been a lot of heated discussion about the British practice of insisting that men should walk into battle. The French advanced in short rushes, with companies leap-frogging each other and providing cover. They had been markedly more successful than the British on the first day of the Somme, when we had lost over 60,000 casualties. By 1918, the British, too, were doing this. Essentially, the British commanders were concerned about maintaining discipline and cohesion in the chaos of battle. Kitchener may have raised a New Army, but Haig's preference was for Old Army discipline.

Each man on 15th September would carry a bandolier of rifle ammunition, two Mills bombs (grenades) and a tool of some kind – spade, pick, etc. The Sherwoods and Suffolks, who were to provide support, would carry two bandoliers of ammunition

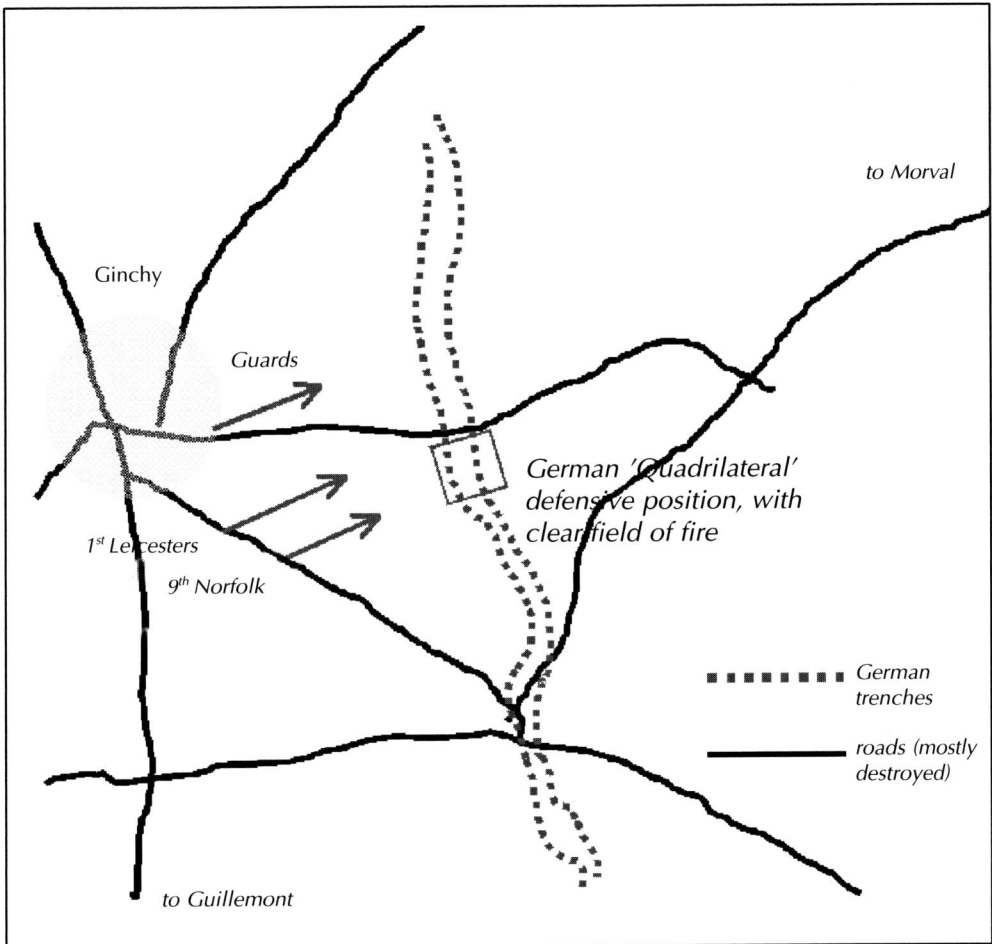

Alfred was mortally wounded, probably between the sunken road and the 'quadrilateral' marked on the map.

each. In the early hours of the morning, the Leicesters passed through the Sherwoods and climbed out of the sunken road , just on the south edge of Ginchy (it is still there, though maybe not quite as deep as in 1916), and moved a couple of hundred yards forward, straddling the Ginchy-Morval road. (*See sketch map.*) At 5.50 a.m.:

> ... a Tank was noticed, going up to enemy lines and enfilading to
> both sides with his MC guns. Enemy fired very heavily with their
> MCs but had little effect.

The tank was probably one of a squadron that headed north, directly to Flers. Nevertheless, it would have been a real morale-booster to the young men of the 1st Leicesters. Zero hour was at 6.20 a.m. and the advance began. They had not gone more than a couple of hundred yards when, despite the covering barrage, they were met with ferocious machine gun fire from a position in front and slightly to the right of them.

> The Bn had not gained the objective being held up by very heavy fire and the very strong and undamaged wire met in front of the trench leading from NW corner of Quadrilateral (a strong point hitherto unknown).

Yet this was precisely the point where, according to the orders received the previous day, the enemy were holding out. There was some good news – the enemy had countered with an artillery barrage, but it was falling on or behind the sunken road which even the support battalions of Sherwoods and Suffolks had now left.

On the other hand, another problem had arisen in the morning mist and the smoke of battle. The troops had been ordered to stay in touch with the units to their right and left, respectively. This they did, so well in fact that a gap opened up in the middle which had to be filled with support companies coming into the front waves. The upshot was that the whole battalion was now pinned down in fairly open country. The leading companies were entrenched – they seem to have got into German trenches that ran north-south above the Ginchy-Morval road, and were directly north of the Quadrilateral position. The companies behind were in shell holes, keeping their heads down against the intensive sniper fire. Under cover of darkness, though, they managed to move forward and establish a line in front of the German wire, which was largely undamaged, despite the British barrage before the attack.

All day on the 16th the battalion huddled in its positions, unable to advance or retreat safely. Around 6.00 pm a German counter-attack was launched on their left, between them and the Guards, but it was driven off with the Guards' machine guns and their own Lewis gun, supported by artillery. At the same time, they were told they would be relieved later that evening. By 1.00 a.m. nothing had happened, so the C.O. and the C.O. of the Sherwoods went to look. They found the relief battalion some two hundred yards to the rear. No one had told them anything about relieving anyone! The C.O. took the decision to evacuate the position – very sensibly, as the Leicesters could make no headway, and were now simply targets. With not a trace of irony the war diary records:

> The Bn now formed up and marched 300yds – 400yds from the trenches an orderly arrived with a message from BOC [Brigade Commanding Officer] stating that we were to evacuate our present position without relief. (It has since been found that this was necessary to enable the Heavy artillery to bombard the Quadrilateral and the West Yorks were in a position to hold the ground evacuated by us, should the enemy attempt to advance).

In other words, they might have stayed there until dawn, without support, only to be told to evacuate, but under extremely dangerous conditions. The battalion, what was left of it, marched to a rest area a mile or so to the rear. 23 officers and 610 men had gone over the top on the 15th. Forty-eight hours later, 14 officers and 410 Other Ranks had become casualties. Two-thirds of the battalion were now out of action. It is highly likely that Alfred Savage was among them.

*Alfred's grave at Grove Town
Cemetery, Meaulte.*

Badly wounded, he would have been taken to the nearest available Casualty
Clearing Station, which was almost certainly at Grove Town. It may well have been
the same station – 34 CCS – that Bramford Sparrow would be taken to four months
later. Grove Town, then an encampment on the bare downs above Meaulte, near
Albert, is a beautiful area in summer, with extensive views towards Albert. In winter,
it is windswept and bleak. It is here, just a few yards from Bramford Sparrow, that
Alfred now rests. It is one of two cemeteries – Estaires, much bigger, is the other –
that hold two Wymeswold men.

In Wymeswold, Alfred is remembered on the three Rolls of Honour – in St Mary's,
the Methodist church, and the Memorial Hall. His brother Herbert returned from the
war, and married Florence Brown in 1919. He at least, was able to lead the normal,
quiet life in England that Alfred must have dreamed of.

Sources

Census records: 1871, 1891, 1901, 1911.

Certificate of Birth, Marriage or Death. General Register Office. Online at:
www.freebmd.org.uk [accessed January 2014].

Wymeswold parish registers. Online at: www.hoap.co.uk/who/localhisregister.htm
[accessed June 2014].

Wymeswold Church of England School: log books and misc papers 1875–1983 (DE7281). The Record Office for Leicestershire, Leicester and Rutland.

Wymeswold vicar's correspondence (DE 1728/37). The Record Office for Leicestershire, Leicester and Rutland.

Commonwealth War Graves Commission. 'Find War Dead' Online at: www.cwgc.org [accessed 7 February 2014].

Map: M/5/005085 Ginchy 57c SW 030916. The Western Front Association.

War Diary 1 Bn Leicestershire Regiment September 1916 (WO/95/1621). The National Archives.

Medal Roll Index Cards (Series WO 373). The National Archives.

www.royalleicestershireregiment.org.uk [accessed 1 April 2014].

Baker, Chris / Milverton Associates, 2014. 'The Long Long Trail: How men joined the British Army'. Online at: www.1914-1918.net/recruitment.htm [accessed 7 June 2014].

Baker, Chris / Milverton Associates, 2014. The Long Long Trail: The Leicestershire Regiment. Online at: www.1914-1918.net/leicesters.htm [accessed 19 July 2014].

Hancock, E., 2001. *Bazentin Ridge*. Pen and Sword.

Kelly, D., 2001. *39 Months with the 'Tigers' 1915–1918*. reprint edn. Naval and Military Press.

Pidgeon, T., 2002. *Flers and Gueudecourt*. Pen and Sword.

Richardson, M., no date.*The Tigers: 6th, 7th, 8th, 9th (Service) Battalions of the Leicestershire Regiment.*

Chapter 24

Walter Foster Simpson

Joseph Simpson, who came to Wymeswold in the mid 1880s, must have had a hard life as a child. One of at least four children of an unmarried mother in East Leake, he had to start work early. At the age of eleven, he was working as a 'Plow Driver'. Anyone who has ploughed with horses, or spoken to someone who has, will know it takes both strength and skill. For an eleven year old, it is quite an achievement.

Joseph stayed at home until at least the age of twenty-one, by which time he was a general labourer. We do not know when he came to Wymeswold, but by 1885 he had married Miriam Spencer, and was certainly resident here six years later. Miriam had been brought up on East Road (then called East Street), the daughter of John Spencer and Harriet Mills. Possibly the Spencers or the Mills helped the young couple find work and accommodation, for by 1891 Joseph and Miriam were living at Dungehill Farm, a mile outside the village, on the Melton road. By this time they already had three children – Alfred (aged four), Mary (aged three) and William (aged one). Seven more were to follow.

The family were at Dungehill farm until at least the end of 1894. That was their address when they had three of their children baptised in the church: William, John Joseph (born 1891) and Frank (born April 1893). It was also their address when little Frank died at the age of 1½. By 1901 the family had moved into the village, and were living in Far Street. Bernard Harry (born 1895), Walter Foster (born 1897), Hilda (born about 1900), Lillian (born 1902) and Harriet (born 1905) all followed on.

Although baptised Walter Foster, the boy was known as Foster from a young age. At the Mixed School , he made his first appearance in the records at the age of eleven, when he won *Our Den* as a prize for Religious Knowledge. Other winners included Eustace Hubbard (*Martin Rattler*) and Foster's sister Hilda (*The Mysterious House'*. It is worth noting that although his sister was four years younger, they were both in the Lower Division – if Foster had been a quick learner, he would have been in the Upper Division with Eustace. These prizes were provided with money sent by the Ferriman family from New Zealand – even today, schools still rely on donations from ex-pupils and well-wishers.

Just over a month later, in July, the headmaster noted the 'weak ones' in Standard iii – Foster was one of them. Additionally, we can speculate that at the age of eleven, he might have been at least a standard higher as progression at this time was not

Foster's father at home in Wymeswold. Photograph courtesy of Lily Simpson.

through classes, but by 'standards' based on performance. In May of the following year, he was one of eight children specifically noted as being absent from school – in his case with a throat complaint. Herbert Orridge, another absentee, had mumps. Absence was a continual trial to the headmaster Mr Bailey. In the time before the welfare state and the National Health Service, children were frequently ill, sometimes because of poor housing, or insufficient food, or lack of treatment. Equally, children were often sent to do seasonal work – primrose picking, blackberry gathering, and corn gleaning after harvest. They were needed to supplement the family income – and most children preferred this work to sitting in school!

In April 1910, just as he was about to reach his thirteenth birthday and leave school, he won his last prize – a copy of *Cared For*. Hilda won *Mattie's Home*. Horace Giles and Herbert Orridge, who both died in 1918, also took away prizes.

Foster would have started immediately in farm work, though in the 1991 census, which followed just nine months or so after his thirteenth birthday, he is not shown as having any occupation. The family is still on Far Street, presumably in the same four-roomed house in which they had brought up at least six of their ten children after leaving Dungehill Farm.

Foster's brother Bernard in the uniform of the Royal Artillery. Photograph courtesy of Simpson family.

On the outbreak of war in August 1914, did Foster enlist right away, like Alfred Savage, or did he wait to be called up? His service records appear to have been destroyed, and his medal card gives no clues. However, according to the 'Soldiers Died in the Great War' database, he enlisted in Newcastle upon Tyne. Frederick Henry Robinson, another soldier on the Wymeswold Roll of Honour, enlisted into the same battalion at Creswell, a village on the coast of Northumberland, about twenty miles north of Newcastle. Why did they both join the Northumberland Fusiliers?

One explanation might be that it was pure chance. The slaughter of July 1st 1916 (the opening day of the battle of the Somme) changed the army's recruitment procedures. It still desperately needed replacements, but it also realised that allowing men to join up together, from villages, factories and church brigades, could be very damaging at home. When they 'went over the top' together, it could result in the loss of a whole community. Consequently, when men were called up they were frequently dispersed to whichever regiments needed men at that time.

The other explanation was that they were both working in the north-east, and decided to join up together. We have no information about Foster's occupation, but we know that Frederick Robinson had moved around a lot on account of his work as a grocery manager, and it is just possible that they were both working in the Newcastle area when they were called up. Both explanations tend to make better sense if they were called up in 1916 or 1917, rather than volunteering before then.

143

One would have thought that, as volunteers, they would have been more likely (as other village men did) to ask to be sent to a local regiment – the Leicesters or the Sherwood Foresters.

Whether he had joined, as seems likely, in late 1916–1917, or had volunteered earlier, Foster would have seen some serious fighting. By the end of 1917, the 1st Battalion Northumberland Fusiliers had been in the battle of Arras, the battle of Polygon Wood (in which Ernest Hubbard and his Australian comrades fought), and the battle of Cambrai – the first major battle with tanks on each side. All these had been British attacks, and all, though they had pushed the Germans back a little, had petered out in the mud and the rain. By March 1918, the battalion knew that there would be a massive German reply. Russia had collapsed into revolution in late 1917, and the Germans and Austrians were able to bring dozens of battle-hardened divisions back to the Western Front.

The British did not know that the Germans had also stripped their factories, schools and colleges of men, in preparation for the *Kaiserschlact* – the Kaiser's Battle. Meanwhile, British politicians and military commanders had been locked in a battle over reinforcements (see the chapter on Frederick Robinson). The only incontrovertible result was that the British were not ready when the Germans struck.

What Haig and his friends declined to discuss was that they knew a German offensive was coming, and they considered they were ready for it. In fact, they may have had enough men – they calculated that there was a man for every yard of British front line. However, many were too far from the front, and others too bunched up in the front line. The defences, hurriedly put together following the German retreat in late 1917, were known to be 'porous' – nothing like the complex trench systems they had left behind. The theory was that if the Germans broke through the series of strong points that marked the front, the troops would retreat to a second line, which would be more secure. The enemy, already tired, would be held up and destroyed by this 'elastic' defence in depth.

It was a good theory, and worked quite well for the Germans as they retreated in late 1918, but the fact was that the British had no experience in these tactics. So far, all their major battles had relied on large formations acting like a single body. This defence would require local initiative and excellent communications between units in order to work. Neither of these happy intentions came to fruition, at least not to any great extent.

At the beginning of March 1918, the 1st Northumberland Fusiliers were in the line just to the west of the village of Fontaine-Les-Croisilles. Their task was to protect the south-eastern approaches to Arras – a key city which had to be defended at all costs. It never did fall into the hands of the Germans. It was obvious that a major attack was coming. Their raids into front line enemy trenches found them empty: the Germans did not want to risk men being taken prisoner and forced to disclose valuable information. They were given demonstrations of low-flying aircraft, and trained in counter-attack.

On the 12th there was a general 'stand-to' at dawn because an attack was thought imminent. Work on defences was pushed forward at speed. Every succeeding day saw another dawn 'stand-to'. Then the hammer-blow fell:

> '21st March. Bn 'stand to' as usual. Enemy put down intense
> barrage of very considerable depth and captured front line of
> entire Bn front: by 9 a.m. the enemy has been thrown out of the
> front line. Enemy attack again shortly before noon and again
> occupy front line. Battle continues.

The next day, the Germans gradually closed in on the Northumberlands' right flank, squeezing their position and threatening to come round behind them. During the night, they were ordered to pull back and re-group. On the 23rd, they took stock. They had suffered 122 casualties. The day was spent resting in the Northumberland lines, while the King's and Royal Fusiliers now came up from reserve, but they were still being shelled.

Four days later they went forward again, relieving the 4th Royal Fusiliers. The next day, the 28th, saw another massive onslaught:

> Enemy attack about 4.30 a.m. and capture front line. Enemy in
> very large numbers and supported immense concentration of
> artillery, low-flying aeroplanes, continue attack but were held up
> by reserve line until 3.30 p.m. in spite of the fact that both flanks
> were in the air [exposed]. Order to evacuate position. This was
> done.

That was the end of the 1st Northumberlands' defence of Arras. The remaining men were marched to the rear to regroup and rest, while a Canadian brigade took over the front. It is likely that Foster's fellow soldier Frederick Robinson – we do not know if they were close comrades, but it is very likely they knew each other in the battalion – was still alive. He was to die of wounds in May. The irony is that the battalion was now being sent to a 'quieter' part of the front. Within a month, with their advance on the Somme grinding to a halt, the Germans would deliver the next brutal assault – codenamed 'Georgette'. The 1st Northumberlands would be right in its path.

The future, however dangerous, was denied to Foster Simpson. He died on the 29th March. The war diary entry is brief and factual:

> Enemy does not renew his attacks: but shells all lines very heavily.
> Div'n relieved by Canadian. Bn marched to Monchiet arriving
> about 6 a.m. 30-3-18.

Monchiet is about thirteen miles to the rear. After fighting all week, with little sleep because of the guns, they must have been exhausted. It is possible that Foster was killed by a stray shell, one of the many that were carpeting the British positions that day. Or perhaps he had died of wounds following the previous day's fighting. He is recorded as missing, so it is unlikely he got as far as the nearest Dressing Station, let

The Simpson family grave in Wymeswold Cemetery.

alone a Casualty Clearing Station, which would have been a couple of miles away. Had he been 'checked in' he would have been registered as 'died of wounds'.

At home in England, there would be tears for him and for the other four men of Wymeswold who died between March 21st and 31st 1918. In total, eleven men of the village were to die in the great German Spring Offensive of March-June.

But the war had not finished with Joseph and Miriam and their family, at home in Clay Street. Foster's brother Bernard survived, but at a cost. He had gone to France in August 1915, with the Royal Artillery. His service records have been destroyed, but his pension records survive. He returned from the war with a damaged leg and 'tremors, hands and legs'. The diagnosis was neurasthesia, or shell shock, as they called it then. Now we call it post-traumatic stress.

Foster is remembered on the wall of the Arras memorial to the 35,000 British and Imperial servicemen who have no known grave. In Wymeswold, his family inscribed his name on the family tomb. Under the name of his baby brother Frank, there is the inscription:

WALTER FOSTER SIMPSON
BORN 23RD MAY 1897
REPORTED MISSING IN THE GREAT WAR
MAR 1918

He is also remembered every Remembrance day, when his and the other twenty-nine names are read. Bernard's suffering, and Joseph and Miriam's, have no memorial. As with all our men, it is a family, not just an individual tragedy.

Sources

Census records: 1861, 1871, 1881, 1891, 1901, 1911

Wymeswold parish registers. Online at: www.hoap.co.uk/who/localhisregister.htm [accessed June 2014].

Wymeswold Church of England School: log books and misc papers 1875–1983 (DE7281). The Record Office for Leicestershire, Leicester and Rutland.

Wymeswold vicar's correspondence (DE 1728/37). The Record Office for Leicestershire, Leicester and Rutland.

Map: M/5/000123 Croisilles_Fontaine Les Croisilles 51bSWSE 57cNWNE 7-3-18, Western Front Association.

War Diary 1 Bn Northumberland Fusiliers March 1918 (WO/95/1430). The National Archives.

War Office Pensions Record: 62749 Bernard Simpson. The National Archives.

Medal Roll Index Cards (Series WO 373). The National Archives.

Corrigan, G., 2003. *Mud, Blood and Poppycock.* Cassell.

Passingham, I., 2008. *The German Offensives of 1918.* Pen and Sword.

Pitt, B., 2003. *1918 The Last Act.* Pen and Sword.

Terraine, J., 1978. *To Win a War.* Cassell Military Paperbacks.

Chapter 25

William Bennett Sissins

William Bennett Sissins came to Wymeswold when he was a young man. Until then, the family had lived in Willoughby since the 1870s, when William's father David had left his native Lincolnshire, presumably to look for work as a driver of the new agricultural engines.

The Sissins had been established in the Saxilby area of Lincolnshire since the late seventeenth century, when they used the more common spelling of Sissons. By the 1750s however, the name Sissins started to be used, and by the 1850s it had become accepted. It does appear to be a unique variant of Sissons, and all the present Sissins seem to be descended from this line.

William's middle name shows how family history (and connection with a 'respectable' family) was enshrined in the names of the children. He had been named after his great-grandmother's family, the Bennetts of Middle Rasen. It appears that when she married Robert Sissins she was disowned by her family, but retained the connection herself by naming her ninth child Bennett. She had named her first son Robinson – her mother's maiden name. After he died as an infant, she named the next son Robinson, too.

The names Robinson and Bennett recur in the Sissins family. Robert and Patience's surviving Robinson lived and died in Lincolnshire. Though he and his wife Mary Ann (or Marianne) had four sons, two died before reaching manhood. One of these was a William Bennett Sissins (not of course to be confused with our William). The two surviving sons, both agricultural engine drivers, moved to Nottinghamshire to look for work. Robert returned to Lincolnshire, but David settled in Willoughby. Both men were to lose sons in the Great War. Robert's son Francis Joseph Sissins, of the 2nd Battalion Lincolnshire regiment, was to die on the first day of the Somme, 1st July 1916. David's son, William Bennett Sissins, survived only another three days before he, too, was killed.

David had married in 1877, and he and his wife Ellen had fourteen children until her death in 1900, giving birth to Robert Leslie (later known, at least in Wymeswold school, as Leslie). The family continued living in Willoughby, and the younger children were looked after (as was so often the case) by the eldest sister, Florence. However, Florence married in 1903, and emigrated to America in 1905. Whether she felt able to go because her father had a new lady friend, or whether David

William's father, David, and stepmother Emma. Photograph courtesy of Linda Dale.

needed a partner to replace Florence, is just speculation. In 1905 David remarried, to Emma Watkin, who took over as the children's stepmother. It is likely that the family left Willoughby sometime between 1906 and 1909, as the children figure in a picture of Willoughby schoolchildren (sadly undated) around that time.

The only mentions of the Sissins family in the Wymeswold Mixed School log books are dated 1912. Leslie would be around twelve years of age at that time, and being the youngest, all the others would have left school. Leslie himself is recorded as being one of those who left between September and December of that year. Another 'graduate' was Herbert Orridge, who died, just eighteen, in the last few months of the war.

William himself then, was not strictly a Wymeswold man. While his older siblings either stayed in Willoughby or emigrated to north America, his surviving younger brothers and sisters variously emigrated, stayed in Nottinghamshire, or in the case of Horace (born 1895) and Leslie, settled in Wymeswold. In the Second World War Horace would go on to become a member of the Royal Observer Corps in Wymeswold, reporting on aeroplane movements to the RAF.

As to William, he seems to have stayed in Nottinghamshire. He may be the William Britt referred to in the 1901 census for Willoughby, and is almost certainly the William Sissons in Basford in 1911. At that time he was working as a brewer's labourer, and lodging with the family of a workmate. It was in Nottingham, according to the Leicestershire Regiment, that he enlisted. The obvious choice would have been the Notts and Derbyshire (Sherwood Foresters), but for some reason – possibly the fact that he lived in Leicestershire, possibly the losses recently suffered by 2nd Battalion Leicesters in April 1915 – he did not serve with the Sherwoods.

There is evidence to suggest that he volunteered. Firstly, the date of his entry into a theatre of war, on 27th May 1915, is almost a year before conscription was introduced. His actual date of enlistment would have been the winter of 1914/15 at the latest, since he would have spent some months in training. Secondly, his service number, taken from his medal card, is a five-digit one. Analysing Great War service numbers is a notoriously inexact science, but the soldiers of Kitchener's New Army on the whole had five-digit numbers. This contrasts with the old four-digit numbers of the militia (Territorials) and the six-digit numbers created in 1917 when the

Territorial Reserve had their four-digit numbers increased by a two-digit prefix. The conclusion then, is that like Alfred Savage and another million men, he had volunteered between August 1914 and January 1915.

William was not the only Sissins man to join up. In addition, his cousin Francis, his brother Horace and cousin Robert also served – Horace in the Leicesters, and Robert with the Leicesters, and then the Machine Gun Corps. The Leicestershire Regiment records that William joined the 2nd Battalion in the field on 30th May 1915. At this time the battalion was recovering from the battering it had taken in the attack on Neuve Chapelle in March. He did not have long to wait before the next 'show'. The battalion, as part of the Garwhal Brigade, Meerut Division, was thrown into the battle of Loos in September. The regimental website refers to him being wounded on 25th September, the opening day of the battle. It is to be hoped that he was spared the rest of the fighting, as the Meerut Division was called into the main action after 29th September. The battle of Loos ended with 61,000 British casualties, of whom nearly 8,000 died. Like Neuve Chapelle, it had not achieved the breakthrough that was hoped for, and massive trench systems on both sides were now even more firmly consolidated.

William must have had some home leave after Loos, because in the final quarter of 1915 he was back in Nottingham, where he married Eva Oxby. The Oxbys were a Lincolnshire family, although two of her siblings had been born in Yorkshire: presumably the family had moved on account of the father's work at the time. Perhaps it was the Lincolnshire connection that brought the two families together.

By the time William had recovered from the Loos experience – he had no time to get used to married life – he would have found himself shipped out to Mesopotamia (Iraq). The 2nd Leicesters were now part of the Tigris Corps, a force assembled to relieve the town of Kut-Al-Amara, in central Iraq. Despite getting within artillery range of Kut, it was unable to break through and Kut fell at the end of April 1916. By July 1916 the battalion was dug in near the river Tigris at Falahiye, about seventeen miles to the north-east of Kut. Conditions were harsh. Temperatures rose to 1150F (46C), dropping to 750F (24C) at night. The Turks on the north bank of the river were very active – there was constant sniper fire, with occasional shelling.

Turkish prisoners were passing through the battalion on their way to prison camps, or one occasion, back to the Turkish trenches (accommodating prisoners must have been very problematical anyway, and this batch had women and children with them). The battalion lived in constant danger, and constant discomfort. It is likely, given the number of times that the war diary mentions snipers, that this is how William died. His body now lies in Amara War Cemetery, Iraq. Sadly, it is still too dangerous to visit.

Eva had scarcely become a wife before she was a widow, and saw her dreams of the future evaporate in the sand of the Middle East. It is likely that she married again, though, as there is a record of an Eva Sissins marrying a George Roebuck at Glandford Brigg, Lincolnshire in 1922. It is to be hoped that she found happiness a second time. Back in Wymeswold, there were many who would have mourned

William. His brothers Leslie and Horace were now fixtures in the village. His cousin Robert also came – for how many years is not known – but he and his wife Annie had their daughter Mary Amanda baptised in St Mary's in 1918. William's place on the Roll of Honour was secure.

Note: I have borrowed quite shamelessly (and with her permission) from the excellent Sissins family history compiled by Linda Dale of Nottingham. I owe her a great debt of thanks.

Sources

Census records: 1891, 1901, 1911.

Wymeswold parish registers. Online at: www.hoap.co.uk/who/localhisregister.htm [accessed June 2014].

Wymeswold Church of England School: log books and misc papers 1875–1983 (DE7281). The Record Office for Leicestershire, Leicester and Rutland.

Wymeswold vicar's correspondence (DE 1728/37). The Record Office for Leicestershire, Leicester and Rutland.

War Diary 2Bn Leicestershire Regiment July 1916 (WO/95/5140). The National Archives.

Medal Roll Index Cards (Series WO 373). The National Archives.

Carver, 2003. *Turkish Front 1914–18*. 2nd edn. Pan Books.

Macdonald, L., 1997. *1915 The Death of Innocence*. Penguin Books.

Nixon, P., 2013. *Army Service Numbers 1881-1914*. Online at: armyservicenumbers.blogspot.co.uk [accessed 18 June 2014].

Chapter 26

Walter Charles Smith

Walter's father, John Smith, was one of the last framework knitters in Wymeswold. The son of a framework knitter, also John Smith, Walter's father had grown up in the trade, which his family ran from their home in Clay Street (known as The Clays in 1851). The family joined in the business, as was the practice in those days. In 1851, John senior was a stocking maker, while his son Edward, aged fourteen, was helping as a cotton winder. In 1861, still in Clay Street, John senior continued to ply his trade as a stocking maker, but had been joined by his son John and a lodger, George Cater. Someone has added the notes 'cotton stockings' to each of them. Presumably it needed to be recorded that they worked in cotton, rather than making the coarser wool worsted stockings made for the poorer classes of society.

John junior soon married, probably in 1865, to Sarah Holwell, of Old Dalby and set up in business in Kirk's Buildings, on Brook Street. Like his father, he was a framework knitter, but by 1891 was back in Clay Street – perhaps moving back to his father's old house. He and Sarah now had six of their seven children, including Walter, still living with them, as well as their grandson, little Arthur aged six months. Perhaps framework knitting was already in substantial decline, because John's eldest son James had not gone into the business – he was an agricultural labourer. His wife Sarah and their daughter Kate earned a living as seamstresses, but all the other children were still at school.

Ten years on, and John was still working at his trade, but James had left home; he had evidently married and had a daughter Marion, born in 1894. Kate had also left and Arthur was now described as John and Sarah's son – the implication being that he was the illegitimate son of one of the children (probably of Kate or Polly), and brought up by his grandparents as their own. The only child missing in 1891 – Polly – had now returned, and was working as a hosiery seamstress – possibly working with her father. John William, now called William, was working in Loughborough, for the Brush Company, which provided work for a number of Wymeswold men. In 1905 he married, and by 1911 was living and working as a crane driver in Loughborough.

In 1911, still in Clay Street, John and Sarah had only their daughter Julia at home. She was now aged twenty-three and a domestic servant. None of the family had gone into the knitting craft, though John was still working at his frame. One wonders

To the left of the telegraph pole is one of several framework knitters' buildings in Wymeswold which still retain the characteristic large first-floor windows. This one is probably Kirk's Buildings. Photographed by Bob Trubshaw in 1993.

how much longer that lasted, in an increasingly industrialised age. Certainly he continued right into and possibly through the First World War. Ellen Smith, in her autobiography, talks about

> an old man named Smith, who lived next door to our builder's yard, had a huge machine that made a dreadful noise, but it was fascinating to watch the stockings appearing down the length of his contraption.

The builder's yard, by the way, was in Clay Street.

Walter had gone to school in Wymeswold, and would have been a direct contemporary of Jack Morris, Bill Collington, David Spicer and Ernest Hubbard. In 1893 he won prizes for Religious Knowledge (as did Ernest Hubbard) and Geography. Nothing more is recorded about him at school. His siblings also escaped mention, with the exception of Julia his younger sister, who 'read very nicely' at her Reading Examination in 1895.

In common with all the village boys he would have left school at thirteen and found work locally, probably on the farms. At the age of seventeen, in 1901, he was living and working as a farm servant for John Baldock in the hamlet of Thorpe in the Glebe, less than a mile from his parents' home. In January 1909, though, he married Annie

153

Adcock at the Primitive Methodist Chapel in Syston. She had been born in Syston, and in 1901 was working as a housemaid in the home of a doctor at Frisby on the Wreake. Just as men were turning to industry, so Annie, at the time of her marriage, had become a stockroom hand at a boot factory. It seems that Walter had moved jobs and then met Annie, as he was living at Rothley when they married. Two years later, their child, also called Walter Charles, was born. Walter was still working as a farm labourer, but now the couple had a house of their own in Martin's Row, Mountsorrel.

Walter would have been thirty at the outbreak of the Great War. Did he volunteer, like Ernest, or was he called up? His service record has been lost, and his medal card gives no clue, except that his service number was not the four-digits of the 'Old Army' or militia, nor the six digits of the post-1917 Territorial Reserve. The medal card does offer another clue: he was enlisted first in the Army Veterinary Corps as Private 23840.

It was common for men to be recruited and allocated to a regiment for basic training, only to be sent to another regiment when required for active service. If the time delay was short, then the period of time on the strength of the first regiment is unlikely to show on the medal card, mostly, in all probability, because the man had not changed his service number. In Walter's case, he ceased at some time to be in the Army Veterinary Corps, and became Lance Corporal 33975 of the Yorkshire Regiment.

It is probable, therefore, that he spent some time working in one of the less glamorous, but essential parts of the army. The Army Veterinary Corps (it only acquired the designation 'Royal' in November 1918) started the Great War as a tiny unit comprising 122 officers and 797 Other Ranks. In 1914 its task was mainly to look after the 53,000 horses of the British Expeditionary Force. However, its remit and staff grew enormously as the war went on. Though combustion engines were being developed and improved very fast, horses were still in most cases more reliable and more adaptable to the mud and shell holes of the Western Front. Although it is likely that Walter would have been looking after horses, the Army Veterinary Corps cared for carrier pigeons, dogs (usually carrying messages), canaries (detecting bad air underground) and cats (keeping down the mice and rats in billets and trenches). In all, 16 million animals were used during the Great War, of which two million were horses. Sadly, over 200,000 horses had to be destroyed in the war, but the Army Veterinary Corps had an impressive record of restoring eighty percent of their charges to active duty.

When and why Walter transferred to the Yorkshires is another mystery. The most obvious theory (but it is only a theory) is that he was needed to fill the losses incurred during the massive British and Allied attacks of 1917 – the battles of Arras, 3rd Ypres and Cambrai.

Historians will argue about the squabbling between the Prime Minister, Lloyd George and the general commanding the Western Front, Sir Douglas Haig over the question of reinforcements (see the chapter on Frederick Robinson). When the blow fell,

Haig's problem was as much where his forces were, as how numerous they were. Walter, of course, was to know nothing of all this. We know that he had been transferred to the Yorkshire regiment by early 1918, because he made his will. It is a normal part of military life, of course, especially when a man is sent into a war zone, but it is significant that he gave his wife's address as ' …Leicester, England'.

This suggests that he was already with his regiment in France or that he was about to be sent overseas. He was also in a different battalion – the 13th. The story of that battalion towards the end of the war is an interesting one. In May 1918 it was reduced to 'cadre' strength – a skeleton staff. As part of 121st Brigade, it had been severely mauled just south of Armentieres during the German offensive, when the Portuguese Division to its right panicked and fled, leaving the British exposed and vastly outnumbered. It may have been that Walter transferred to the 9th Battalion in May. Had he stayed, Walter would have found that the 13th Battalion was rebuilt and sent off to Murmansk in September, to fight in north Russia!

Whenever Walter transferred, he would have endured some fierce, not to say desperate battles. If he had been with the 13th until May, he would have gone through the 'meat grinder' of the German Offensive. If he had transferred any time before September 1918, he would have been fighting in the mountains of northern Italy – the very battleground that claimed the life of Wilfred Brookes in August. As it was, that same month saw the turning of the tide on the Western Front. The British and Imperial troops had regrouped and large numbers of reinforcements were coming in from Britain. The Americans were now battle-ready and in position, mostly in the French sector of the front. The Allied onslaught began on 8th August; 'a black day' for the German army, as its commander Ludendorff noted. From then on, the story was one of steady advances. As soon as the old battlegrounds of the Somme had been crossed, the fighting was largely in open country, and movement was rapid, compared to the previous four years.

In October 1918 the 9th Battalion, Yorkshire Regiment had reached Moislains, on the eastern part of the Somme, about thirteen miles from Albert. The British had already advanced as far as in the previous four years, and had regained almost all the ground lost in the spring. On the 3rd, they marched another twelve miles from Moislains, leaving Epehy, the scene of ferocious fighting in 1917 and 1918, off to their left, and arrived at lines just south of Le Catelet, a couple of miles to the west of the village of Beaurevoir.

After a couple of days' rest, they attacked the village. Though they were held up by machine gun fire, the Warwickshires got into the village and took it, leaving the Yorkshires to dig in on its eastern edge and secure the area. After another couple of days in support, they pushed on about eight miles to the north-east and on the 9th seized a position just south of Honnechy, allowing the cavalry to pass through them, presumably to harass the retreating enemy. At last, the generals' idea of letting the cavalry sweep forward was coming true, if in a limited way.

Since 1914, the British High Command, (mostly ex-cavalrymen) had hoped that the German line would be broken and that the cavalry would surge through to break up

Walter's grave at St Sever Cemetery Extension, Rouen. Photograph copyright The War Graves Photographic Project; reproduced with permission.

and destroy the fleeing enemy. Now that the war was being fought in open conditions, the cavalry could be used much more, but the German army was no pushover. Outnumbered, low on food and material, the men nevertheless stood and fought, even if they then retreated by night.

There was one more attack before the 9th Battalion was relieved. The battalion war diary reads:

> 10-10-18. Moved off to attack about 0200 hours and reached
> position S.W. of ST BENIN where we dug in. Captured ST BENIN
> about 1500 hours, and dug in just outside the village.

For the next week or so, the battalion was resting about six miles or so to the west, behind the lines. In this period, on the 18th, Walter died.

The Commonwealth War Graves Commission records that Walter died of wounds. The location of his burial confirms this. He was not buried near the scene of any recent actions, but at St Sever Cemetery Extension, in Rouen. The city was home to more British hospitals (sixteen, at one time or another) than any other part of the Western Front, and the St Sever cemetery was the main burial ground for the men who died while being treated.

That he, and tens of thousands of others, got this far, was testament to the untiring work of the 113,000 men and women of the Royal Army Medical Corps. Though many died, the RAMC estimates that it saved some 1,600,000 men. It is not possible to say when Walter was wounded. The RAMC had a very effective and comprehensive system of evacuation, from the front line Regimental Aid Posts, through Casualty Clearing Stations, to specialist hospitals in France or Britain, as described in the chapter on Frederick Robinson.

Walter may therefore have just reached Rouen after a journey of a few days, or he might have been hospitalised for weeks. His will, like that of many British soldiers, was on a form inside his 'AB 64' Paybook. It read simply:

> In the event of my death, I give the whole of my property and
> effects to my wife, Mrs Annie Maud Smith, 23 Lower Free Lane,
> Charles Street, Leicester, England.

It was taken from his paybook by an administrative officer and processed by the army. At least Annie could be sure of quick access to any savings or property he had – not all widows were so lucky.

With such a common name as hers, it has just not been possible to trace the progress of Annie or her daughter. We hope that they were able to rebuild their lives.

In the village, his family here would have mourned him. His parents were still living, although it is likely that most, if not all his siblings had moved away through marriage, or to find work. Old John Smith had joined other fathers of Wymeswold like David Sissins, John and Thomas Clarke, the two John Collingtons, 'Billy' Dykes and others – 'an old man weeping, just an old man in pain' for a son that would not come home again.

Sources

Census records: 1851, 1861, 1871, 1891, 1901, 1911.

Wymeswold parish registers. Online at: www.hoap.co.uk/who/localhisregister.htm [accessed June 2014].

Wymeswold Church of England School: log books and misc papers 1875–1983 (DE7281). The Record Office for Leicestershire, Leicester and Rutland.

Wymeswold vicar's correspondence (DE 1728/37). The Record Office for Leicestershire, Leicester and Rutland.

Smith W.C. Will FAEJ722316. HM Government / Department of Justice,

Soldier's service and pay book - Army Book 64 (AB64). Trustees of the King's Own Royal Regiment Museum Online at: www.kingsownmuseum.plus.com/ab64.htm [accessed 19 June 2014].

War Diary 9Bn Yorkshire Regiment October 1918 (WO/95/2247). The National Archives.

Medal Roll Index Cards (Series WO 373). The National Archives.

Brown, M., 1999. *1918 Year of Victory*. Pan Books.

Chris Baker/Milverton Associates Ltd, no date.'The Long Long Trail: The Base Hospitals in France and Flanders'. Online at: www.1914-1918.net/hospitals.htm [accessed 19 June 2014].

Corrigan, G., 2003. *Mud, Blood and Poppycock*. Cassell.

Janman, B., 2007. 'The RAMC Chain of Evacuation'. Online at: www.ramc-ww1.com/ [accessed 19 June 2014].

Laughead, G., 2013. 'The Medical Front WW1'. Online at: www.vlib.us/medical/ [accessed June 2014].

Mackintosh William Ewart. 'In Memoriam'. Online at: www.greatwar.co.uk/ poems/ewart-alan-mackintosh-in-memoriam.htm [accessed July 2014].

Passingham, I., 2008. *The German Offensives of 1918*. Pen and Sword.

Payne, D. D., 2008. 'The Royal Army Veterinary Corps and the Animals Employed by the British Army on the Western Front in the Great War'. Online at: www.westernfrontassociation.com/great-war-on-land/general-interest/357-army-vets.html [accessed 19 June 2014].

Pitt, B., 2003. *1918 The Last Act*. Pen and Sword.

Smith, E., 1983. *Memories of a Country Girlhood*. Published by author.

Winter, D., 2004. *Haig's Command: A Reassessment*. Pen and Sword.

Chapter 27

Bramford Sparrow

The Sparrows were a Lincolnshire family: Bramford's grandfather, John Sparrow, was born in Cabourn, and became a sergeant in the county police. At the age of thirty-six he married Jane Bramford. The couple and their children evidently moved around the county, presumably according to John's postings. The eldest, Elizabeth, was born in Scotter, her mother's native village. Martha was born in Nettleham and Gertrude in Weeby. Mary and William Henry were born in Caistor.

The young William did not follow in his father's footsteps, but became a wheelwright – a good, skilled trade in the late nineteenth century. In 1884 he married Harriet Flintham, and at some point moved to Wymeswold. By this time, 1901, he had become a cabinet maker. There is evidence to suggest that he moved around, probably according to his work. In 1908, for example, the Mixed School head wrote:

> Jan 10th... this week Beatrice Sparrow is leaving as her father has obtained a situation in Belfast.

Whether the move to Belfast actually happened, Beatrice was in Wymeswold school two years later. William and Harriet are also recorded as living in London after Bramford died. This comes from an entry in the cemetery records at Meaulte, where Bramford is buried, so it probably dates to the early 1920s. On the other hand, a newspaper article at the time of their son's death gives their address as High Street, Loughborough.

To add to the picture of William moving around, he is absent from the family home when the 1911 census was taken. His absences may not have been just due to work. When Bramford enlisted in 1912, he gave his mother's address as Far Street, Wymeswold, but his father's address as 'unknown'.

Though William and Harriet's two eldest children Beatrice and Bramford were born in Caistor, Lincolnshire (1894 and 1895 respectively), Lenora, the youngest came along in 1907 in Wymeswold, where she was baptised on 8th September.

Given that the family was in Wymeswold from at least 1901 onwards, all the children would have regarded Wymeswold as home, and their friends would have been the other local children who lived nearby in Brook Street. Bramford would have played with George and John Spicer who lived next door; George was a couple of years older, but his brother John just a year younger than Bramford.

Beatrice did well at school, winning prizes for Religious Knowledge in 1904, 1905 and 1906. In that year her brother Bramford also won, along with Jesse Mills and Eric Evans. Not many children are recorded by name as leaving school, but Beatrice was one:

> 1908 May 15 A girl, Beatrice Sparrow, aged 14, has left this week, and gone into service.

This was probably with the James family of Hoby, with whom she was a housemaid in 1911. Given that she could have left at thirteen, either her parents were in no hurry to see her start work, or she had been encouraged to stay, or both. She certainly appears to have been a good pupil.

Bramford only figures twice in the Mixed School records. The first is for that prize, and the second mention is on the list, drawn up in 1914, of school 'old boys' who had already joined the army.

Bramford started his working life as a farm boy. He must have been working locally, because at the 1911 census he was still living at home in Far Street (the family had moved). However, in just over a year, in December 1912, he joined the Grenadier Guards. In doing so, he joined a list of five Wymeswold men (Bill Collington, John Lamb, James Collington, George Williams) who were pre-war, professional soldiers, but who did not survive the Great War.

Soldiering was not an unusual occupation for a Wymeswold lad, at a time when conditions were hard and work was not always available. Mr Bailey, the redoubtable head of the Mixed School , recorded some of them at the time of the South African War in 1900:

> John Wood (Fort Artillery), William Allen Leicestershire Regiment in Transvaal, George Allen Leicestershire Regiment in Transvaal, John Tyler (jnr) and John Tyler (Snr) and Alf Tyler, Arthur Morris died of fever in the Mediterranean Feb 1900, Ernest Brookes, Samuel Knifton, Albert Basford (Fort Artillery), Alexander Sheppard, died of fever in India 1898.

Though joining the army was not unusual, being assigned to a Guards regiment was unexpected. True, Amos Clarke had joined the Coldstream Guards, and later his younger brother Thomas (perhaps with a recommendation from Amos) did the same. Amos returned to the school several times in 1903 and 1904, and took the children for drill and marching, favourite forms of physical exercise in the Mixed School . Perhaps it was Amos' example that gave young Bramford the idea of joining the Guards. There was also a history of men named Sparrow in the Grenadiers; a P. Sparrow had served in South Africa, while a James and a Joseph Sparrow had fought in the Crimea.

Bramford in the uniform of the Grenadier Guards. Photograph courtesy of Loughborough Roll of Honour.

Bramford's attestation papers have survived (unlike other regiments, the Guards kept their records in their own archives). Bramford volunteered on the 7th December 1912, giving his age as 18 years and 5 months. This was not true. He was in fact 17 years and 5 months old. The recruiting sergeant for the Guards countersigned the document. He had obviously been in prior contact with him, as he had sent Bramford a formal Notice in advance of the Attestation hearing, but had evidently not enquired too closely about his age. Bramford's medical examination shows that he was big for his age – 5 feet 87/8 inches tall, and 154 pounds, with a chest measurement of 38 inches – an ideal recruit.

His records go on to show that he was among the very first of the British Expeditionary Force to go to France. He left England on 11th August 1914, just eight days after war was declared. Consequently, he would be entitled not just to the 1914–15 Star, but to the clasp as well. Had he survived, he would have been one of the 'Old Contemptibles' who led the march past at the Cenotaph for nearly fifty years after the war. His Casualty Form lists his postings and health issues. Unlike the newspaper report of his death, which claimed he had been wounded twice, the record shows that he been wounded once, in May 1915, but that it was 'slight'. He had been hospitalised twice, though. Firstly for the wound, and secondly for scarlet fever, which he contracted in January 1916.

His war had been eventful, to say the least. He would have been with the battalion at the First Battle of Ypres, when it lost all but four officers and 140 men. In May 1915 the battalion had been rotating between the front line and billets at Le Casan, just a few miles south east of the spot near Mt Bernanchon where Jesse Mills was to die three years later. They moved up to the front line again on 17th, and attacked on the 18th. The war diary records:

> The attack was a failure owing to flatness of country swept by machine gun fire and enfilade artillery fire.

The next day:

> Battalion buried British and German dead all night and in the
> early morning. Heavy shelling all day with every description of
> shell some very big.

This was when Bramford was first wounded. He was back at base depot though
within a fortnight and was assigned duties as a transport driver until October, when
he rejoined the battalion. After a spell in hospital with scarlet fever in January 1916,
he returned to the Guards' division base, at Harfleur, and from there was reassigned
to an entrenching battalion in the field, in April 1916. His record does not show
exactly when he returned to his battalion in the field, but he was certainly with his
old comrades – what were left of them – in January 1917.

The winter of 1916–17 was very cold. The 2nd Battalion Grenadier Guards saw the
New Year in at Bronfay, on the Somme, and marched on New Year's Day to
Meaulte, a little village to the south of Albert. They spent several weeks there,
keeping themselves occupied all day, every day. The first thing they had to do was
to clean their arms and equipment, and then began the normal rounds of training in
'musketry', bombing (grenades) and Lewis gunnery. There were route marches if
nothing else presented itself. Men were detailed off to fatigue parties, building horse
standings and other works. Men were sent up to work on the light railway on the
nearby plateau.

In the midst of all this, they managed to put on a concert, together with 3rd Battalion
Coldstream Guards in the YMCA hut at Meaulte. (Thomas Clarke would come out to
join the same Battalion the following August.) On the 24th they were told they would
be moved by bus and lorry up to Priez Farm, about halfway between Combles and
Rancourt. The new location was more or less on the front line, and about eleven
miles north-east of their present position. The next day, about half of the promised
transport arrived, so a large part of the battalion had to march. At Priez Farm, they
were 'accommodated' in dugouts, which they set about improving. On the 27th,
their second full day at Priez, the war diary noted:

> Fine but very cold. Work continued on dugouts. The filling of
> sandbags very difficult, as frost is nearly two feet into the ground.
> Shelled in the morning, not very heavily, but very unluckily. One
> shell falling among our cookers. Casualties, 2 killed, 3 wounded
> and 1 slightly wounded. The latter remained at Duty. One
> watercart was blown up. 2 other men slightly wounded during the
> day.

This was the day that Bramford was mortally wounded. There is some inconsistency,
however, between this description and the nature of his wounds. Bramford was
evacuated, presumably via the Regimental Aid Post to the nearest Casualty Clearing
Station, at Grove Town, about two miles south-east of the billets he had left at
Meaulte only two days before.

Bramford's grave at Grove Town, Meaulte.

According to the officer commanding 34 Casualty Clearing Station at Grove Town, Bramford died "g.s.w. leg (R) hand (R)". A gunshot wound (g.s.w.) is definitely not a shell fragment wound, and the officer would have known that. He may of course have been injured by shrapnel bullets from the shells, or have been one of the two men whose wounds were originally thought to be 'slight'.

Whatever the records say, they agree that he was wounded on the 27th, and recorded dead on the 28th. His body was buried in the cemetery just outside the Clearing Station. It is one of two cemeteries on the Western Front – Estaires is the other – that hold the bodies of two Wymeswold men.

His death was reported by the *Leicester Mercury* on 7th February 1917:

> Pte Bramford Sparrow, of the Grenadier Guards, died on January 28 from wounds received the previous day. Deceased was the son of Mrs Sparrow ,of High Street, Loughborough. He joined the Grenadier Guards over four years ago and went to the front in August, 1914. He was twice wounded.

The Loughborough Roll of Honour adds, quoting from the *Loughborough Echo*:

> Before joining the regular army he lived at Wymeswold, where he
> was well known. His mother has been residing in Loughborough
> for some time, and lived in the High Street.

We do not know who requested his inclusion on the Wymeswold Roll of Honour. His parents lived in Loughborough, and we last heard of his sister Beatrice in Hoby. Whoever it was, they did the right thing. Bramford was a true son of Wymeswold, and his memory has been kept alive at home.

Sources

Census records: 1881, 1891, 1901, 1911.

Wymeswold parish registers. Online at: www.hoap.co.uk/who/localhisregister.htm [accessed June 2014].

Wymeswold Church of England School: log books and misc papers 1875–1983 (DE7281). The Record Office for Leicestershire, Leicester and Rutland.

Wymeswold vicar's correspondence (DE 1728/37). The Record Office for Leicestershire, Leicester and Rutland.

Loughborough Roll of Honour. Online at: loughborough-rollofhonour.com/page44.htm [accessed 20 June 2014].

Map: WO 297/1560 Sheet 62c NW2 29-08-1916. The National Archives.

Service Record: 16175 Bramford Sparrow, Grenadier Guards archive.

War Diary 2Bn Grenadier Guards August 1914 to December 1915 (WO 95/1342/1). The National Archives.

War Diary 2Bn Grenadier Guards January 1917 (WO/95/1215). The National Archives.

Laughead, G., 2013. 'The Medical Front WW1'. Online at: www.vlib.us/medical/ [accessed June 2014].

Macdonald, L., 1997. *1915 The Death of Innocence.* Penguin Books.

Nixon, P., 2013. 'Army Service Numbers 1881–1914'. Online at: armyservicenumbers.blogspot.co.uk [accessed 18 June 2014].

Chapter 28

David Spicer

David's grandfather, also David Spicer, had arrived in Wymeswold between 1859 and 1865. He was already married to Mary, a Wymeswold woman, and they settled here, raising seven children, including Thomas (Tom, born about 1859) and George (born about 1868). Like his father William before him, David was a farm labourer. Curiously, William, by now in his mid-sixties, described himself as a Chelsea Pensioner at the 1851 census. This indicates a connection with the army which was to resurface with at least two of his great-grandsons.

David's son Tom took after his father, working on the land, and married Elizabeth Dexter in St Mary's church in May 1883. In an age when writing was less important than it is now, spelling tended to follow pronunciation. Probably because they pronounced their name as if it had a 'z', the family was being referred to as 'Spizer' or 'Spiser' in the census records, right up to 1881. Tom's marriage in 1883 seems to be the first time that the present spelling was used in an official document.

Children followed immediately. Tom and Elizabeth's first child, David, was born later the same year, with Harriet in 1887, Annie 1890, Thomas 1892, Frederick 1893, Percy 1896 and Edward in 1901. Three children also died in infancy, including little Mary, aged eleven months, whose burial was recorded in St Mary's church in 1889. None of the children are mentioned in the school log books, except Harriet, who attracts some very blunt comments about her lack of ability. As the family grew, Tom changed his occupation. He moved away from the land, and became a bricklayer/labourer. His son David may have started on the land when he left school, but by the age of eighteen he was following the same trade, and probably working with his father.

Another change came in the 1890s, when the family moved to Salmon Street in Loughborough. It probably happened as a result of Tom taking a job in one of the local engineering factories. By 1911 the transformation of the family from a rural economy to an urban one was complete. Most of the men worked for an engineering company, though not necessarily the same one. Tom was a labourer, as was Thomas junior, now twenty. Fred (eighteen) was a moulder, and Percy (sixteen) a riveter. David, aged twenty-eight and still unmarried was a domestic chauffeur.

Due to the bombing by the Luftwaffe in 1940, most of the First World War service records were destroyed. David Spicer's seems to have been among them. We do not

David Spicer in the uniform of the Notts and Derby Regiment. Photograph courtesy of Winnie Sleath.

know therefore, when he joined up, or which regiment he was initially sent to. His service number – 24369 – suggests that he enlisted directly into the regular army, rather than the Territorials. It is not possible to say either whether he was a volunteer or a conscript. Although a million men had volunteered in 1914–15, the army needed more, and from March 1916 every man between the ages of 19 and 41 was 'deemed to have enlisted' unless he could show he was involved in a trade that would preclude him from fighting. This does not mean that everyone who joined after March 1916 was a conscript: prior to that, 'Lord Derby's Scheme' allowed men to volunteer, but stay in civilian life until they were required. His number is not, however, a militia or Territorial number.

Before the war, the 'old' army and Territorials mostly had four-digit numbers that were allocated by the regiments, and re-used as necessary. In 1917, the Territorial units were given two-digit prefixes in order to cope with the increasing numbers, and the problem of duplication. On the other hand, if a man transferred from a Territorial unit into a 'Regular' army battalion, he would be allocated a new number. Interpreting First World War service numbers is complex, to say the least. However, the army was assiduous in keeping records, including the entitlement of soldiers to campaign and gallantry medals. David's medal card shows no indication that he served with any but the 15th Battalion, Notts and Derby Regiment (the Sherwood Foresters). If that is the case, then unlike his two cousins back in Wymeswold, he had not been in the Territorial army, and had enlisted or been sent directly into the battalion.

Another set of possibilities as to his date of enlistment comes from a history of the 15th Battalion. It had been raised in 1915 as a 'Bantam Battalion' – a unit comprised of men who were below the height of 5 feet 3 inches normally regarded as the minimum for service. It fought in the early battles of the Somme in the summer of 1916, taking heavy casualties. In late 1916:

> … the division received new drafts of men to replace losses suffered on the Somme, but the commanding officer soon discovered that these new recruits were not of the same physical standard as the original Bantams, being men of small stature from the towns, rather than the miners and farm workers who had joined up in 1915. A medical inspection was carried out and 1,439 men were transferred to the Labour Corps. Their places were taken by men transferred from the disbanded yeomanry regiments, who underwent a quick training course in infantry methods at a Divisional depot set up specifically for that purpose.

Unfortunately, we know nothing of David's height. Had he been one of those original Bantam volunteers? Or was he one of the bigger, later recruits in late 1916? After his death, the village headmaster was under the impression that he had served with the 6th Leicesters. If this were the case, then almost certainly David would have been one of those many men who were initially allocated to a local regiment – and 6th Leicesters would make sense – before being sent on to their 'destination' regiment.

In the late autumn of 1916, the battle of the Somme was drawing to an uncertain close in the mud, wind and rain on the Transloy Ridges, but the 15th Sherwoods had been sent up to the Arras sector. They were holding trenches just north of the city. Today the area is easily identified on Google Earth, just north of the suburbs of St Nicolas and St Laurent-Blangy. It is roughly bounded on the south by the D950 dual carriageway, on the east by the D919 and on the west by an unnamed track. In 1916 it formed part of the outer defences of Arras, and faced eastwards, just a hundred yards or so to the German lines.

On 25th October, a company of the battalion had carried out a raid on the German lines, in order to obtain prisoners, if possible, and any other information. Badges, papers, weapons, even identity discs were to be stripped from corpses and brought back for analysis. The artillery put down a barrage, and the other companies of the battalion kept up covering fire with Lewis guns, rifle grenades and rifle fire. The raid was launched in the evening and the war diary reported a success:

> One prisoner was taken and a great deal of damage done to Enemy Trenches.

David's grave at the Faubourg d'Amiens Cemetery, Arras (the Arras Memorial).

However, the detailed report reveals that only one of the three 'bombing' parties detailed to assault the enemy trenches actually got through, and the total cost was heavy: three killed, nineteen wounded and five missing.

No activity was reported for the next few days, but on the 2nd November, the enemy became very active:

> 7 a.m. Bombardment of JII Sector by Enemy Heavy T.M.s [trench mortars]. 9 a.m. Heavy T.M.s ceased but Medium T.M.s and Rifle Grenades were troublesome until 1.p.m. 1 p.m. to 4 p.m. Heavy T.M.s again bombarding causing considerable damage to Front Line and SUPPORT Trenches. At 4 P.M. our Artillery and T.M.s in a combined operation silenced the Enemy – Situation Normal during the night 2nd–3rd.

The battalion was relieved the next day, 3rd November. It was a relief that David Spicer would not see. He had died the previous day, almost certainly a victim of the artillery fire that accounted for around fifty-eight percent of the casualties of the fighting on the Western Front.

Back home in England, the news quickly filtered through to Wymeswold, probably through his cousins. William Bailey, the headmaster of the Mixed School , wrote:

Nov 17. We have just heard that another of our 'Old Boys', David Spicer, of the VI Leicesters, has given up his life for his Country, in N.E. FRANCE. He worked on the land before he enlisted.

Mr Bailey's facts may have been out of date, or even wrong, but having read his log books I think that his words were written with sadness and reverence.

David now lies not far from where he fell. His grave is in the cemetery at the Faubourg d'Amiens in Arras. It lies in the shadow of the great memorial to the 35,000 men of the British and Imperial forces who have no known grave. David is in good company. Facing towards his grave is the name of John William ('Bill') Collington. Other names that look down from the walls are Foster Simpson, Albert Bacon and William Wilson.

Note: The photograph that accompanies this chapter has been kindly donated by Winnie Sleath. In the family, it had been referred to as a picture of David's cousin George. However, he is wearing the uniform of the Sherwood Foresters. Since David was in that regiment, and George was not, I have assumed it to be of David.

Sources

Census records: 1841, 1851, 1871, 1881, 1891, 1901, 1911.

Certificate of Birth, Marriage or Death. General Register Office. Online at: www.freebmd.org.uk [accessed January 2014].

Wymeswold parish registers. Online at: www.hoap.co.uk/who/localhisregister.htm [accessed June 2014].

Wymeswold Church of England School: log books and misc papers 1875–1983 (DE7281). The Record Office for Leicestershire, Leicester and Rutland.

Wymeswold vicar's correspondence (DE 1728/37). The Record Office for Leicestershire, Leicester and Rutland.

Commonwealth War Graves Commission. 'Find War Dead.' Online at: www.cwgc.org [accessed 7 February 2014].

Map: WO 297/1188 Sheet 51b NW 200916. The National Archives.

War Diary 15Bn Sherwood Foresters October to November 1916 (WO/95/2488). The National Archives.

Loughborough Roll of Honour. Online at: loughborough-rollofhonour.com/page44.htm [accessed 20 June 2014].

'Remember Loughborough'. Online at: www.facebook.com/pages/Remember-Loughborough/562549607110527 [accessed 21 June 2014].

Baker, Chris / Milverton Associates, 2014. 'The Long Long Trail: Renumbering of the Territorial Force in 1917'. Online at: www.1914-1918.net/renumbering.htm [accessed 6 June 2014].

Corrigan, G., 2003. *Mud, Blood and Poppycock.* Cassell.

Chapter 29

The Spicer Brothers: George and John Edward

George and John Spicer are the only brothers from Wymeswold to be killed in the First World War. The family was especially hard hit as their cousin David was also killed. The two families must have been closely linked, as David's parents lived for many years in Wymeswold, and most of their children spent their early lives here. George and John shared a grandfather – also called David – with their cousin. The elder David had been brought up in Asfordby, and moved to Wymeswold in the mid-eighteenth century, after his marriage to Mary Coddington in St Mary's in 1854. From then on, the family settled in Wymeswold, until David's son Tom moved to Loughborough at the end of the 1890s.

Tom's brother George remained in Wymeswold, marrying Alice Basford Fletcher in 1892. The couple had six children – George William (about 1894) Mary (1895), John Edward (1896), Christopher (1898; died in infancy), Bertie (1900) and Hilda (1902). During the 1890s, both families lived in Brook Street. George and Alice lived next door to the Sparrows (their son Bramford died in January 1917), while Thomas and Elizabeth lived two doors from the Savages (Alfred Savage was to die in 1916). For a number of years, the children would have mixed and played together. George's family never moved from Wymeswold, but stayed, working on the land.

George followed his father to become a farm labourer, and unlike his elder brother, Thomas, he remained in that occupation all his life. His sons George and John both took after him. George and Alice's children had their share of prizes at school, though not all the entries in Mr Bailey's log were complimentary. In 1893, George was said to be a weak reader – but within two years, his attainment must have improved, since in 1905 he won a prize for Religious Knowledge (*Stories From Acts*), as did Mary (*Jessica's First Prayer*). He also won a prize for good attendance (*Robinson Crusoe*). Jesse Mills also won a prize for Religious Knowledge, while Alf Savage and William Wilson were rewarded for good attendance.

It was a small community, and the losses of 1914–18 would leave great gaps in Wymeswold's social fabric. However 1905 was a good year for the Spicer children, as young Bertie, now in the Infant School , also won a prize for attendance. George and John continued their winning streak in 1906, with prizes for attendance – John got a copy of the *World Wide Atlas of England and Wales,* while George got the *British Isles* equivalent. Other recipients of atlases were George Marriott, Eric Evans and Alfred Savage. None of them would return from the war.

George and John's parents with sister Hilda and William Selby Fletcher, son of James Fermer Fletcher. Photograph taken around 1914. Courtesy of Linda Ward.

That year was probably George's last at school – most young lads were eager for their thirteenth birthday, when they could finally leave school and start working, like their fathers. John would have left a couple of years later, but attracted no more attention, and it was just Bertie and Hilda who picked up prizes (Bertie in 1910 and 1911, Hilda in 1911). The last of the Spicer children, Hilda, left the school in 1915: 'Jan 18 Hilda Spicer left; she was 13 last Nov'. Schooldays were over for all of them, and the serious business of making a living was just beginning.

Within a few years of leaving school, George was establishing a career in farming. In 1911 he was living and working with Herbert Emmerson at Manor Farm, Wymeswold. George was now a cowman, not simply a labourer. He was becoming a skilled, and valuable, worker. Working alongside him was the farm's waggoner, William Clarke, the brother of John Clarke, who was to die during the Arras offensive of spring 1917.

While George's career was just starting to take shape, John, in 1911, was living at home and working as a farm labourer. He was just fourteen, only a year out of school. At the outbreak of war in 1914, George was twenty-two, while John was barely of military age (he turned eighteen in October 1914). Both young men, however, joined the Territorial forces, ready to serve their country. George's service record has survived, though much damaged in 1940 by enemy bombing and the water used to put out the fires. He attested (presented himself) for the Leicester Territorial regiment in August 1915, and was allocated to the 3/5th battalion.

Private 4591 Spicer, George was taken on the strength of the 3/5 Leicesters and sent for training. It was a new battalion, formed at Loughborough earlier in the year;

171

George Spicer. Photograph courtesy of Winnie Sleath.

George must have responded to the call for men that saw around a million enlist in the first year of the war. In December he was sent out to France, where he was transferred to the 1/5th.

The 1/5th Leicesters had been involved in the battle of Hooge and the attack on the Hohenzollern Redoubt, and they were still up in the northern sector, manning trenches just south of Souchez, a little village about seven miles north of Arras. The area is now better known for being just to the west of the famous Vimy Ridge, which was taken by the Canadians in 1917.

In March 1916 they were in and out of the front line trenches. Like all units, they would spend several days in the front line before being relieved, and passing into support lines, or further back into reserve. On the 9th they took over trenches from the French 68th Regiment. All was quiet for a couple of days until, at 10.30 p.m. on the 10th, sporadic rifle grenade attacks began. These were followed the next day with more serious explosions, when the enemy blew in one of the Leicesters' 'saps' – trenches pushed out towards the enemy lines and used for observation or to launch raids. So began several days of minor attacks and counter-attacks.

On the 13th the Leicesters exploded a 'Camouflet' between the lines. A Camouflet is an underground explosive charge, used either to destroy an enemy tunnel, or to create confusion and localised damage above ground. They surprised themselves by its ferocity. Though they had used the prescribed charges, it created a crater forty feet deep and thirty-five yards across. It also blew down between twenty and twenty-five yards of the German parapet.

The response was predictable, and much bombing and counter-bombing ensued. The battalion was relieved on the 15th and did not return to the trenches until the 21st. On the 22nd, the enemy began using trench mortars and kept up a four-hour bombardment. Six rounds of artillery from the British side had no effect as retaliation, but things quietened down.

John Spicer. Photograph courtesy of Winnie Sleath.

A similar pattern developed on the 23rd. The enemy continued targeting the British front line trenches on the 24th. At this point, the war diary notes that:

> Considerable damage was done to this piece of trench. One dugout was blown in. Casualties were:- Sergt Staniforth wounded. One man killed. Capt Williamson killed. One man wounded.

The 'one man killed' must have been George Spicer. In a most unusual entry, probably because the casualties were so few, the war diary for March 1916 ends by naming the four men who were struck off the strength of the battalion by reason of being casualties. Pte Spicer G.W. was one of them.

His body now lies in the Military Cemetery at Ecoivres. It is some twenty miles west of Souchez, and was a cemetery that the North Midland Division had recently taken over from the French, who had already interred around a thousand men in the adjoining Communal Cemetery. Using a French military tramway, the North Midland and succeeding divisions – including the Canadians, after Vimy Ridge – brought a total of over 1,700 bodies to be buried there.

John, meanwhile, had joined the South Notts Hussars. Without his service records, which have been lost, we cannot be sure where or exactly when he joined the regiment. However, there are a number of pointers that can lead us some way to understanding what happened. The South Notts Hussars was (and is – it survives as a battery of the Royal Artillery) originally a militia regiment, founded in the days before the police force existed. The militia, or Yeomanry Cavalry, were volunteers,

George Spicer's grave at Ecoivres.

usually paid for by local landowners or businessmen, and could be called out to restore order at times of public unrest or riots.

The South Notts Hussars could trace their origins back to the Nottingham Town Troop of Yeomanry Cavalry, which was used to help suppress food riots in Nottingham in 1795 and 1800, and the dispersal of Luddite rioters in 1811. It may well be that by the time war broke out John Spicer was no longer working as a general farm worker, but had some daily contact with horses. It would have been natural for him to have volunteered to a cavalry regiment, and equally naturally for them to have accepted him. One has to wonder whether he had been working on a farm in one of the nearby Nottinghamshire villages – Willoughby, say, or Wysall or Rempstone – which led him to volunteer for a Nottinghamshire unit rather than a Leicestershire one.

The evidence for the date he volunteered is in his medal card. It shows that he first entered a 'theatre of war' on 12th September 1915. This would be the date his unit disembarked – in this case, in Egypt. His service number there is given as 1770. This is fairly unambiguous. It is an example of how the 'old army' regiments and the Territorial Forces had allocated their own numbers. On 1st April 1917. a major renumbering of the Yeomanry came into effect. All units received six digit numbers, and the block of numbers allocated to the South Notts Hussars was from 280001 to 285000. There was no set rule that told each regiment how to distribute its numbers, but John was an early recipient – he was given the service number 280691.

John disembarked in Egypt in September 1915, but according to the regimental histories, the South Notts were being withdrawn from Gallipoli at the time, and did not reach Egypt until December. It seems likely that John was occupied in non-active service duties until joining his regiment, as there is a note on his medal card first awarding him the 1915 Star, then cancelling it. The best explanation I can find for this is that the 1915 Star was given to everyone who served in an active theatre of war before 1916. It may be that John had been given some non-combatant role that kept him away from his active service regiment until early 1916, and when the army realised that, it withdrew the medal.

John would however have had plenty of action later with the regiment, which had an eventful time on the Eastern Front. Deployed in Egypt, some elements were included in the Desert Column which successfully attacked the Senussi tribesmen and relieved Sidi Barrani in December 1915 and January 1916. The divison to which it belonged was broken up at this time, and it was sent to Salonika as part of 7th Mounted Brigade, but was back in Egypt by June 1917. It had been sent to Gallipoli as dismounted infantry, but now General Allenby, needing the speed and manoeuvrability of cavalry, had them remounted and brought them into his new Desert Mounted Corps. Most of the cavalry in the Corps was armed with rifles, but the 7th Brigade, and the Yeomanry Division, were armed with swords. They were with the Corps when it captured Beersheba at the end of October 1917, and initiated the change from fighting a defensive war in Palestine to an advance that continued until the end of the war.

By mid-November the cavalry was badly in need of rest. They had covered 190 miles of rocky, hilly terrain in hot and dry conditions; the retreating Turks had done their best to make the wells unuseable, and both horses and men were tired and thirsty. The Turkish army was retreating, and the British harried them with attack after attack. Frequently the Turks would counterattack to protect their withdrawal. It was exhausting for horses and men. On the 19th the weather broke and the rains came:

> ... this added to the difficulties of the cavalry, turning the valley bottoms into a sea of viscid, black mud, and the beds of the ravines into rushing torrents. The sudden drop in temperature which accompanied the rain was a severe trial to our troops, who were dressed in light, khaki-drill clothing, and had no blankets, greatcoats, or tents.

These were the conditions when the South Notts Hussars relieved the Sherwood Rangers in the rocky hills north of Jerusalem. The battle of Nebi Samwil, as it is now known, lasted a week. At the end of it, the British had captured the gateway to Jerusalem, which was to fall within a month. But at a cost. Repeated Turkish counterattacks had taken their toll, and amongst the wounded of the campaign was John Spicer.

The immediate evacuation from the front line would have been very difficult, through the hills, and into the valleys deep in mud. He may have made it all the way to the large hospital base at Kantara in Egypt, or he may have died at one of the

175

The Spicer family grave in Wymeswold Cemetery

smaller hospitals in Palestine. The cemeteries attached to these units were cleared after the war and the bodies relocated to Kantara, where John now lies.

George, like many soldiers going into a war zone, even today, had made a will. It was short and to the point. 'In the event of my death I give the whole of my property and effects to my mother'. It was written on 9th December 1915, when he was still with the 3/5th Leicesters, and just before he went to France. That meant of course, that she was the one who had to sign the correspondence with the army, and supply supporting documentation, such as the names and addresses of George's surviving relatives, in order to receive his death plaque and scroll. By this time, July 1919, her son John had also died, of course. If his records were available, we should see the same heart rending process being drawn out a second time.

John had also made a will. We do not know when he made it, as there is a large military stamp across the date. However, it was written when he was still Pte 1770, i.e. before he was renumbered in the spring of 1917. Like his brother, he probably wrote it when he was sent overseas in 1915. Like his brother too, he left everything to his mother.

Alice Spicer grieved for two sons, but thankfully Bertie came home. From family photographs he was also working with horses, probably as a driver with the 4th Battalion (Transport Section) Middlesex regiment, though no records have been found to date. Alice herself did not live to see the world torn apart by war a second time. She died in 1929 at the age of fifty-nine. Her husband George put up a tombstone to remember both her and the two sons he lost in the war. It is still in Wymeswold Cemetery, on Rempstone Road. And it now has his name as well.

Sources

Census records: 1851, 1871, 1891, 1901, 1911.

Wymeswold parish registers. Online at: www.hoap.co.uk/who/localhisregister.htm [accessed June 2014].

Wymeswold Church of England School: log books and misc papers 1875–1983 (DE7281). The Record Office for Leicestershire, Leicester and Rutland.

Wymeswold vicar's correspondence (DE 1728/37). The Record Office for Leicestershire, Leicester and Rutland.

Spicer G W Will FAEJ728911, London: H M Government/ Department of Justice.

Spicer J E Will FAEJ943761, London: H M Government/ Department of Justice.

Map: M/89/000382 Souchez 36c SW3. Western Front Association.

Service Record: 4591 George William Spicer. The National Archives.

War Diary 1/5 Bn Leicestershire Regiment March 1916 (WO/95/2690). The National Archives.

The Queen's Royal Lancers and Nottinghamshire Yeomanry Museum. Online at: www.qrlnymuseum.co.uk/snhhist1.htm [accessed 21 June 2014].

'Tunneling Companies in the Great War'. Online at: www.tunnellersmemorial.com/ tunnelling-companies/ [accessed July 2014].

Baker, Chris / Milverton Associates, 2014. 'The Long Long Trail: How men joined the British Army'. Online at: www.1914-1918.net/recruitment.htm [accessed 7 June 2014].

Baker, Chris / Milverton Associates, 2014. 'The Long Long Trail: Renumbering of the Territorial Force in 1917'. Online at: www.1914-1918.net/renumbering.htm [accessed 6 June 2014].

Lock, M. H. O., 1919. *With the British Army in the Holy Land,* Robert Scott. Online at server16040.contentdm.oclc.org

Nixon, P., 2013. 'Army Service Numbers 1881–1914'. Online at: armyservicenumbers.blogspot.co.uk [accessed 18 June 2014].

Preston, L. C. R. M. P. D., 1921. *The Desert Mounted Corps,* Houghton Mifflin. Online at www.archive.org

Chapter 30

George Williams

George was born in 1889, the fourth child of Frederick and Emma Elizabeth Williams. Rather like Colin Bramall, whose father became a farm manager at Stapleford near Melton Mowbray, George's father Frederick was a farm bailiff. Unlike the Bramalls, who were from Yorkshire, Frederick came from Lincolnshire. Indeed, the three younger children had been born in East Drayton, just on the Nottinghamshire side of the border with Lincolnshire while William, the eldest, was born just down the road in Headon cum Upton. George's mother came from Markham Field, a couple of miles south of East Drayton.

Like Joseph Bramall, Frederick Williams would have had to move around if he were to follow a career in farm management. Unfortunately for Frederick, his career seems not to have taken off, because in 1901 he was a 'cattle man on farm'. He and the family were at Highthorne Farm in Wymeswold, and it appears that this is where George grew up. The family must have arrived at Wymeswold sometime in 1898 or early 1899, as the Reverend Green noted in the Infant School log for June 8th 1899:

> One new boy Frank Williams seems very backward for his age
> (just six), as he does not know how to form simple letters, as B
> and S. He does not seem deficient, but has been probably taught
> nothing. Two older brothers in the National School, of the same
> family, are similarly backward.

It would seem that the Williams family hadn't had much schooling until then.

George had either caught up with his education, or found that the army was less interested in academic subjects than the Reverend Green, because 1911 found him in the Notts and Derbyshire Regiment. He had been posted to India, and Lance Corporal George Williams was included in the census with the other men of 1st Battalion, The Sherwood Foresters. This was the same battalion as John James Collington and, although James had been out of the army for three years by 1911, there is a possibility that they had known each other as fellow soldiers.

His family's fortunes had continued to decline it seems, as his father is described in 1911 as 'farm labourer, former bailiff'. George's parents had moved yet again, and were back in their native area, at Edwinstowe, near Newark. More children had been born; in total the Williams had twelve children, of whom eight were still living. We do not know their conditions or standards of living, but they had lost a third of their children, which suggests that their life was a hard one.

The Williams' youngest child Doris was four in 1911, and had been born in Wymeswold, so they must have left between 1907 and 1911. It means that the family had lived eight to ten years here, and had presumably become quite established. On the other hand, it does seem that by 1911 the Williams family had been dispersed quite widely. None of the male Williams was resident in Wymeswold. Frank was a cowman in Pallerton near Chesterfield, John may also have been a cowman in Willoughby, and William was possibly the same William Williams recorded as a newly married 'shoe clicker' (leather cutter) in Rothley.

It seems that George's parents moved again, this time back to his mother's home area near East Retford, in north-east Nottinghamshire. There is a reference to the death of Frederick Williams in the area in 1915, and George's next of kin (so far as the Commonwealth War Graves Commission is concerned – i.e. after the war) was his mother, living in East Retford.

George's service records have not survived, so we do not know whether he was still in the army at the outbreak of war in 1914, or whether, like John James Collington, he was on the reserve list, having completed his service. His unit, the 1st Battalion Sherwood Foresters, was in India in 1914, but was brought back to Europe in the October, and found itself in France in November. Perhaps George and James were reunited at this point, as James was mobilized in August 1914, and was posted in the October.

The battalion was quickly in action, and helped to stop the advancing German army in the 'Race to the Sea' – the attempt to get around the British Expeditionary Force and cut it off from the English Channel. By Christmas, the battalion was in the trenches near Richebourg, close to Arras. The war diary remarks that Christmas Eve:

> ... was kept by the Battn as Xmas day, owing to Battn going into
> the trenches on 25th. G.O.C. 8th Division Gen DAVIES came
> round to wish the Battn a happy Xmas etc. Men started on some
> of 1100 plum puddings sent by county and city of Nottingham.

Not all days were so pleasant. Apart from the winter weather, casualties were mounting. Between their arrival at the front at the end of November, and 1st March, the battalion had suffered severe casualties: 74 dead and 298 wounded. On that day they received a letter from the Officer Commanding IV Corps, praising them and their neighbouring battalion, the 2nd East Lancashires. '... their casualties have been high', he wrote,

> but they have stuck to a difficult and dangerous task with a
> determination worthy of all praise and have expended an amount
> of physical labour in the construction of the lines which does
> them high credit.

By this time, of course, James Collington was already dead - shot in the head on 27th January. Worse suffering for the battalion was not far away. On 10th March, they were a little north east of Richebourg, about twenty miles north of Arras and five miles south of Estaires. At 7.30 a.m.

> Battn stood to arms. Weather fine but dull. Terrific bombardment
> opened on enemy lines by our artillery . Receive news that
> German trenches for a front of 4000 yards carried.

Gradually, inexorably, the battalion moved closer to the fighting as the day wore on. One by one, staging posts that were to become familiar to millions of men, were passed: Pont du Hem, Red Barn, Rouge Croix, Pont Logis, until at 5.30 p.m.

> Battn moved to cross roads N of NEUVE CHAPELLE and deployed
> for attack of points 85 and 86 N.E. of that village and advance to
> a position facing S.E. and about 1000 yards N.E. of NEUVE
> CHAPELLE being held up by a strongly fortified breastwork. Battn
> entrenched so as to make good ground gained.

A brief enough description of their part in the battle of Neuve Chapelle, the British army's first major attack of the war. In this attack and the subsequent German counter-attack, the battalion suffered 96 killed and 275 wounded, as well as 87 missing. Neuve Chapelle had accounted for nearly half the battalion's fighting strength. The total casualties in France now stood at 171 killed, and 581 wounded. Without the reinforcements it had received, and wounded men coming back, the battalion would have been all but wiped out.

Neuve Chapelle had been an attempt to cut through the German lines and cut off a large salient (bulge) that was pointing towards the British positions. 40,000 men had attacked on a two-kilometre front. Over 11,000 of them became casualties, but the attack was a success, if a limited one. It showed that major defence lines could be breached. However, it also showed that breaking through the lines into open country was quite another matter. The artillery failed to destroy the enemy's second line defences. The problem of what to bombard, and for how long, would bedevil British commanders for the rest of the war.

All of which was of no concern, or use, to George Williams. He had been fatally wounded somewhere between Pont du Hem and Neuve Chapelle village, in that flat landscape, criss-crossed by drainage ditches, damp trenches and water-filled trench holes. Somehow, his comrades must have got him back to a Regimental Aid Post, and possibly even to a Casualty Clearing Station, because he is recorded as having died of wounds. Quite possibly he was taken to the same 25th Field Ambulance Station that had tried to save James Collington's life, because he is buried in the same cemetery that it used. Both he and James now rest in Estaires British cemetery. Only two cemeteries on the Western Front hold the bodies of two Wymeswold men: Grove Town, at Meaulte, is the other.

The obvious question, in researching this book, was 'Why was George Williams included on the Roll of Honour list?' His family did not come from Wymeswold; it

George Williams' grave in Estaires Cemetery. James Collington lies in a small enclave of British graves on the other side of the cemetery.

had only lived here a few years, and George had spent much of that time in the army. The answer lies with his elder sister Maria. She had left home while the family was still in Wymeswold, and had gone to work for the Hardy family as a domestic servant; aged fourteen, she was with them at the time of the 1901 census. In 1907 she married William Tomlinson of Wymeswold, and they set up home in a cottage just beside the Maltby family on Clay Street. The front walls of those cottages still exist as the front wall of Wootton's timber workshop. Her husband, William Tomlinson, volunteered in December 1915.

This was no knee-jerk reaction to George's death in March. As a thirty-two year old father of three, William had responsibilities, and going to war was a serious matter. As it happened, he was not called for until June 1916, when he was sent to the Royal Garrison Artillery. (This is the arm of the artillery that deals with the heaviest guns. It originated as the force defending Britain's coasts, which necessitated long range guns, against ships. During the First World War, the technology and the need for heavy guns increased dramatically, making the RGA an integral part of the Royal Artillery.) William served in France with several units – 178th, 175th, and 116th Heavy Batteries. He was hospitalised in mid-1917 with influenza, and sent back to England, but returned to France in November, and appears to have served the rest of the war with 76th Siege Battery.

He eventually came home to Maria and the children in February 1919. He was one of the lucky ones. By the time of his return, people were starting to think about a memorial to the dead, and the first public meeting was held in May 1919. It looks as though Maria was very fond of her brothers, especially perhaps George. Her first child was called Rebecca, her second John, but her third child, born in April 1911, was called George William Tomlinson. No doubt she was anxious that her brother should be remembered and indeed he appears on the original list in the deeds of the Memorial Hall in 1922. George Williams may not have spent much time in Wymeswold, but memorials are as much about the living as the dead. They are somewhere that relatives can focus both their grief and their happy memories. For succeeding generations like us, we become inheritors for a time of the place we live in and all the stories that have gone before us. George Williams' name on the Roll of Honour is testament not only to him, but to Maria's grief, her worry over her absent husband, and her joy at his return. He deserves his place.

Sources

Census records: 1891, 1901, 1911.

Certificate of Birth, Marriage or Death. General Register Office. Online at: www.freebmd.org.uk [accessed January 2014].

Commonwealth War Graves Commission. 'Find War Dead' Online at: www.cwgc.org [accessed 7 February 2014].

Map: M/001475 36cSW3 Richebourg. Western Front Association.

Map: WO 297/340 Sheet 36 SW 1_3 Neuve Chapelle. The National Archives.

War Diary 1Bn Sherwood Foresters September 1914 to October 1915 (WO 95/1721/1). The National Archives.

Service Record: 89031 Tomlinson, William. The National Archives.

Medal Roll Index Cards (Series WO 373). The National Archives.

Laughead, G., 2013. 'The Medical Front WW1'. Online at: www.vlib.us/medical/ [accessed June 2014].

Macdonald, L., 1997. *1915 The Death of Innocence*. Penguin Books.

Winter, D., 2004. *Haig's Command: A Reassessment.* Pen and Sword.

Chapter 31

William Wilson

William Wilson was probably named after his grandfather, a miller in Wymeswold. Old William had been born in Keyworth, two villages away, but his wife Sarah was from Wymeswold, and it was here that they settled. In 1881 they were living in East Street with two children; Robert William ('Miller's son') and his sister Mary – both aged eleven. Were they twins? It seems possible, because twenty years later, Robert William was to include two sons – James Redvers, and Walter Baden, both four months old – on his 1901 census return.

With the Boer war still grinding on, Robert William must have responded to the call of patriotism to name his new twins after the two most famous British commanders of the time – Sir Henry Redvers Buller and Lord Robert Baden-Powell. Also in that census is William, son of Robert William and grandson of the miller. Aged eight, William was the second eldest of seven children.

The children had mixed fortunes in the local schools. At the age of five, in 1898, 'May 9th William Wilson was taken ill and went home at 2.56.' Later, in the Mixed School he came twelfth in the attendance lists, and was a given a book as a prize. His younger brother Frank did better – he came third! In fact, Frank is credited as having won two more book prizes during his time at the school. The older children seem to have had a less happy time than their younger siblings – Richard 'reads badly' wrote the headmaster in 1901. Adela and her parents had a major problem with her attendance. The school log book observes in 1902:

> Jan 17th The Attendance Officer visited the school this morning.
> He told us he had a summons for the parents of a girl named
> Adela Wilson who has lately been attending little better than half-
> time.

Within a couple of weeks, however, the headmaster noted: 'The Wilson case noted above was remanded for a month, to give the parents a chance of sending the girl to school.' Nothing more was recorded, so presumably the threat of prosecution worked! There was no suggestion that Adela was ill, so it may well be that as an elder daughter, she was kept at home to help in the house as there are occasional references to this practice.

The twins, James Redvers and Walter Baden, did quite well. Both won prizes (*Children of the New Testament*) for Religious Knowledge, and turned in Arithmetic and Spelling performances that were fairly low down on the class list but above the bottom performers. Their careers were similar to Ellen's – she won a Scripture prize (*Pilgrim Street*), but did not do too well in the other subjects. Florry and Rose are recorded for their absences; in 1905, the school log tersely observes 'April 7th Rose E. Wilson has gone to live in Nottingham'. She was only six years old; was she sent because there were too many mouths to feed, and she was neither too young to go, nor economically useful? In 1914, Florence was absent too 'Oct 9, Florry Wilson absent all week; she is staying with her married sister in Yorkshire'. Adela would be the only sister of marriageable age; she was twenty-four by now.

In both the 1901 and 1911 censuses, Robert is described as a journeyman bricklayer – a self-employed tradesman, who worked for Thomas Warner Wooton during the First World War. By 1911 he and his wife Mary had ten children, and successfully reared nine of them; a good track record when infant mortality nationally was approximately 154 per 1000 live births. The older children had left to make their own way in life, though five, including the twins, were still at home. No wonder Mary had to get a job as a school cleaner. She described herself as a 'school caretaker' but someone, probably the enumerator Mr Dawson, had edited the entry. Curiously, for one who had had at least one run-in with the attendance authorities, Mrs Wilson had also been the school cleaner for eleven years – right up to February 1914. William's sister Florence ('Florrie') would stay at home and look after their mother until she died.Then she would continue to live in the same cottage on East Road until her own death. William's father would acquire a certain reputation among the children of Wymeswold. Known as 'Drummer' Wilson because of the instrument he played in the Wymeswold band, the village children would deliberately annoy him because they knew he had a fierce temper. The fact that sometimes he caught one and administered a good hiding seemed to encourage them all the more!

Outside of school, the children would have been looking to get work as soon as they were thirteen. Undoubtedly, William and his elder brother Richard found work on the land as soon as they were able. In the 1911 census, William, now nineteen, was a farm labourer, living and working just a mile or so from his family. His employer was Tom Shaw, the farmer at Thorpe in the Glebe, a medieval settlement that nowadays is just one house.

Both William and his elder brother Richard Edward would go on to serve in the next war – Richard however would survive. By 1916, with the war demanding even more men to go to the front, boys as young as twelve were released to work on the farms in their holidays – among them Bernard, William's youngest brother.

William was the first of the brothers to enlist. In fact, it looks as though he was among the first thirty or so men to leave the village – his name is on the school Roll of Honour, which seems to have been compiled in 1914. His army medal card shows that he went to France in August 1915, while Richard attested at Derby in February 1916. If Richard's description of himself as a corn dealer is accurate, then

William's name on the Arras Memorial.

enlisting must have been quite a wrench; his career was evidently taking off. The fact that his residence at the time was the Jolly Sailor in Hemington could lend itself to quite a few interpretations, though.

We do not have a physical description of William, but we know about his brother Richard from his army service record. Richard was not tall at 5 feet 5 inches, but he was stocky – a chest measurement of 38 inches (good for those days). He attested in Derby in February 1916, and by May had joined his unit – the Royal Field Artillery (27th Battery). In November he was posted with an Expeditionary Force to Salonika. By 1919 Driver Richard Wilson was discharged, suffering from malaria; a 30 percent disability, it was judged, which entitled him to a pension of twelve shillings a week. On discharge, his home address was given as East Street, Wymeswold – his parents' home.

William's story was very different. He had joined the Notts and Derby Regiment – the Sherwood Foresters. Although his contemporaries George Williams, David Spicer, Robert Ovendale and John James Collington all served in the same regiment, William was the only one in the 2nd Battalion. It had been raised in 1914, in Sheffield, and was sent with the Expeditionary Force to France, where it was plunged into ferocious fighting at the Aisne. Having lost over two hundred casualties, it was reinforced and took part in a desperate defence at Ennetiere in October 1914 against vastly superior German numbers. In so doing, it took over seven hundred casualties – out of a nominal strength of around nine hundred. Such was William's introduction to the war. He was to survive another three and a half years.

The Battalion was one of six battalions in the 71st Brigade, which also contained 1st Leicesters – Bill Collington's battalion. The 2nd Sherwoods started March 1918 in reserve trenches, at rest, but in preparation for the German offensive that was to come, they were sent up the line to front line trenches on the 11th. They were still there on the 21st, when the offensive began. This was relatively unusual, as most deployments into the front line lasted less than a week. Even so, commanders managed some 'rotation', putting 'C' and 'D' companies into reserve trenches and putting 'A' and 'B' companies into the firing trenches on the 14th.

Everyone knew that a major attack was coming, and for the troops in the 'firing line' the tension must have been excruciating. This was going to be a Big Show. On the 21st, at 5 p.m. the enemy opened up 'with every description of shell, including Gas shells', and the bombardment 'remained on our lines until 9.30 a.m.'

The battalion's war diary goes on to say that:

> The enemy came on in mass formation, and though the Battalion
> had suffered heavy casualties during the Bombardment, he was
> held in check until 10 p.m. …

The 2nd Battalion had almost been destroyed. When it was relieved on the 23rd; at the end of two days' maniacal defence, there was no longer an eight hundred strong fighting unit. 'After relief, the remainder of the Battn (4 officers and 110 O.R.) marched back …..' wrote Lt. Colonel H Milward, Commanding 2nd Battalion Sherwood Foresters, just before he signed the war diary for the month.

On the 21st, the battalion had been less than a mile to the north-east of Bill Collington's Leicesters. When the Germans broke through on their left, capturing Lagnicourt and attacking the Leicesters, the 2nd Sherwoods were forced back towards the same Vaulx-Morchies line that Bill's men so desperately tried to hold on to. Both battalions, to a greater or lesser degree, were overwhelmed. George and Bill were to die within a mile of each other, on the same day.

William never got to see the massed formations in their field-grey, coming through the mist and the dust. He had died in that great bombardment – one of the 'heavy casualties' of the early morning on the 21st March. As well as Bill Collington, he was in company with George Marriott and John Robert Ovendale, who also died that day.

Sources

Census records: 1891, 1901, 1911.

Certificate of Birth, Marriage or Death. General Register Office. Online at: www.freebmd.org.uk [accessed January 2014].

Wymeswold parish registers. Online at: www.hoap.co.uk/who/localhisregister.htm [accessed June 2014].

Wymeswold Church of England School: log books and misc papers 1875–1983 (DE7281). The Record Office for Leicestershire, Leicester and Rutland.

Commonwealth War Graves Commission, 2014. 'Find War Dead'. Online at: www.cwgc.org [accessed 2014].

Map: M/010634 Beugny 57c SW July 1918. The Western Front Association.

Map: M/000646 Vaulx-Vraucourt 57c NW 210318. Western Front Association.

War Diary 2Bn Sherwood Foresters March 1918 (WO 95/1624). The National Archives.

Service Record: 140972 Williams, Richard. The National Archives.

Passingham, I., 2008. *The German Offensives of 1918.* Pen and Sword.

Pitt, B., 2003. *1918 The Last Act.* Pen and Sword.

R. I. Woods, P. A. W. a. J. H. W., 1988. 'The Causes of Rapid Infant Mortality Decline in England and Wales, 1861- 1921 Part I'. *Population Studies*, Vol. 42:3 (Nov)

Smith, E., 1983. *Memories of a Country Girlhood.* Published by author.

Chapter 32

Wymeswold's Memorial Hall

The first official record of discussing a war memorial for Wymeswold comes in May 1919. It is written, not in the minutes of the Parish Council, but in the Church Parish Meetings and Vestry Minutes. A parish meeting had been convened, with Mr Reuben Charles in the chair. The minutes note briefly 'Principal business – should there be a War Memorial? Motion carried'. That decision was taken on 22nd May, and the meeting went on to discuss what sort of memorial would be fitting. However, there are some other records that provide a background to what followed next.

The war had resulted in many social changes in the country. Hundreds of thousands of men were due to be demobilised, but the army was very slow to respond. There were some good reasons for this. Firstly, it was by no means certain that the German army would accept the Armistice (it had not surrendered). Secondly, Russia had collapsed into civil war, and Britain was firmly against the 'Reds' (Bolsheviks). British troops had already been sent to Murmansk, and there was a definite possibility that the army would be required in another major conflict.

There were also some less good reasons. The sheer magnitude of demobilisation was a problem, as was deciding who should be sent home first. Another problem was working out how to cope with a huge influx of men onto the labour market. War had brought with it a boom in manufacturing – munitions, clothing, processed food and so on. Steel production and coal mining had been doing well. With the Armistice, many of those industries had to contract enormously, and far too quickly. It was a perfect recipe for social unrest. Just ten months after the Armistice, there were still a million men in uniform. Small mutinies were breaking out, as men refused to accept the unquestioning and, to them, pointless, military discipline.

As 1919 progressed, the wartime boom turned to bust , and the already saturated labour market was swamped by ex-soldiers. There were riots in Liverpool – tanks were called in and a battleship sent to the river Mersey. Shots were fired over the heads of the rioters and 370 people were arrested. Women, regarded as heroines and indispensable workers during the war, were now publicly criticised for occupying jobs that men might take.

There is no evidence of this level of discontent in Wymeswold, though Peggy Mills does report that her father remembered food being in shorter supply in the First World War than in the Second. The vicar, Rev Claud Edmunds, did report some changes, though, in response to his Bishop's visitation in 1921. Sadly, we do not have the Bishop's questionnaire but Rev Edmunds began by observing:

> (ii) (a) I think on the whole the war has been unfavourable to religion. Many of the men who served seem to have no use for it: those who were Churchworkers have become less regular and reliable.

He also listed among the 'Hindrances' (presumably hindrances to increasing his flock):

> The increased pressure in domestic life owing to general lack of servants.

An interesting comment. Even though times were hard, people were not going back into service. Perhaps the well-to-do had less money, or perhaps the poorer classes were not prepared to take that type of work. It certainly seems that, to the vicar at least, some fundamental changes were at work. True, when he listed 'A reaction from religious exercises on the part of the faithful, since the end of the war', he did follow it up with the hope that 'Time will presumably supply the remedy for them'. This expressed wish was typed on a separate line, and stands curiously alone – whether for emphasis, or whether he himself did not really believe it, is hard to say. Granted, these are just one man's reports – but they are carefully thought through, by an educated and sensitive observer of the times.

Against this backdrop, the vicar received a letter written on 22nd March 1919 by the County Secretary of the Young Men's Christian Association, P. Escott-North. The YMCA had been started in 1844 by young male shop workers who met for Bible readings and prayer. In the mid-1800s it had grown rapidly to become an international organisation. During the war, it had been very active in providing rest and recreation facilities for the troops behind the lines. The YMCA was quick to respond to the welfare needs of the troops, and the first centre was opened in June 1915. The same month saw the opening of a hostel in France for the relatives of wounded soldiers.

The YMCA centres – sometimes just a makeshift shelter within the range of enemy guns – were all staffed by volunteers. Most of the staff were women, but there were also a number of men who were either too old or physically unfit for active service. At any one time, there were as many as 1500 volunteers on the Western Front. The YMCA logo – the 'Red Triangle' – was distinctive, trusted and held in great affection by the men. In particular, the YMCA had acquired great experience in providing 'YMCA huts' – or 'Institutions' as the YMCA called them – that the soldiers relied on for tea and sandwiches, and conversation. They were islands of rest in a sea of destruction and confusion. (The description of a concert held at the YMCA in Meaulte on the Somme found its way into the war diary of 2nd Battalion, Grenadier Guards – see the chapter on Bramford Sparrow).

Escott-North's letter of 22nd March seems to have been unsolicited – we might even call it 'junk mail' today. There is no suggestion that he knew Rev Edmunds. He opens

189

by explaining that the 'enclosed literature' (which may be a document in the same folder of papers – see below) shows how the YMCA is taking 'immediate steps to meet the expressed needs of the smaller communities'. Wymeswold itself had not expressed any needs to the YMCA, because he goes on to say:

> I do not know if any steps have as yet been taken in Wymeswold
> to mark the appreciation of its inhabitants of the self-sacrifice of
> those of its sons who have fallen in the terrible strife of the last
> few years, but the probability is that if you are not already
> considering a War Memorial , you soon will be, and I beg
> therefore to draw your attention to the enclosed particulars of our
> Scheme which will acquaint you with it in broad outline.

The YMCA was certainly in tune with the mood of the country. At least, with the mood of the civilian population. There is a lot of evidence to suggest that many ex-servicemen were less enthusiastic for monuments and memorials. For four years, millions of young men had been trained to kill. Their lives had been dominated by anger, fear, and the indescribable sights and sounds of violent and bloody death. There are many accounts of former soldiers who would remember their comrades over a pint with other veterans, but who saw little point in the vast public outpouring of grief. Nevertheless, the move towards remembrance was powerful and unstoppable. The Cenotaph was unveiled in London in 1920 – the same year that the Unknown Warrior was laid to rest in Westminster Abbey.

The red poppy as a symbol of remembrance had been introduced in 1918 by an American YMCA worker, Moina Michael. She had been inspired by John McRae's poem 'In Flanders Fields', and her campaign for an international symbol was later taken up in France by Mme. Anna Guerin, a French YMCA worker, who had the idea of making artificial poppies for sale. It was she who enlisted the help of Sir Douglas Haig, formerly Commander in Chief of British Forces on the Western Front. By 1921, the British Poppy Appeal had been launched.

Escott-North's letter also appealed to the practical nature of the British:

> I take it that Wymeswold, in common with most other places,
> would desire something of a utilitarian type rather than a
> memorial that was merely ornamental, and when considering any
> project or perhaps number of Schemes that may be in mind for
> this purpose, it would doubtless be a help towards choosing the
> best and most useful Memorial if, along with the others, the
> enclosed Scheme were discussed.

The language is not exactly the hard-hitting marketing speak of the twenty-first century, but it is clear that the YMCA had a 'Scheme' that it wanted to spread around the country. Even without the literature to hand, subsequent correspondence and YMCA history explains the scheme. It was to build YMCA Institutes across the country, for the benefit of young people. Then, as now, the YMCA was committed to providing places and activities that young people could enjoy safely, and that would give them opportunities to relax, make contacts and have fun.

The letter seems to have inspired Rev Edmunds. Maybe he had already been discussing a memorial with villagers – maybe some had even come to him, as a village leader, to ask what should be done. The village losses had been terrible. At least a quarter of those who fought had died; 1918 had seen sixteen young men killed; around twenty of the war dead came from families that were related to other families in the area. He wrote back on the 25th, thanking Scott-North for his letter.

> Our returned lads say there is nothing they miss at home more
> than the Y.M.C.A., and are very keen on having an Institute in the
> village, if possible.

Clearly, he had been canvassing opinion in the intervening forty-eight hours. He wasted no time in getting the ball rolling:

> Could you come over one evening in the week after next? ... and
> discuss the matter with some of us? ... we shall be glad to give
> you supper before the meeting at the Vicarage.

A printed explanation of the county YMCA's scheme is included in Rev Edmunds' papers. It may not be the original enclosure, but it gives sufficient background to understand what was going on. The YMCA was aware that before the war, its activities were mostly confined to towns and cities. The scheme was intended to change that:

> The war has altered all this. The men who are coming back
> expect to find a Y.M.C.A. everywhere! ... Enquiries from all parts
> of the country are pouring in...

Leicester's YMCA secretary, Mr H.E. Smith had been appointed chairman of a new committee, and he had secured the service of Mr Escott-North to get the project under way. The document continues:

> Mr Smith will have the active help of Mr Escott-North, just
> returned from military service, who has had world-wide
> experience in Y.M.C.A. and organising work. Mr North is a man
> of strong initiative and energy, and his extensive soldiering
> experience has brought him into living with touch and
> understanding with men of all shades of opinion and outlook.

The scheme was to build institutes as war memorials, funded by the local community, but with advice and expertise supplied by the YMCA. The concept was for a large hall, with separate women's and men's areas, though the men's area was to have a concert platform and could be used for community functions. Interestingly, the concept included not only toilets but baths. This was an age when hygiene and cleanliness were not only beginning to be understood as healthy, but were also a moral duty. Given that many homes were without flushing toilets, let alone baths, these facilities would have been very much in demand in many parts of the country. The cost, however, was considerable. To build the 'complete package' was estimated at between £3,000 and £5,000 and 'was being adopted in scores of large villages throughout the country.'

The proposals were careful to include conventional war memorials within the plans:

> Memorial Tablets, Shrines, or other suitable means are adopted to
> place on permanent record the names of those who have given
> their lives in the great war.

Mr Escott-North wrote back directly. The letterhead he used had 'Leicester Young Men's Christian Association' at the top, but directly underneath was a banner that read 'The Y.M.C.A. with H.M. Troops' and featured the silhouette of a British soldier against the background of a burning and devastated landscape, with a YMCA hut in the right foreground. He would bring Mr Smith with him, and was comfortable about finding the vicarage – he mentioned that he had several times called upon the previous vicar, and enquired whether it was correct that Mr Campion ('of cycle fame') had come to live in the village.

The meeting evidently took place and it appears that a building had been identified. However, a letter from Joseph Wootton a few days later informed the YMCA that his tenant was not prepared to leave. This appears to have been the building in question, because Escott-North now wrote to Rev Edmunds , remarking that there now seemed 'no alternative to endeavour to secure a site, and transfer an Army Hut to your village'. He continued with the suggestion that a suitable site might be found, and that 'this might arise if we had a large village meeting sometime early next month, and put the whole thing before your people, endeavouring to get everybody there'.

This was the background to the village meeting in May 1919. The YMCA proposal was not the only one on the table. The vestry records show that there were at least three options that were seriously canvassed:

> (a) a Village Hall, (b) a Fixed Cross with the names of the fallen (c)
> a row of trees down the centre of Brook Street.

The vicar's notes also allow for the possibility of a memorial in the church alone, or a memorial in the village, and one in the church. Serious thought had evidently been given to the idea of a cross opposite the church. The same set of notes considers the possibility that it could be a cross on a series of steps, with a 'recessed tomb', and again 'regimental devices... Inscriptions'. A cost of £100–£300 had already been put down beside the idea, so it had obviously been thought about in some detail.

In the event, Mr James proposed a hall, and was seconded by Mr Watson. However, no vote was taken, since no costs were available. Therefore a committee was formed, comprising Rev C.H. Edmunds, R.W. Charles, J.W. Wootton, W. Woolley, E.W. Campion, E.F. Hayes and W. Taylor. Rev Edmunds and Joseph Wootton have already been mentioned; E.W. Campion, too, as the cycle manufacturer who had come to live at Wymeswold Hall during the war. The vicar's notes also included 'Site:- Enquire as Parish Ground', and then underneath, 'Sound College'. Most likely this is a note to 'sound out' Trinity College, the largest landowner in the village, to see if it would make a site available.

There followed more correspondence between Rev Edmunds and Mr Escott-North. The YMCA was very keen on getting this moving, and finding an army hut to bring to Wymeswold. Rev Edmunds, however, had to dampen their enthusiasm:

> We had a village meeting' [i.e. the 22nd May] 'on the subject last Thursday, and appointed a Committee to report on the cost of building a hall. The meeting was so decidedly against erecting a wooden structure of any kind as a permanent war memorial, that I don't think it is worth considering a hut.

Within days the YMCA had offered to provide the vicar with all the information he required to build a hall. He accepted gratefully – adding the proviso, of course 'I take it you submit these *gratis*'.

The next crucial meeting took place on 17th June 1919. Another village meeting was held, with about thirty people attending, and the Vicar in the chair. This time Mr Escott-North was invited to attend, and was able to present the idea directly to the villagers. He had brought with him costs and plans, so the meeting was in a position to make a decision. And it did. Mr Escott-North's message was simple and direct:

> There could not be a better type of War Memorial, since a worthy memorial should be costly, and do something to achieve the object for which our men died, of making the country better and happier. The names of all the men who had served should be inscribed in each institute.

He offered two suggestions, both for a solid construction of brick or concrete with concrete floor and asbestos roof forty feet by twenty feet, at about £550, or sixty feet by thirty feet at £1200. Furnishing would be extra. These would definitely be Christian clubs, but not denominational. 'Gambling and strong drinks were not allowed'.

The vicar, as chairman, was in agreement.

> A Village Hall would be an appropriate Thankoffering to the men who had returned, and a sphere for united Christian work.

Other questions persisted, though. Some villagers had evidently wanted a memorial in the church. Rev Edmunds was supportive of that idea as well. 'In any case,' he told the meeting, 'the wishes expressed by many that there should be a memorial to the fallen in the Parish Church would be carried out.'

There only remained the problem of finding a site. Some people had obviously wanted to use the village Shrubbery. This appears to have been situated on what is now known as Queen's Park, at the bottom of the Stockwell. The Parish Council had agreed its use as a village amenity back in 1905. Although it appears to have been regarded as village 'property', and therefore subject to the decisions of a village meeting (held, as this one was, under the auspices of the Parochial Church Council), the formal agreement of the Parish Council would be required for any change of use.

In fact, the Parish Council had met the previous week, and agreed to defer a decision on handing over the Shrubbery until the outcome of the village meeting was known.

With the exact location of a hall being put to one side, the motion was carried unanimously, and a Committee was formed. Those 'founding fathers' of the Memorial Hall were:

> Messrs Campion, Watson, H. Emmerson, Garner, J. James Senr,
> Burrows, Hayes, F. Bailey, Taylor, W. Wootton, F. Jalland, Everard
> Collington, T.G. Brown, Dr Tawse, J. James Jnr, J. Smith, Woolley,
> Baker, C. Mills, Jas Wootton, Jas Smith, P. Brown, F. James, C.
> Hubbard and the vicar.

The meeting minutes add, almost as an afterthought 'It was decided also that a Ladies' Committee should be formed'.

Several Committee members demonstrated their enthusiasm with very generous donations (bearing in mind that a modest house could be bought for a few hundred pounds). Mr Campion donated £100, the chairman (vicar) £10, Mr Hayes £10, and Mr James Senr £10. The project was off to a good start.

With that, the Memorial Hall disappears from the public records for nearly five years. This does not mean to say that nothing was being done. Ellen Smith, in *Memories of a Country Girlhood*, says:

> Eventually, after many garden fetes, concerts, dances, whist drives
> and sewing parties, the hall was built.

The next official document seems to be the indenture (deed) recognising that a Memorial Hall charity exists, and 'conveying', in lawyers' speak, the property to the charity. The Indenture is a handsome work in its own right. Handcrafted, with a large and florid capital 'I' at the beginning, it really looks more like a Victorian document than a twentieth century one.

The village had identified a plot of land – two roods and twenty perches to be precise – just off Clay Street. The land was used as allotment gardens at the time, and was owned, as was much of Wymeswold as a whole, by Trinity College, Cambridge. Trinity College (legally 'the Master Fellows and Scholars of the college of the Holy and Undivided Trinity within the town and University of Cambridge of King Henry the Eighth's Foundation') had owned land in the village for centuries, and still held the 'living' – the right to appoint the vicar – as well as being responsible for the maintenance of the chancel in St Mary's church. The college sold off its landholding *en bloc* to a consortium of tenant farmers in the mid-1950s, but its connection with the village still survives in the street name 'Trinity Crescent'.

The indenture and the deed of conveyance are dated 26th September 1922 and obviously part of the same deal. No record survives of the discussions or correspondence which must have gone back and forth between the Hall Committee and the college, but they must have been extensive, since the two documents are very detailed. The documents also contain a declaration by the Bursar of Trinity that

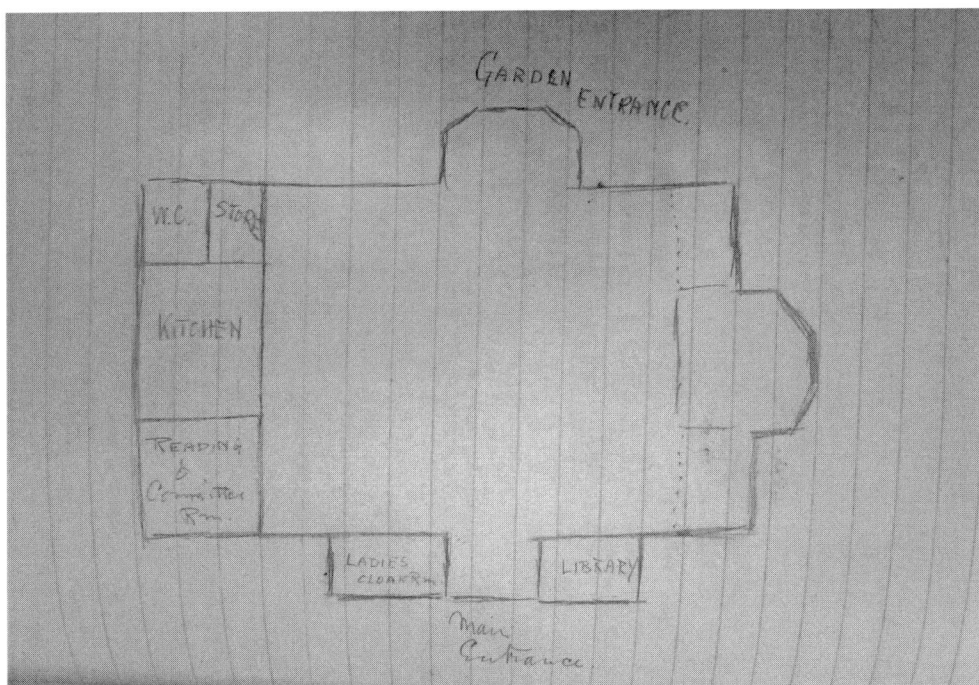

How Wymeswold Memorial Hall might have been. A pencil sketch from the notes taken at the time.

the land actually belonged to the college (presumably the college had owned the land for so long that all proof of ownership was lost in the mists of time).

It would appear that Edwin Campion, the owner of Wymeswold Hall at the time, was the leader of the charity's trustees, since his name heads the list, which in itself is interesting, as it lists their occupations as well: Edwin William Campion, Motor Cycle Manufacturer, Reubon William Charles, Farmer, William Garner (a space has been left against his name, and someone has written 'Grazier' in pencil), Thomas Warner Wootton, Builder, Thomas Glover Brown, Grocer, Edward Frederick Hayes, Blacksmith and John James the Elder, Farmer.

From the original committee three years before, there had been one addition – Reubon Charles – and nineteen had dropped out. That is not to say, of course, that they no longer had anything to do with the project. A committee of twenty-six would have been very unwieldy in getting decisions made, whereas a trustee board of seven made very good sense. It was these seven men who had paid over the sum of £62 10s to the Ministry of Agriculture and Fishery, at the request of Trinity College, to secure the purchase of the land. (It seems that the money had to be administered by the Ministry under the Universities Estates Acts.) The actual sum of money was not a problem – more than double that had been raised at the first meeting back in 1919 – but the negotiations must have taken some time. And of course, someone had to pay the lawyers' fees!

Wymeswold Memorial Hall. Photographed in 1991 by Bob Trubshaw.

The indenture made very clear that:

> The Charity hereby created shall be known as 'The Wymeswold
> Memorial Hall' and is created with the object and intention of
> perpetuating the memory of the brave men of Wymeswold who
> gave their lives for their King and Country in the Great War...

There follows a list of twenty-seven men. All twenty-seven are still commemorated today, but have been joined by Albert Bacon, William Dykes, and Frederick Robinson. Albert Bacon's family was primarily associated with Loughborough, and his father had moved to Leicester after the war. William Dykes had been mostly associated with Wymeswold through his stepmother, Harriet Morris, though the family seem to have moved to Wymeswold latterly (possibly after William had enlisted). Frederick Robinson had lived and worked in Wymeswold for some time before joining the army, but his wife had moved back to Loughborough. The relatives of these men must have come forward in the years between the founding of the charity and Amos Clarke's gift of the Roll of Honour to St Mary's church.

The land and any buildings erected on it was clearly intended as a village resource:

> ... to be used and enjoyed in perpetuity by the inhabitants of the
> Parish of Wymeswold aforesaid as a public hall and/or reading

The Roll of Honour inside Wymeswold Memorial Hall.

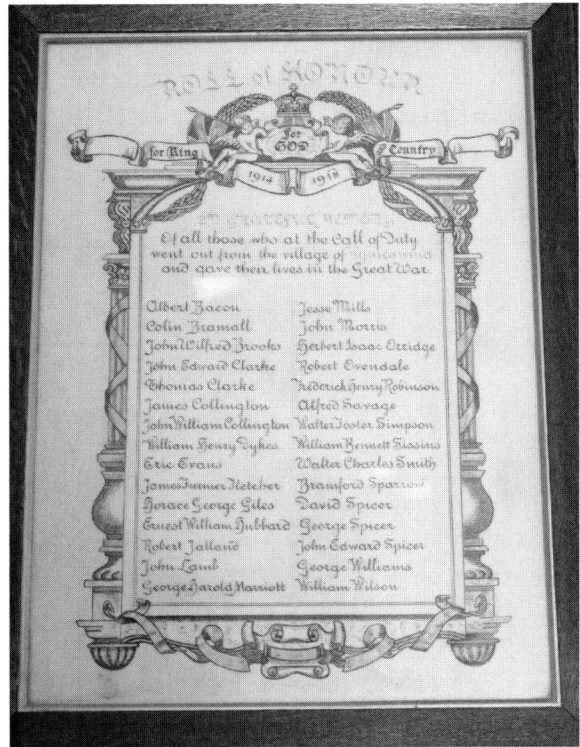

room and/or recreation rooms or for any other purposes allowed by law for the benefit of the said inhabitants …

This expansive view of the purposes of the hall was limited by a proviso which years later, had to be changed if the hall were to attract paying users:

… that the hereditaments hereby assured shall not in any circumstances be used for the sale or consumption of intoxicating drinks and such drinks shall not in any circumstances be sold or consumed therein.

The Trustees were not killjoys; they were responding both to the initial impetus and help from the YMCA, which was teetotal, and to a strong current of feeling within the country that alcohol was the cause of many of the social and healthcare problems of the day. That debate still continues, though now it tends to be more about the cost to the NHS of alcohol-related disease and accidents.

Within three years the village had gone from some general ideas about a memorial to a piece of land, owned by a charity, and dedicated to the benefit of the future generations of Wymeswold. All that remained was to build the hall. Back in 1919, Mr Escott-North had offered a suggested plan (see diagram). The structure that was built turned out to be the longer of his suggestions. By the standards of the time, it was a magnificent building for a small village. Internally, the main hall was forty-eight feet long and twenty-seven feet wide, with a stage area of twenty-seven by twelve feet. The stage itself was set three feet six inches above the floor – higher than it needed to be, but the extra height allowed for a large amount of storage underneath. The ground slopes away quite steeply, so the builders were able to use that to create a large basement. The hall had toilets for both sexes, and a kitchen that was big enough to cater for any village event.

In just two years the last of the money had been raised and the hall had been completed. Apparently some of the money at least was lent to the Committee. Ellen Smith (then Ellen Wootton) noted that:

> I believe it took nearly a decade before everything was paid off in
> full. My father [Thomas Warner Wootton] was one of the men
> who lent money, interest free, and these men were made the
> trustees of the hall.

On 12th March 1924, the Mixed School 'closed at midday for the Opening of the War Memorial Hall'. The headmistress of the Infant School was more descriptive in her log book: 'March 12th:

> A holiday was given this afternoon for the opening by Colonel
> Martin of the Village Hall. This is the War Memorial for those who
> fell in the Great War 1914-1918.

And it still is.

Sources

Wymeswold Church of England School: log books and misc papers 1875–1983 (DE7281). The Record Office for Leicestershire, Leicester and Rutland.

Wymeswold vicar's correspondence (DE 1728/37). The Record Office for Leicestershire, Leicester and Rutland.

Memorial Hall Deeds (copy in Wolds Historical Organisation Archives).

'The Great War 1914–1918: The Story Behind the Remembrance Poppy'. Online at: www.greatwar.co.uk/article/remembrance-poppy.htm [accessed 24 June 2014].

Loughborough Roll of Honour. Online at: loughborough-rollofhonour.com/page44.htm [accessed 20 June 2014].

University of Birmingham Cadbury Research Library. Online at: calmview.bham.ac.uk/ [accessed 24 June 2014].

Arthur, M., 2010. *The Road Home*. Phoenix.

Baker, C., 2010. 'The Long Long Trail: YMCA and other Volunteer Organisations.' Online at: www.1914-1918.net/ymca.htm [accessed 24 June 2014].

Brown, M., 1999. *1918 Year of Victory*. Pan Books.

Moretti, Alec, 1998, 'Widows Close', *WHO Newsletter*. Online at: http://www.hoap.co.uk/who/who24.htm

Smith, E., 1985. *Many Fingers In The Pie*. Published by author.

Smith, E., 1983. *Memories of a Country Girlhood*. Published by author.

Smith, E., 1984. *Seven Pennies in My Hand*. Published by author.

Van Emden, R. a. H. S., 2003. *All Quiet on the Home Front*. Headline.

Verleyen, H., 2002. *In Flanders Fields*. 4 edn. De Klaproos.

Chapter 33

The effect on the village:
wives, children and loved ones

Of course, with the end of the war, the village, like all communities in Britain, celebrated. Ellen Smith recalled:

> The peace rejoicing in Wymeswold took the form of a party for
> everyone. The village brass band marched around the streets,
> followed by all who could walk, while others sat at their doors
> watching the proceedings. Most people wore fancy dress. Games,
> races and all kinds of sports were enjoyed.

Such was a child's impression of events. It must have been a time of mixed emotions for the adults; the band was without John Robert Ovendale, and 'Drummer' Wilson had lost a son. The procession would have passed many homes that had lost someone in the war.

It is difficult, now that a hundred years have passed, and all the actors in this drama are dead, to assess the effect on Wymeswold. Maybe it was not as marked as it could have been. A number of the widows moved away from the village, like Elizabeth Bramall and Beatrice Robinson. Their husbands had come to Wymeswold to work, and now there was nothing to tie them to the village. Others, like Julia Collington and Annie Smith, had never really lived in Wymeswold at all. Others, like Mary Ovendale, stayed, either because they had family here or there was nowhere else to go. The parents would have been in a similar position. For most of them, Wymeswold was their home, and the place where they had raised all their children, not just the ones who died. The presence of daughters and surviving sons, even for George and Alice Spicer, who lost both George and John, must have been some comfort.

Ellen Smith reported that after the war, life gradually got back to normal, though towards the end, food had been in short supply. Things did not improve immediately: 'The blackout was lifted, but food supplies were slow in returning to pre-war standards'. In her autobiography she also gives an insight into some of the difficulties that returning soldiers – even those with jobs to go to – faced.

The Peace Celebrations outside the Three Crowns in Wymeswold, probably 19th July 1919. Photograph courtesy of Nigel and Elizabeth Sykes..

> Our workman, Bill Tomlinson, who had fought all through the
> war, came home without a scratch, but he said war left its mark.
> He had got out of the habit of sleeping in a bed, so he slept on the
> floor for several nights.

Bill Tomlinson was almost certainly the William Tomlinson who was the brother-in-law of George Williams, and who lived next door to the Wootton's bulder's yard.

In some ways, life continued much as it had. The Rev Claud Edmunds was fairly philosophical about pre-marital sex in his 1921 report to the Bishop:

> Pre-Nuptial Sin. Very prevalent... The great difficulty is that
> parental control is lax, and the parents are in many cases known
> to have gone astray themselves.

Nor had the work pattern of the village changed much: 'This village is almost entirely agricultural...'

Yet there were deeper changes under way. In 1914, Britain had a two-party political system, Conservatives and Liberals. During the war they governed in coalition, and maintained that alliance, under a Liberal Prime Minister (David Lloyd George) until 1922. Following the war, the new Labour Party rapidly gained popularity, forming its first government, with Liberal support, in 1924.

The old social structures, too, were breaking down. We have seen how the Rev Edmunds was concerned about the effects on organised religion. He also observed that 'the example of the well-to-do is growing increasingly lax.' True, he was talking in the context of church life, but it is another indicator that the 'social glue' that held together the old ways of doing things was gradually dissolving.

Agricultural communities were also going through massive changes due to mechanisation. This was not caused solely by the war – men like Charles and Ted Morris and David Sissins, had been 'engine drivers' for years. The need however to manage with fewer men had given an impetus to the introduction of machinery. Men like James Collington and Walter Smith were moving off the land and into urban jobs. Others continued to live in Wymeswold, but were increasingly dependent on income from factories like the Brush, in Loughborough.

Again, all these trends had been present before the war, but government attempts to stimulate the economy and to increase housing for workers (the Labour/Liberal government of 1924 started a programme of building half-a-million council houses) were mostly directed at the towns, not the villages. It would be another thirty to forty years before the villages would see a resurgence. By then Britain would be entering an age of affluence, and people would start moving out of the towns to find more attractive areas to live in.

Though this book has been about the men who died, the great majority of men returned from the 'Great War' and took up their lives again. Around eighty men of Wymeswold are known to have served, and there must be some more who are not mentioned in the village records. In the research that I have done for this book, I have not heard of any who talked extensively about his experiences at the front. Quite the reverse, in fact. This is something that they shared with most returning servicemen. They might reminisce over a drink with other ex-soldiers, but the experiences they had been through, and the sights they had seen, were so far removed from the understanding of civilians that there was no common ground, no shared vocabulary, to discuss them.

And so, quietly and slowly, the cataclysmic events of 1914–18 faded from public consciousness. Except for one day, every year. The fighting had stopped at 11.00 a.m., on 11th November, the 11th month, in 1918. In May 1919, an Australian journalist proposed a short period of silence to honour the dead, and on 7th November 1919 George V made his famous proclamation:

> All locomotion should cease, so that, in perfect stillness, the
> thoughts of everyone may be concentrated on reverent
> remembrance of the glorious dead.

The two-minute silence, and Armistice Day, was born. 11th November would become recognised as the national day of remembrance, and services held on the nearest Sunday.

In 1920, the Cenotaph was unveiled in London, and a national tradition of Armistice Day services, and commemorations, began. Since the Second World War, the name gradually changed to Remembrance Day, to accommodate the fallen of that war, and then the Korean War, and the subsequent conflicts in which British servicemen have given their lives.

There is no reference to a special Armistice Day service in Wymeswold immediately after the First World War, but there is no reason to assume it did not happen. Certainly, the service of Remembrance in St Mary's church is something that all the elder people of the village remember as a 'permanent' event.

For today's villagers, it is easy to see the Roll of Honour in the churches as an interesting curiosity, and the Memorial Hall as a convenient and useful village amenity. And so they are. Yet, behind that lies a community tragedy on a scale that this area had not seen since perhaps the Black Death six hundred hundred years before. How would we react now if, over the next four years, we saw one-in-three of our young men die? It says a lot for the cohesion of the community, and for the resilience of the women and children who were left, that the community held together.

This book was not written to critique the great patterns of history. It takes no sides in the debates over the conduct of the war, or the merits or otherwise of the Allies' case. Those are issues for other books. This book is about human beings. Men who had wives, sisters, brothers, parents and children. The men have some memorial to their passing. Their relatives made sure of that when they clubbed together to build the Memorial Hall. Those same sisters, mother, fathers had no memorial, yet they had to carry on without their loved ones.

Laurence Binyon said of the Fallen 'They shall grow not old, as we who are left grow old'. Yet the other side of the coin is that those at home had to grow old, knowing their sons and husbands would never have the chance to grow old. After a hundred years, and before it is too late, we can now honour those families, as well as the sons of Wymeswold.

Sources

Wymeswold vicar's correspondence (DE 1728/37). The Record Office for Leicestershire, Leicester and Rutland.

Wartime Memories Project. Online at: www.wartimememoriesproject.com /greatwar/allied/westyorkshireregiment11.php [accessed 12 February 2014].

'Ninety Years of Remembrance'. Online at: www.bbc.co.uk/remembrance/ [accessed July 2014].

'Remember Loughborough'. Online at: www.facebook.com/pages/Remember-Loughborough/562549607110527 [accessed 21 June 2014].

The First World War Poetry Digital Archive. Online at: www.oucs.ox.ac.uk/ww1lit/collections [accessed July 2014].

Smith, E., 1983. *Memories of a Country Girlhood*. Published by author.

Van Emden, R. a. H. S., 2003. *All Quiet on the Home Front*. Headline.